Conference of the North American Chapter of the Association for Computational Linguistics: Human Language Technologies 2016 (NAACL HLT 2016)

Student Research Workshop

San Diego, California, USA
12 – 17 June 2016

ISBN: 978-1-5108-2514-7

NAACL HLT 2016

**The 2016 Conference of the
North American Chapter of the
Association for Computational Linguistics:
Human Language Technologies**

Proceedings of the Student Research Workshop

June 12-17, 2016
San Diego, California, USA

Introduction

Welcome to the NAACL-HLT 2016 Student Research Workshop.

This year, we have three different kinds of papers: research papers, thesis proposals, and undergraduate research papers. Thesis proposals were intended for advanced students who have decided on a thesis topic and wish to get feedback on their proposal and broader ideas for their continuing work, while research papers describe completed work or work in progress with preliminary results. In order to encourage undergraduate research, we offered a special track for research papers where the first author is an undergraduate student.

We received 11 research papers, 5 thesis proposals, and 8 undergraduate research papers – making the total number of submissions 24. We accepted 9 research papers, 2 thesis proposals, and 6 undergraduate research papers (17 accepted in total). This translates to an acceptance rate of 81% for research papers, 40% for thesis proposals, and 75% for undergraduate research papers (70% overall). This year, all the SRW papers will be presented at the main conference evening poster session. In addition, each SRW paper is assigned a dedicated mentor. The mentor is an experienced researcher from academia or industry who will prepare in-depth comments and questions in advance for the poster session and will provide feedback to the student author. Thanks to our funding sources, this year's SRW covers registration expenses and provides partial travel and/or lodging support to all student first authors of the SRW papers. We gratefully acknowledge the support from the NSF and Google. We thank our dedicated program committee members who gave constructive and detailed feedback for the student papers. We also would like to thank the NAACL-HLT 2016 organizers and local arrangement chairs.

Organizers:

    Jacob Andreas, University of California Berkeley
    Eunsol Choi, University of Washington
    Angeliki Lazaridou, University of Trento

Faculty Advisors:

    Jacob Eisenstein, Georgia Institute of Technology
    Nianwen Xue, Brandeis University

Program Committee:

    Amjad Abu-Jbara, Microsoft
    Bharat Ram Ambati, Apple
    Gabor Angeli, Stanford University
    Yoav Artzi, Cornell University
    Daniel Bauer, Columbia University
    Yevgeni Berzak, Massachusetts Institute of Technology
    Arianna Bisazza, University of Amsterdam
    Shu Cai, University of Southern California
    Hiram Calvo, Instituto Politécnico Nacional, Mexico
    Dallas Card, Carneige Mellon University
    Asli Celikyilmaz, Microsoft
    Danqi Chen, Stanford University
    Jesse Dodge, University of Washington
    Raquel Fernandez, University of Amsterdam
    Thomas Francois, UC Louvain
    Lea Frermann, University of Edinburgh
    Daniel Fried, University of California Berkeley
    Annemarie Friedrich, Saarland University
    Yoav Goldberg, Bar Ilan University
    Amit Goyal , Yahoo! Labs
    Michael Hahn, University of Edinburgh
    David Hall, Semantic Machines
    Eva Hasler, University of Cambridge
    Luheng He, University of Washington
    John Henderson, MITRE Corporation
    Derrick Higgins, Civis Analytics
    Dirk Hovy, University of Copenhagen.
    Yuening Hu, Yahoo! Labs
    Philipp Koehn, University of Edinburgh
    Lingpeng Kong, Carneige Mellon University
    Ioannis Konstas, University of Washington

Jonathan K. Kummerfeld, University of Berkeley
Kenton Lee, University of Washington
Tal Linzen, Ecole Normale Supérieure
Fei Liu, University of Central Florida
Adam Lopez, University of Edinburgh
Nitin Madnani, ETS
Shervin Malmasi , Harvard University
Diego Marcheggiani, University of Amsterdam
Karthik Narasimhan, Massachusetts Institute of Technology
Arvind Neelakantan, University of Massachusetts Amherst
Denis Paperno, University of Trento
Adam Pauls, University of California, Berkele
Ted Pedersen, University of Minnesota Duluth
Barbara Plank, University of Groningen
Christopher Potts, Stanford University
Daniel Preoţiuc-Pietro, University of Pennsylvania
Preethi Raghavan, IBM T.J. Watson Research Center
Roi Reichart, Technion
Tim Rocktäschel, University College London
Roy Schwartz, The Hebrew University
Minjoon Seo, University of Washington
Kairit Sirts, Tallinn University of Technology
Huan Sun, University of Washington
Swabha Swayamdipta, Carneige Mellon University
Kapil Thadani, Columbia University
Travis Wolfe, Johns Hopkins University
Luke Zettlemoyer, University of Washington

Table of Contents

Conference Program

Monday June 13th

An End-to-end Approach to Learning Semantic Frames with Feedforward Neural Network
Yukun Feng, Yipei Xu and Dong Yu

Analogy-based detection of morphological and semantic relations with word embeddings: what works and what doesn't.
Anna Gladkova, Aleksandr Drozd and Satoshi Matsuoka

Argument Identification in Chinese Editorials
Marisa Chow

Automatic tagging and retrieval of E-Commerce products based on visual features
Vasu Sharma and Harish Karnick

Combining syntactic patterns and Wikipedia's hierarchy of hyperlinks to extract meronym relations
Debela Tesfaye Gemechu, Michael Zock and Solomon Teferra

Data-driven Paraphrasing and Stylistic Harmonization
Gerold Hintz

Detecting "Smart" Spammers on Social Network: A Topic Model Approach
Linqing Liu, Yao Lu, Ye Luo, Renxian Zhang, Laurent Itti and Jianwei Lu

Developing language technology tools and resources for a resource-poor language: Sindhi
Raveesh Motlani

An End-to-end Approach to Learning Semantic Frames with Feedforward Neural Network

Yukun Feng, Yipei Xu and Dong Yu[*]
College of Information Science
Beijing Language and Culture University
No.15 Xueyuan Rd., Beijing, China, 100083
`{fengyukun,xuyipei,yudong}@blcu.edu.cn`

Abstract

We present an end-to-end method for learning verb-specific semantic frames with feedforward neural network (FNN). Previous works in this area mainly adopt a multi-step procedure including part-of-speech tagging, dependency parsing and so on. On the contrary, our method uses a FNN model that maps verb-specific sentences directly to semantic frames. The simple model gets good results on annotated data and has a good generalization ability. Finally we get 0.82 F-score on 63 verbs and 0.73 F-score on 407 verbs.

1 Introduction

Lexical items usually have particular requirements for their semantic roles. Semantic frames are the structures of the linked semantic roles near the lexical items. A semantic frame specifies its characteristic interactions with things necessarily or typically associated with it (Alan, 2001). It is valuable to build such resources. These resources can be effectively used in many natural language processing (NLP) tasks, such as question answering (Narayanan and Harabagiu, 2004) and machine translation (Boas, 2002).

Current semantic frame resources, such as FrameNet (Baker et al., 1998), PropBank (Palmer et al., 2005) and VerbNet (Schuler, 2005), have been manually created. These resources have promising applications, but they are time-consuming and expensive. El Maarouf and Baisa (2013) used a bootstrapping model to classify the patterns of verbs from Pattern Dictionary of English[1] (PDEV). El Maarouf et al. (2014) used a Support Vector Machine (SVM) model to classify the patterns of PDEV. The above supervised approaches are most closely related to ours since PDEV is also used in our experiment. But the models above are tested only on 25 verbs and they are not end-to-end. Popescu used Finite State Automata (FSA) to learn the pattern of semantic frames (Popescu, 2013). But the generalization ability of this rule-based method may be weak. Recently, some unsupervised studies have focused on acquiring semantic frames from raw corpora (Materna, 2012; Materna, 2013; Kawahara et al., 2014b; Kawahara et al., 2014a). Materna used LDA-Frame for identifying semantic frames based on Latent Dirichlet Allocation (LDA) and the Dirichlet Process. Kawahara et al. used Chinese Restaurant Process to induce semantic frames from a syntactically annotated corpus. These unsupervised approaches have a different goal compared with supervised approaches. They aim at identifying the semantic frames by clustering the parsed sentences but they do not learn from semantic frames that have been built. These unsupervised approaches are also under a pipeline framework and not end-to-end.

One related resource to our work is Corpus Pattern Analysis (CPA) frames (Hanks, 2012). CPA proposes a heuristic procedure to obtain semantic frames. Most current supervised and unsupervised approaches are under similar pipeline procedure. The procedure can be summarized as follows with an example sentence "The old music deeply moved

---

[*]The corresponding author.

[1]`http://pdev.org.uk/`

Proceedings of NAACL-HLT 2016, pages 1–7,
San Diego, California, June 12-17, 2016. ©2016 Association for Computational Linguistics

the old man":

step 1 Identify the arguments near "moved", which can be expressed as (subject:music, object:man)

step 2 Attach meanings to above arguments, which can be expressed as (subject:Entity, object:Human)

step 3 Clustering or classifying the arguments to get semantic frames.

However, step 1 and 2 are proved to be difficult in SemEval-2015 task 15 [2] (Feng et al., 2015; Mills and Levow, 2015).

This paper presents an end-to-end approach by directly learning semantic frames from verb-specific sentences. One key component of our model is well pre-trained word vectors. These vectors capture fine-grained semantic and syntactic regularities (Mikolov et al., 2013) and make our model have a good generalization ability. Another key component is FNN model. A supervised signal allows FNN to learn the semantic frames directly. As a result, this simple model achieves good results. On the instances resources of PDEV, we got 0.82 F-score on 63 verbs and 0.73 on 407 verbs.

The contributions of this paper are summarized as follows:

- Semantic frames can be learned with neural network in an end-to-end map and we also analysed our method in detail.

- We showed the power of pre-trained vectors and simple neural network for the learning of semantic frames. It is helpful in developing a more powerful approach.

- We evaluate the learned semantic frames on annotated data precisely and got good results with not much training data.

2   Model Description

2.1   Overview

Our model gets verb-specific semantic frames directly from verb-specific sentences. A running ex-

<hr>

[2]http://alt.qcri.org/semeval2015/task15/

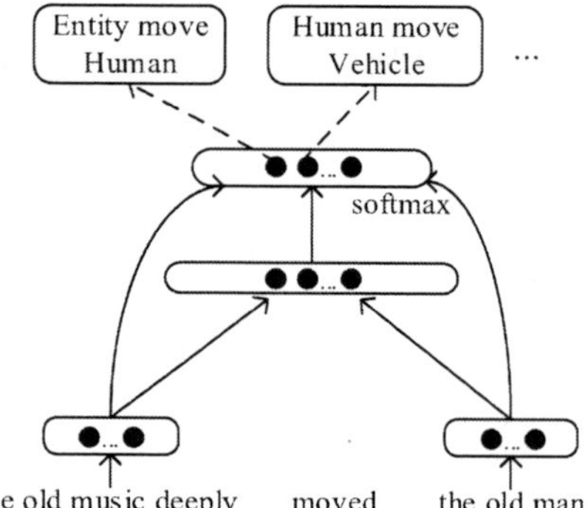

Figure 1: Model architecture for an example of learning semantic frames directly from verb-specific sentence. The sentence is divided into two windows. "The old music deeply" is in the left window and "the old man" is in the right window. The target verb "moved" is not used in the input. The input is connected to output layer. Each unit of output layer corresponds to one semantic frame of the target verb.

ample of learning semantic frames is shown in Figure 1. Our FNN model can be regarded as a continuous function

$$c = f(x). \tag{1}$$

Here $x \in \mathbb{R}^n$ represents the vector space of the sentence and c represents the index of the semantic frame. Instead of a multi-step , FNN model directly maps the sentence into semantic frame. In the training phrase "The old music deeply moved the old man" is mapped into vector space and "Entity move Human" is learned from the vector space. In the testing phrase, an example result of FNN model can roughly expressed as "Entity move Human" $= f$("The fast melody moved the beautiful girl") $=$ which is an end-to-end map.

2.2   Feedforward Neural Network

Denote $C_{i:j}$ as the concatenation of word vectors in a sentence. Here i and j are word indexes in the sentence. The input layer is divided into two windows (padded with zero vector where necessary), which are called left window and right window. The input for FNN is represented as

$$x = C_{v-lw:v-1} \oplus C_{v+1:v+rw}, \tag{2}$$

where v denotes the index of target verb in the sentence, $\oplus$ is the concatenation operator, lw is the length of left window and rw is the length of right window. Both lw and rw are hyperparameters. The target verb can be ignored by the input layer because the arguments of it lie on the left and right windows. W, U and V respectively represent the weight matrix between input and hidden layer, hidden and output layer and input and output layer. d and b respectively represent the bias vector on hidden and output layer. We use hyperbolic function as our activation function in hidden layer. Using matrix-vector notation, the net input of softmax layer of FNN can be expressed as:

$$a = \lambda(U\tanh(Wx + d) + b) + (1 - \lambda)Vx. \quad (3)$$

Here λ controls the relative weight of the two items in the above formula. FNN will have three layers when λ is set to 1 and two layers without bias when λ is set to 0. Then a softmax function is followed for classification:

$$p_i = \frac{e^{a_i}}{\sum_i e^{a_i}}. \quad (4)$$

Here p_i represents the probability of the semantic frame i given x. The cost we minimize during training is the negative log likelihood of the model plus the L2 regularization term. The cost can be expressed as:

$$L = - \sum_{m=1}^{M} \log p_{t_m} + \beta \mathrm{R}(U, W, V). \quad (5)$$

Here M is number of training samples and t_m is the index of the correct semantic frame for the m'th sample. R is a weight decay penalty applied to the weights of the model and β is the hyperparameter controlling the weight of the regularization term in the cost function.

2.3 Model Analysis

We extend equation 1 as

$$c = f(w_{v-lw}, ...w_i..., w_{v+rw}). \quad (6)$$

w_i is the i'th word vector in the input vector space above. Note f is a continuous function and similar words are likely to have similar word vectors. That is to say, if $c_1 = f(w_{v-lw}, ...w_i..., w_{v+rw})$ we usually have $c_1 = f(w_{v-lw}, ...sw_i..., w_{v+rw})$ with w_i similar to sw_i. One obvious example but roughly expressed is if "Entity move Human" $=$ f("The","old","music","the","old","man"), then it will have "Entity move Human" $=$ f("The","fast","melody","the","beautiful","girl"). Because "music" and "melody" can be regarded as similar words, which is also the case for "man" and "girl". Since one of the critical factors for semantic frame is semantic information in specific unit (e.g., subject and object), the pre-trained vectors can easily capture what this task needs. Thus pre-trained vectors can have a good generalization ability for semantic frame learning. In the training phrase, FNN can learn to capture the key words which have more impact on the target verb. This will be shown later in the experiment. Because the input of FNN is a window with fixed length, this would cause a limited ability of capturing long-distance key words. Despite this weakness of this model, it still got good results.

3 Experiments

3.1 Task and Datasets

SemEval-2015 Task 15 is a CPA (Hanks, 2012) dictionary entry building task. The task has three subtasks. Two related subtasks are summarized as follows [3]:

- CPA parsing. This task requires identifying syntactic arguments and their semantic type of the target verb. The result of this task followed by our example sentence can be "The old [subject/Entity music] deeply moved the old [object/Human man]". The syntactic arguments in the example are "subject" and "object" respectively labelled on the word "music" and "man". Their semantic types are "Entity" and "Human". Thus a pattern of the target verb "move" can be "[subject/Entity] move [object/Human]".

- CPA Clustering. The result of the first task give the patterns of the sentences. This task aims at clustering the most similar sentences according to the found patterns. Two sentences which belong to the similar pattern are more likely in the same cluster.

---

[3] Subtask 3 is CPA Automatic Lexicography. Since we have nothing to do with this task, we don't make a introduction.

Datasets Statistics				B-cubed or micro-average F-score of Methods			
	Verb number	Training data	Testing data	Semantic frame number	FNN	SEB	DULUTH	BOB90
MTDSEM	4	136.5	159	4.86	0.7	0.59	0.52	**0.74**
	3	1546.33	214.67					
PDEV1	407	373.49	158.32	6.53	0.73	0.63	-	-
PDEV2	63	1421.22	606.60	9.60	0.82	0.64	-	-

Table 1: Summary statistics for the datasets (left) and results of our FNN model against other methods (right). On the right side, MTDSEM is evaluated by B-cubed F-score for clustering. On PDEV1 and PDEV2, FNN model is evaluated by micro-average F-score. SEB is always evaluated by B-cubed F-score as the base score. DULUTH and BOB90 are Participant teams in 2015.

SemEval-2015 Task 15 has two datasets which are called Microcheck dataset and Wingspread dataset. The dataset of SemEval-2015 Task 15 was derived from PDEV (Baisa et al.,). That is to say, all the sentences in SemEval-2015 Task 15 are from PDE-V. These datasets have a lot of verbs and have many sentences for each verb. Each sentence of each verb corresponds to one index of the semantic frames. Note that the semantic frames are verb-specific and each verb has a close set of its own semantic frames. Thus in our experiment we build one model for each verb. Our task is to classify each sentence directly into one semantic frame which is different from C-PA clustering, but we will also test our model with clustering metric against other systems. We only remove punctuation for these datasets. To test our model we split these datasets into training data and testing data. Summary statistics of the these datasets are in Table 1. In Table 1, Figure 2 and Table 3, Verb number is the number of verbs, Training data and Testing data represent the average number of sentences for each verb and Semantic frame number is the average number of semantic frames for each verb. Details of creating the datasets are as follows:

- **MTDSEM**: Microcheck test dataset of SemEval-2015 Task 15. For each verb in MTDSEM we select training sentences from PDEV that doesn't appear in MTDSEM.

- **PDEV1**: For each verb, we filter PDEV with the number of sentences not less than 100 and the number of semantic frames not less than 2. Then we split the filtered data into training data and testing data, respectively accounted for 70% and 30% for each semantic frame of each verb.

- **PDEV2**: Same with PDEV1, but with the difference of threshold number of sentences set to 700. PDEV2 ensures that the model has relatively enough training data.

- **MTTSEM**: Microcheck train dataset and test dataset of SemEval-2015 Task 15. We split MTTSEM as above to get training data and testing data for each verb. The summary statistic of this dataset is separately shown in Table 3.

We use the publicly available word2vec vectors that were trained through GloVe model (Pennington et al., 2014) on Wikipedia and Gigaword. The vectors have dimensionality of 300. The word vectors not in pre-trained vectors are set to zero.

3.2 Experimental Setup

We build one model for each verb. Training is done by stochastic gradient descent with shuffled mini-batches and we keep the word vectors static only update other parameters. In our experiments we keep all the same hyperparameters for each verb. we set learning rate to 0.1, lw and rw to 5, minibatch size to 5, L2 regularization parameter β to 0.0001, the number of hidden unit to 30 and λ to 0. Because of limited training data, we do not use early stopping. Training will stop when the zero-one loss is zero over training data for each verb. The official evaluation method used B-cubed definition of Precision and Recall (Bagga and Baldwin, 1998) for CPA clustering. The final score is the average of B-cubed F-scores over all verbs. Since our task can be regarded as a supervised classification, we also use the micro-average F-score to evaluate our results.

3.3 Experimental Results

Table 1 shows the results on MTDSEM with supervised and unsupervised approaches. SemEval-2015 Task 15 baseline (SEB) clusters all sentences together for each verb. That is to say, SEB assigns the

Verb-specific Sentences	Verb-specific Semantic Frames
Mary resisted the temptation to answer her back and after a moment's silence	[[Human 1]] answer ([[Human 2]]) back [[Human 1]]
Pamala Klein would seem to have a lot to answer for.	[[Human]] have a lot to answer for [NO OBJ]
and I will answer for her safety	[[Human]] answer [NO OBJ] for [[Eventuality]]
he cannot answer for Labour party policies	[[Human]] answer [NO OBJ] for [[Eventuality]]
it is fiction and can not be made real by acting it out	[[Human]] act [[Event or Human Role or Emotion]] out
You should try to build up a network of people you trust	[[Human]] build ([[Entity]]) up

Table 2: Example results of our FNN model mapping verb-specific sentences to semantic frames on PDEV.

same cluster to all the sentences and is evaluated by B-cubed F-score for clustering. So its score depends on the distribution of semantic frames. The higher the score is, the more concentrated the distribution of semantic frames is. SEB to get higher score usually indicates other methods are more likely to get high scores, so we use it as a base score. DU-LUTH (Pedersen, 2015) treated this task as an unsupervised word sense discrimination or induction problem. The number of semantic frames was predicted on the basis of the best value for the clustering criterion function. BOB90 [4] used a supervised approach to tackle the clustering problem (Baisa et al., 2015) and get the best score on MTDSEM. An example result of FNN model on PDEV is shown in Table 2

4 Discussions

4.1 Large vs. Small Training Data

MTDSEM is divided into two parts to report on the left part of Table 1. One part has larger training data while the other part has little. Our FNN model gets a relatively lower score, mainly because the part of training data is too small. FNN got 0.88 B-cubed F-score on the larger training data part and 0.57 on the other part. In order to show the real power of our model, PDEV1 and PDEV2 were made which have much more training data than MTDSEM and more verbs to test. It shows a better result on hundreds of verbs. We also made Figure 2 to show the performance of FNN model when the training data size increases. As a result, our method can perform really well on sufficient training data.

4.2 The Direct Connection

Our FNN model has a direct connection from input to output layer controlled by λ in the second term

---

[4]BOB90 did not submit an article

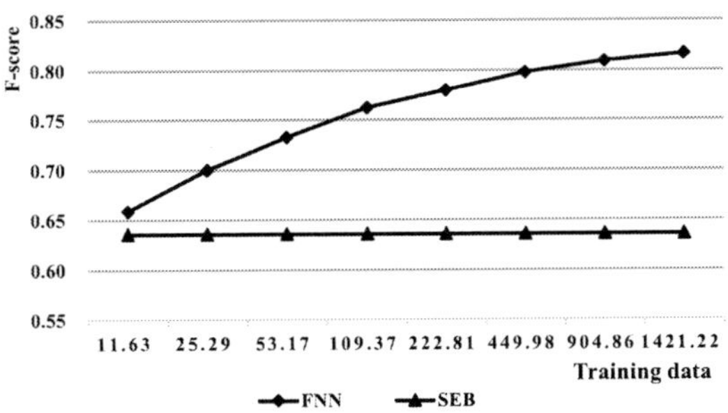

Figure 2: Results of FNN on PDEV2. The testing data is fixed at 606.60. The training data increases two times at each step. Y-axis represents B-cubed F-score for SEB and micro-average F-score for FNN.

of the equation 3. It is designed to speed up the convergence of training (Bengio et al., 2006), since the direct connection allows the model fast learning from the input. But In our experiments the number of epoch before the convergence of training is very close between FNN with two layers and FNN with three layers. On the contrary, we observed that FNN with two layers where λ is set to zero got a slightly better F-score than FNN where λ is set to 0.5 and 1. This may suggest FNN with two layers is good enough on PDEV.

4.3 The Ability of Capturing Key Words

FNN have the ability to capture the key words of the target verb. To show this, we test our FN-N model on MTTSEM with different preprocessing shown in Table 3. We only remove the punctuation of MTTSEM1 which is same as before. MTTSEM2 only contains the gold annotations of syntactic arguments provided by CPA parsing. Note that MTTSEM2 only contains the key words for each target verb and ignore those unimportant words in the sentences. MTTSEM3 is same as MTTSEM2 but with the difference of the arguments for each target verb provided by Stanford Parser (De Marneffe et al., 2006). Dependents that have the following relations to the target verb are extracted as arguments:

nsubj, xsubj, dobj, iobj, ccomp, xcomp, prep_*

As a result, FNN reasonably gets the best score on MTTSEM2 and FNN also gets a good score on MTTSEM1 but much lower score on MTTSEM3. This shows that FNN would have the ability to capture the key words of target verb. The result on MTTSEM1 and MTTSEM3 shows that our FNN model captures the key words more effectively than the parser for this task.

	MTTSEM1 (verb-specific sentences)	MTTSEM2 (gold annotations)	MTTSEM3 (automatic annotations)
Verb number	28		
Training data	111.25		
Testing data	46.39		
FNN	0.76	**0.82**	0.67
SEB	0.62		

Table 3: Results on MTTSEM with different preprocessing.

5 Conclusion

This paper has described an end-to-end approach to obtain verb-specific semantic frames. We evaluated our method on annotated data. But we do not identify the semantic roles for target verbs and the verb-specific model suffers not enough training data. A promising work is to merge these semantic frames over multiple verbs which can greatly increase the training data size. Also, convolutional layer can be applied on the input vector to extract features around verb and more powerful neural network can be used to model the verb.

Acknowledgments

We would like to thank the anonymous reviewers for their helpful suggestions and comments.

References

Keith Alan. 2001. In *Natural Language Semantics*, page 251. Blackwell Publishers Ltd, Oxford.

Amit Bagga and Breck Baldwin. 1998. Entity-based cross-document coreferencing using the vector space model. In *Proceedings of the 17th international conference on Computational linguistics-Volume 1*, pages 79–85. Association for Computational Linguistics.

Vít Baisa, Ismaïl El Maarouf, Pavel Rychlỳ, and Adam Rambousek. Software and data for corpus pattern analysis.

Vıt Baisa, Jane Bradbury, Silvie Cinková, Ismaıl El Maarouf, Adam Kilgarriff, and Octavian Popescu. 2015. Semeval-2015 task 15: A corpus pattern analysis dictionary-entry-building task.

Collin F Baker, Charles J Fillmore, and John B Lowe. 1998. The berkeley framenet project. In *Proceedings of the 17th international conference on Computational linguistics-Volume 1*, pages 86–90. Association for Computational Linguistics.

Yoshua Bengio, Holger Schwenk, Jean-Sébastien Senécal, Fréderic Morin, and Jean-Luc Gauvain. 2006. Neural probabilistic language models. In *Innovations in Machine Learning*, pages 137–186. Springer.

Hans Christian Boas. 2002. Bilingual framenet dictionaries for machine translation. In *LREC*.

Marie-Catherine De Marneffe, Bill MacCartney, Christopher D Manning, et al. 2006. Generating typed dependency parses from phrase structure parses. In *Proceedings of LREC*, volume 6, pages 449–454.

Ismaıl El Maarouf and Vıt Baisa. 2013. Automatic classification of patterns from the pattern dictionary of english verbs. In *Joint Symposium on Semantic Processing.*, page 95.

Ismail El Maarouf, Jane Bradbury, Vít Baisa, and Patrick Hanks. 2014. Disambiguating verbs by collocation: Corpus lexicography meets natural language processing. In *LREC*, pages 1001–1006.

Yukun Feng, Qiao Deng, and Dong Yu. 2015. Blcunlp: Corpus pattern analysis for verbs based on dependency chain. *Proceedings of SemEval*.

Patrick Hanks. 2012. How people use words to make meanings: Semantic types meet valencies. *Input, Process and Product: Developments in Teaching and Language Corpora*, pages 54–69.

Daisuke Kawahara, Daniel Peterson, and Martha Palmer. 2014a. A step-wise usage-based method for inducing polysemy-aware verb classes. In *ACL (1)*, pages 1030–1040.

Daisuke Kawahara, Daniel Peterson, Octavian Popescu, Martha Palmer, and Fondazione Bruno Kessler. 2014b. Inducing example-based semantic frames from a massive amount of verb uses. In *EACL*, pages 58–67.

Jiří Materna. 2012. Lda-frames: An unsupervised approach to generating semantic frames. In *Computational Linguistics and Intelligent Text Processing*, pages 376–387. Springer.

Jiří Materna. 2013. Parameter estimation for lda-frames. In *HLT-NAACL*, pages 482–486.

Tomas Mikolov, Wen-tau Yih, and Geoffrey Zweig. 2013. Linguistic regularities in continuous space word representations. In *HLT-NAACL*, pages 746–751.

Chad Mills and Gina-Anne Levow. 2015. Cmills: Adapting semantic role labeling features to dependency parsing. *SemEval-2015*, page 433.

Srini Narayanan and Sanda Harabagiu. 2004. Question answering based on semantic structures. In *Proceedings of the 20th international conference on Computational Linguistics*, page 693. Association for Computational Linguistics.

Martha Palmer, Daniel Gildea, and Paul Kingsbury. 2005. The proposition bank: An annotated corpus of semantic roles. *Computational linguistics*, 31(1):71–106.

Ted Pedersen. 2015. Duluth: Word sense discrimination in the service of lexicography. In *Proceedings of the 9th International Workshop on Semantic Evaluation (SemEval 2015)*, pages 438–442, Denver, Colorado, June. Association for Computational Linguistics.

Jeffrey Pennington, Richard Socher, and Christopher D Manning. 2014. Glove: Global vectors for word representation. In *EMNLP*, volume 14, pages 1532–1543.

Octavian Popescu. 2013. Learning corpus patterns using finite state automata. In *Proceedings of the 10th International Conference on Computational Semantics*, pages 191–203.

Karin Kipper Schuler. 2005. Verbnet: A broad-coverage, comprehensive verb lexicon.

Analogy-based Detection of Morphological and Semantic Relations With Word Embeddings: What Works and What Doesn't.

Anna Gladkova
Department of Language
and Information Sciences
The University of Tokyo
Tokyo, Japan
gladkova@phiz.c.u-tokyo.ac.jp

Aleksandr Drozd
Global Scientific Information
and Computing Center
Tokyo Institute of Technology
Tokyo, Japan
alex@smg.is.titech.ac.jp

Satoshi Matsuoka
Global Scientific Information
and Computing Center
Tokyo Institute of Technology
Tokyo, Japan
matsu@is.titech.ac.jp

Abstract

Following up on numerous reports of analogy-based identification of "linguistic regularities" in word embeddings, this study applies the widely used vector offset method to 4 types of linguistic relations: inflectional and derivational morphology, and lexicographic and encyclopedic semantics. We present a balanced test set with 99,200 questions in 40 categories, and we systematically examine how accuracy for different categories is affected by window size and dimensionality of the SVD-based word embeddings. We also show that GloVe and SVD yield similar patterns of results for different categories, offering further evidence for conceptual similarity between count-based and neural-net based models.

1 Introduction

The recent boom of research on analogies with word embedding models is largely due to the striking demonstration of "linguistic regularities" (Mikolov et al., 2013b). In the so-called Google analogy test set (Mikolov et al., 2013a) the task is to solve analogies with vector offsets (a frequently cited example is *king - man + woman = queen*). This test is a popular benchmark for word embeddings, some achieving 80% accuracy (Pennington et al., 2014).

Analogical reasoning is a promising line of research, since it can be used for morphological analysis (Lavallée and Langlais, 2010), word sense disambiguation (Federici et al., 1997), and even for broad-range detection of both morphological and semantic features (Lepage and Goh, 2009). However, it remains to be seen to what extent word embeddings capture the "linguistic regularities". The Google analogy test set includes only 15 relations, and Köper et al. (2015) showed that lexicographic relations such as synonymy are not reliably discovered in the same way.

This study systematically examines how well various kinds of linguistic relations can be detected with the vector offset method, and how this process is affected by window size and dimensionality of count-based word embeddings. We develop a new, more balanced test set (BATS) which includes 99,200 questions in 40 morphological and semantic categories. The results of this study are of practical use in real-world applications of analogical reasoning, and also provide a more accurate estimate of the degree to which word embeddings capture linguistic relations.

2 Related work

Current research on analogical reasoning in word embeddings focuses on the so-called "proportional analogies" of the *a:b::c:d* kind. The task is to detect whether two pairs of words have the same relation. A recent term is "linguistic regularity" (Mikolov et al., 2013b), used to refer to any "similarities between pairs of words" (Levy et al., 2014). Analogies have been successfully used for detecting different semantic relations, such as synonymy and antonymy (Turney, 2008), ConceptNet relations and selectional preferences (Herdadelen and Baroni, 2009), and also for inducing morphological categories from unparsed data (Soricut and Och, 2015).

The fact that analogies are so versatile means that to make any claims about a model being good at

Proceedings of NAACL-HLT 2016, pages 8–15,
San Diego, California, June 12-17, 2016. ©2016 Association for Computational Linguistics

analogical reasoning, we need to show what types of analogies it can handle. This can only be determined with a comprehensive test set. However, the current sets tend to only include a certain type of relations (semantic-only: SAT (Turney et al., 2003), SemEval2012-Task2 (Jurgens et al., 2012), morphology-only: MSR (Mikolov et al., 2013b)). The Google analogy test (Mikolov et al., 2013a) contains 9 morphological and 5 semantic categories, with 20-70 unique word pairs per category which are combined in all possible ways to yield 8,869 semantic and 10,675 syntactic questions.[1]

None of the existing tests is balanced across different types of relations (word-formation getting particularly little attention). With unbalanced sets, and potentially high variation in performance for different relations, it is important to evaluate results on all relations, and not only the average.

Unfortunately, this is not common practice. Despite the popularity of the Google test set, the only study we have found that provides data for individual categories is (Levy et al., 2014). In their experiments, accuracy varied between 10.53% and 99.41%, and much success in the semantic part was due to the fact that the two categories explore the same *capital:country* relation and together constitute 56.72% of all semantic questions. This shows that a model may be more successful with some relations but not others, and more comprehensive tests are needed to show what it can and cannot do.

Model parameters can also have a major impact on performance (Levy et al., 2015; Lai et al., 2015). So far they have been studied in the context of semantic priming (Lapesa and Evert, 2014), semantic similarity tasks (Kiela and Clark, 2014), and across groups of tasks (Bullinaria and Levy, 2012). However, these results are not necessarily transferable to different tasks; e.g. dependency-based word embeddings perform better on similarity task, but worse on analogies (Levy and Goldberg, 2014a). Some studies report effects of changing model parameters on

general accuracy on Google analogy test (Levy et al., 2015; Lai et al., 2015), but, to our knowledge, this is the first study to address the effect of model parameters on individual linguistic relations in the context of analogical reasoning task.

3 The Bigger Analogy Test Set (BATS)

We introduce BATS - the Bigger Analogy Test Set. It covers 40 linguistic relations that are listed in table 1. Each relation is represented with 50 unique word pairs, which yields 2480 questions (99,200 in all set). BATS is balanced across 4 types of relations: inflectional and derivational morphology, and lexicographic and encyclopedic semantics.

A major feature of BATS that is not present in MSR and Google test sets is that morphological categories are sampled to reduce homonymy. For example, for verb present tense the Google set includes pairs like *walk:walks*, which could be both verbs and nouns. It is impossible to completely eliminate homonymy, as a big corpus will have some creative uses for almost any word, but we reduce it by excluding words attributed to more than one part-of-speech in WordNet (Miller and Fellbaum, 1998). After generating lists of such pairs, we select 50 pairs by top frequency in our corpus (section 4.2).

The semantic part of BATS does include homonyms, since semantic categories are overall smaller than morphological categories, and it is the more frequently used words that tend to have multiple functions. For example, both *dog* and *cat* are also listed in WordNet as verbs, and *aardvark* is not; an homonym-free list of animals would mostly contain low-frequency words, which in itself decreases performance. However, we did our best to avoid clearly ambiguous words; e.g. prophet Muhammad was not included in the E05 *name:occupations* section, because many people have the same name.

The lexicographic part of BATS is based on SemEval2012-Task2, extended by the authors with words similar to those included in SemEval set. About 15% of extra words came from BLESS and EVALution. The encyclopedic section was compiled on the basis of word lists in Wikipedia and other internet resources[2]. Categories E01 and E10

[1]For semantic relations there are also generic resources such as EVALution (Santus et al., 2015), and semantic similarity sets such as BLESS and WordSim353 (Baroni and Lenci, 2011), which are sometimes used as sources for compiling analogy tests. For example, (Vylomova et al., 2015) presents a compilation with 18 relations in total (58 to 3163 word pairs per relation): 10 semantic, 4 morphological, 2 affix-derived word relations, animal collective nouns, and verb-object pairs.

[2]E06-08: `https://en.wikipedia.org/wiki/List_of_animal_names`
E02: `http://www.infoplease.com/ipa/A0855611.html`

Category	Subcategory	Analogy structure and examples
Inflections	Nouns	I01: regular plurals (*student:students*)
		I02: plurals - orthographic changes (*wife:wives*)
	Adjectives	I03: comparative degree (*strong:stronger*)
		I04: superlative degree (*strong:strongest*)
	Verbs	I05: infinitive: 3Ps.Sg (*follow:follows*)
		I06: infinitive: participle (*follow:following*)
		I07: infinitive: past (*follow:followed*)
		I08: participle: 3Ps.Sg (*following:follows*)
		I09: participle: past (*following:followed*)
		I10: 3Ps.Sg : past (*follows:followed*)
Derivation	No stem change	D01: noun+less (*life:lifeless*)
		D02: un+adj. (*able:unable*)
		D03: adj.+ly (*usual:usually*)
		D04: over+adj./Ved (*used:overused*)
		D05: adj.+ness (*same:sameness*)
		D06: re+verb (*create:recreate*)
		D07: verb+able (*allow:allowable*)
	Stem change	D08: verb+er (*provide:provider*)
		D09: verb+ation (*continue:continuation*)
		D10: verb+ment (*argue:argument*)
Lexicography	Hypernyms	L01: animals (*cat:feline*)
		L02: miscellaneous (*plum:fruit, shirt:clothes*)
	Hyponyms	L03: miscellaneous (*bag:pouch, color:white*)
	Meronyms	L04: substance (*sea:water*)
		L05: member (*player:team*)
		L06: part-whole (*car:engine*)
	Synonyms	L07: intensity (*cry:scream*)
		L08: exact (*sofa:couch*)
	Antonyms	L09: gradable (*clean:dirty*)
		L10: binary (*up:down*)
Encyclopedia	Geography	E01: capitals (*Athens:Greece*)
		E02: country:language (*Bolivia:Spanish*)
		E03: UK city:county *York:Yorkshire*
	People	E04: nationalities (*Lincoln:American*)
		E05: occupation (*Lincoln:president*)
	Animals	E06: the young (*cat:kitten*)
		E07: sounds (*dog:bark*)
		E08: shelter (*fox:den*)
	Other	E09: thing:color (*blood:red*)
		E10: male:female (*actor:actress*)

Table 1: The Bigger Analogy Test Set: categories and examples

are based on the Google test, and category E09 - on the color dataset (Bruni et al., 2012). In most cases we did not rely on one source completely, as they did not make the necessary distinctions, included clearly ambiguous or low-frequency words, and/or were sometimes inconsistent[3] (e.g. *sheep:flock* in EVA-Lution is a better example of *member:collection* relation than *jury:court*).

Another new feature in BATS, as compared to the Google test set and SemEval, is that it contains several acceptable answers (sourced from WordNet),

---

E03: `http://whitefiles.org/b4_g/5_towns_to_counties_index/`

L02: `https://www.vocabulary.com/lists/189583#view=notes`

L07: `http://justenglish.me/2012/10/17/character-feelings`

[3]No claims are made about our own work being free from inconsistencies, as no dictionary will ever be so.

where applicable. For example, both *mammal* and *canine* are hypernyms of *dog*.

4 Testing the test

4.1 The vector offset method

As mentioned above, Mikolov et al. (2013a) suggested to capture the relations between words as the offset of their vector embeddings. The answer to the question "a is to b as c is to $?d$" is represented by hidden vector d, calculated as $argmax_{d \in V}(sim(d, c - a + b))$. Here V is the vocabulary excluding words a, b and c and sim is a similarity measure, for which Mikolov and many other researchers use angular distance: $sim(u, v) = cos(u, v) = \frac{u \cdot v}{||u||||v||}$.

Levy and Goldberg (2014b) propose an alternative optimization objective: $argmax_{d \in V}(cos(d - c, b - a))$ They report that this method produces more accurate results for some categories. Essentially it accounts for $d - c$ and $b - a$ to share the same direction and discards lengths of these vectors.

We supply the BATS test set with a Python evaluation script that implements both methods.[4] We report results calculated by the Mikolov's method for the sake of consistency, but some authors choose the best result for each category from each method (Levy and Goldberg, 2014b).

4.2 Corpus and models

One of the current topics in research on word embeddings is the (de)merits of count-based models as compared to the neural-net-based models. While some researchers find that the latter outperform the former (Baroni et al., 2014), others show that these approaches are mathematically similar (Levy and Goldberg, 2014b). We compare models of both types as a contribution to the ongoing dispute.

Our count-based model is built with Pointwise Mutual Information (PMI)frequency weighting. In the dimensionality reduction step we used the Singular Value Decomposition (SVD), raising Σ matrix element-wise to the power of a where $0 < a \leq 1$ to give a boost to dimensions with smaller variance Caron (2001). In this study, unless mentioned otherwise, $a = 1$. The co-occurrence extraction was performed with the kernel developed by Drozd et al. (2015).

---

[4]`http://vsm.blackbird.pw/bats`

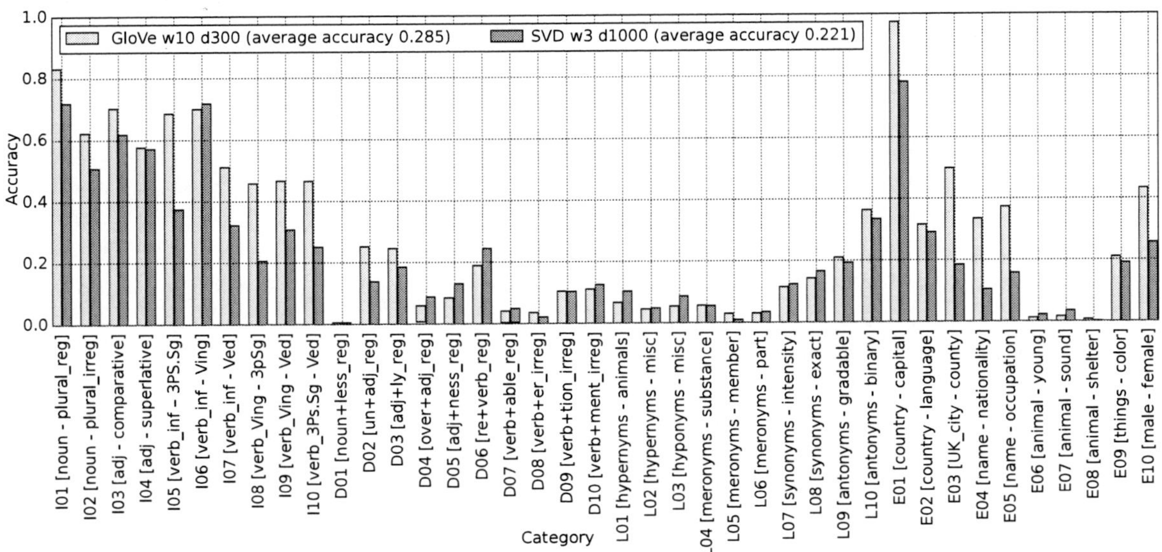

Figure 1: GloVe and SVD: accuracy on different types of relations

As a representative of implicit models we chose GloVe (Pennington et al., 2014) that achieved the highest performance on the Google test set to this date. Our source corpus combines the English Wikipedia snapshot from July 2015 (1.8B tokens), Araneum Anglicum Maius (1.2B) (Benko, 2014) and ukWaC (2B) (Baroni et al., 2009). We discarded words occurring less than 100 times, resulting in vocabulary of 301,949 words (uncased).

To check the validity of our models we evaluate it with the Google test set for which there are numerous reported results. For GloVe we used the parameters from the original study (Pennington et al., 2014): 300 dimensions, window 10, 100 iterations, $x_{max}= 100$, $a = 3/4$, sentence borders ignored. For comparison we also built an SVD model with 300 dimensions and window size 10. On our 5 B corpus GloVe achieved 80.4% average accuracy (versus 71.7% on 6 B corpus in the original study). The comparable SVD model achieved 49.9%, as opposed to with 52.6% result reported by Levy et al. (2015) for 500 dimensions, window size 10 on 1.5 B Wikipedia corpus.

To evaluate effects of window size and dimensionality we built 19 SVD-based models for windows 2-8 at 1000 dimensions, and for dimensions 100-1200 for window size 5.

5 Results and discussion

5.1 Word category effect

Figure 1 presents the results of BATS test on the GloVe model (built with the parameters from the original study (Pennington et al., 2014)), and the best performing SVD model, which was the model with window size 3 at 1000 dimensions. The model built with the same parameters as GloVe achieved only 15.9% accuracy on BATS, and is not shown.

While GloVe outperforms the SVD-based model on most categories, neither of them achieves even 30% accuracy, suggesting that BATS is much more difficult than the Google test set. Many categories are either not captured well by the embedding, or cannot be reliably retrieved with vector offset, or both. The overall pattern of easier and more difficult categories is the same for GloVe and SVD, which supports the conclusion of Levy and Goldberg (2014b) about conceptual similarity of explicit and implicit models. The overall performance of both models could perhaps be improved by parameters that we did not consider, but the point is that the current state-of-the-art in analogical reasoning with word embeddings handles well only certain types of linguistic relations, and there are directions for improvement that have not been considered so far.

The high variation we observe in this experiment

is consistent with evidence from systems competing at SemEval2012-Task2, where not a single system was able to achieve superior performance on all sub-categories. Fried and Duh (2015) also showed a similar pattern in 7 different word embeddings.

As expected, inflectional morphology is overall easier than semantics, as shown even by the Google test results (see Skip-Gram (Mikolov et al., 2013a; Lai et al., 2015), GloVe (Pennington et al., 2014), and K-Net (Cui et al., 2014), among others). But it is surprising that derivational morphology is significantly more difficult to detect than inflectional: only 3 categories out of ten yield even 20% accuracy.

The low accuracy on the lexicographic part of BATS is consistent with the findings of Köper et al. (2015). It is not clear why lexicographic relations are so difficult to detect with the vector offset method, despite numerous successful word similarity tests on much the same relations, and the fact that BATS make the task easier by accepting several correct answers. The easiest category is binary antonyms of the *up:down* kind - the category for which the choice should be the most obvious in the semantic space.

A typical mistake that our SVD models make in semantic questions is suggesting a morphological form of one of the source words in the *a:b::c:d* analogy: *cherry:red :: potato:?potatoes* instead of *potato:brown*. It would thus be beneficial to exclude from the set of possible answers not only the words *a*, *b* and *c*, but also their morphological forms.

5.2 Window size effect

Evaluating two count-based models on semantic and syntactic parts of the Google test set, Lebret and Collobert (2015) shows that the former benefit from larger windows while the latter do not. Our experiments with SVD models using different window sizes only partly concur with this finding.

Table 2 presents the accuracy for all categories of BATS using a 1000-dimension SVD model with window size varying between 2 and 8. The codes and examples for each category are listed in table 1. All categories are best detected between window sizes 2-4, although 9 of them yield equally good performance in larger windows. This indicates that there is not a one-on-one correspondence between "semantics" and "larger windows" or "mor-

	2	3	4	5	6	7	8		2	3	4	5	6	7	8
I01	62	**71**	70	68	67	65	58	L01	**11**	10	9	8	7	6	6
I02	41	**50**	47	44	42	40	34	L02	**5**	4	4	4	4	**5**	4
I03	57	**61**	58	52	47	41	32	L03	**10**	8	8	8	7	6	4
I04	49	**57**	51	45	40	35	25	L04	5	**5**	**5**	**5**	**5**	**5**	4
I05	27	37	**39**	36	34	32	29	L05	**2**	0	1	1	1	1	1
I06	62	**71**	67	63	60	58	53	L06	3	3	**4**	3	3	3	3
I07	26	**32**	**36**	**36**	**36**	**36**	34	L07	**13**	12	9	7	6	5	4
I08	**21**	20	19	18	18	18	16	L08	**19**	16	13	12	10	9	6
I09	23	30	34	35	**36**	**36**	35	L09	15	**19**	17	14	12	11	9
I10	**25**	**25**	23	21	19	19	17	L10	32	**33**	30	28	27	25	24
D01	0	0	0	0	0	0	0	E01	69	77	**79**	77	74	71	69
D02	12	**13**	12	12	11	10	9	E02	**29**	**28**	24	22	21	20	17
D03	10	18	**20**	**20**	**20**	**20**	19	E03	11	**18**	**18**	**18**	**18**	**18**	17
D04	**12**	8	6	5	4	3	2	E04	**19**	10	3	3	3	3	4
D05	7	**13**	**13**	11	9	8	5	E05	**20**	15	15	14	14	13	13
D06	15	**24**	18	13	10	8	5	E06	**2**	**2**	1	1	1	1	1
D07	**4**	**4**	3	2	2	1	1	E07	2	**3**	**3**	2	2	1	1
D08	1	2	**2**	2	1	1	1	E08	0	0	0	0	0	0	0
D09	6	10	**11**	**11**	**11**	**11**	10	E09	**19**	18	**19**	18	18	**19**	18
D10	3	**12**	**12**	10	10	9	9	E10	20	**25**	**25**	**25**	24	23	21

Table 2: Accuracy of SVD-based model on 40 BATS categories, window sizes 2-8, 1000 dimensions

phology" and "smaller windows". Also, different categories benefit from changing window size in different ways: for noun plurals the difference between the best and the worse choice is 13%, but for categories where accuracy is lower overall there is not much gain from altering the window size.

Our results are overall consistent with the evaluation of an SVD-based model on the Google set by Levy et al. (2015). This study reports 59.1% average accuracy for window size 2 yields, 56.9% for window size 5, and 56.2% for window size 10. However, using window sizes 3-4 clearly merits further investigation. Another question is whether changing window size has different effect on different models, as the data of Levy et al. (2015) suggest that GloVe actually benefits from larger windows.

5.3 Vector dimensionality effect

Intuitively, larger vectors capture more information about individual words, and therefore should increase accuracy of detecting linguistic patterns. In our data this was true of 19 BATS categories (I01-02, I04, I06, D02-03, D05-07, E01, E03, E07, E10, L03-04, L07-10): all of them either peaked at 1200 dimensions or did not start decreasing by that point.

However, the other 20 relations show all kinds of patterns. 14 categories peaked between 200 and 1100 dimensions, and then performance started decreasing (I03, I05, I07-10, D01, D04, D09, E02, E05, E09, L1, L6). 2 categories showed negative effect of higher dimensionality (D08, E04). Finally, 2 categories showed no dimensionality effect (E08,

L05), and 3 more - idiosyncratic patterns with several peaks (D10, E02, L06); however, this could be chance variation, as in these categories performance was generally low (under 10%). Figure 2 shows several examples of these different trends[5].

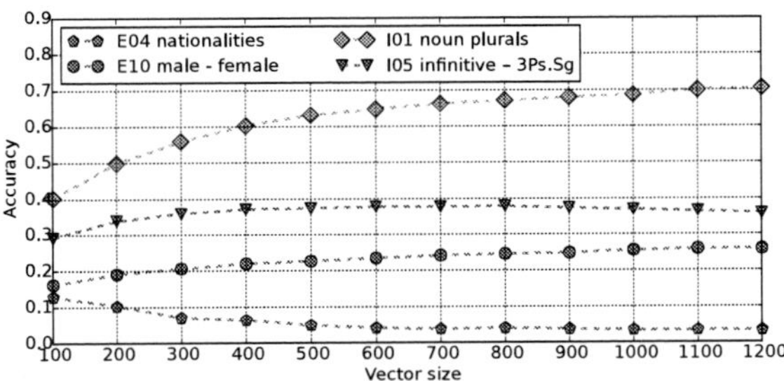

Figure 2: Effect of vector dimensionality: example categories

The main takeaway from this experiment is that, although 47.5% of BATS categories do perform better at higher dimensions (at least for SVD-based models), 40% do not, and, like with window size, there is no correlation between type of the relation (semantic or morphological) and its preference for a higher or low dimensionality. One possible explanation for lower saturation points of some relations is that, once the dimensions corresponding to the core aspects of a particular relation are included in the vectors, adding more dimensions increases noise. For practical purposes this means that choosing model parameters would have to be done to target specific relations rather than relation types.

5.4 Other parameters

In scope of this study we did not investigate all possible parameters, but our pilot experiments show that changing the power a for the Σ matrix of the SVD transformation can boost or decrease the performance on individual categories by 40-50%. Smaller value of a gives more weight to the dimensions which capture less variance in the original data, which can correspond to subtle linguistic nuances. However, as with windows and dimensions, no setting yields the best result for all categories.

A big factor is word frequency, and it deserves more attention than we can provide in scope of this paper. Some categories could perform worse because they contain only low-frequency vocabulary; in our corpus, this could be the case for D01 and D04-06[6]. But other derivational categories still do not yield higher accuracy even if the frequency distribution is comparable with that of an "easier" category (e.g. D8 and E10). Also, SVD was shown to handle low frequencies well (Wartena, 2014).

6 Conclusion

This study follows up on numerous reports of successful detection of linguistic relations with vector offset method in word embeddings. We develop BATS - a balanced analogy test set with 40 morphological and semantic relations (99,200 questions in total). Our experiments show that derivational and lexicographic relations remain a major challenge. Our best-performing SVD-based model and GloVe achieved only 22.1% and 28.5% average accuracy, respectively. The overall pattern of "easy" and "difficult" categories is the same for the two models, offering further evidence in favor of conceptual similarity between explicit and implicit word embeddings. We hope that this study would draw attention of the NLP community to word embeddings and analogical reasoning algorithms in context of lexicographic and derivational relations[7].

Our evaluation of the effect of vector dimensionality on accuracy of analogy detection with SVD-based models shows that roughly half BATS categories are best discovered with over 1000 dimensions, but 40% peak between 200 and 1100. There does not seem to be a correlation between type of linguistic relation and preference for higher or low dimensionality. Likewise, our data does not confirm the intuition about larger windows being more beneficial for semantic relations, and smaller windows - for morphological, as our SVD model performed best on both relation types in windows 2-4. Further research is needed to establish whether other models behave in the same way.

---

[5]All data for all categories can be found at `http://vsm.blackbird.pw/bats`

[6]Data on frequency distribution of words in BATS categories in our corpus can be found at `http://vsm.blackbird.pw/bats`

[7]BATS was designed for word-level models and does not focus on word phrases, but we included WordNet phrases as possible correct answers, which may be useful for phrase-aware models. Also, morphological categories involving orthographic changes may be of interest for character-based models.

References

Marco Baroni and Alessandro Lenci. 2011. How we BLESSed distributional semantic evaluation. In *Proceedings of the GEMS 2011 Workshop on GEometrical Models of Natural Language Semantics*, GEMS '11, pages 1–10. Association for Computational Linguistics.

Marco Baroni, Silvia Bernardini, Adriano Ferraresi, and Eros Zanchetta. 2009. The wacky wide web: a collection of very large linguistically processed web-crawled corpora. *Language Resources and Evaluation*, 43(3):209–226.

Marco Baroni, Georgiana Dinu, and Germn Kruszewski. 2014. Dont count, predict! a systematic comparison of context-counting vs. context-predicting semantic vectors. In *Proceedings of the 52nd Annual Meeting of the Association for Computational Linguistics*, volume 1, pages 238–247.

Vladimír Benko. 2014. Aranea: Yet another family of (comparable) web corpora. In Petr Sojka, Aleš Horák, Ivan Kopeček, and Karel Pala, editors, *Text, speech, and dialogue: 17th international conference, TSD 2014, Brno, Czech Republic, September 8-12, 2014. Proceedings*, LNCS 8655, pages 257–264. Springer.

Elia Bruni, Gemma Boleda, Marco Baroni, and Nam-Khanh Tran. 2012. Distributional semantics in technicolor. In *Proceedings of the 50th Annual Meeting of the Association for Computational Linguistics: Long Papers-Volume 1*, pages 136–145. Association for Computational Linguistics.

John A. Bullinaria and Joseph P. Levy. 2012. Extracting semantic representations from word co-occurrence statistics: stop-lists, stemming, and SVD. *Behavior Research Methods*, 44(3):890–907.

John Caron. 2001. Computational information retrieval. chapter Experiments with LSA Scoring: Optimal Rank and Basis, pages 157–169. Society for Industrial and Applied Mathematics, Philadelphia, PA, USA.

Qing Cui, Bin Gao, Jiang Bian, Siyu Qiu, and Tie-Yan Liu. 2014. Learning effective word embedding using morphological word similarity.

Aleksandr Drozd, Anna Gladkova, and Satoshi Matsuoka. 2015. Python, performance, and natural language processing. In *Proceedings of the 5th Workshop on Python for High-Performance and Scientific Computing*, PyHPC '15, pages 1:1–1:10, New York, NY, USA. ACM.

Stefano Federici, Simonetta Montemagni, and Vito Pirrelli. 1997. Inferring semantic similarity from distributional evidence: an analogy-based approach to word sense disambiguation. In *Proceedings of the ACL/EACL Workshop on Automatic Information Extraction and Building of Lexical Semantic Resources for NLP Applications*, pages 90–97.

Daniel Fried and Kevin Duh. 2015. Incorporating both distributional and relational semantics in word representations.

Ama Herdadelen and Marco Baroni. 2009. BagPack: A general framework to represent semantic relations. In *Proceedings of the Workshop on Geometrical Models of Natural Language Semantics*, GEMS '09, pages 33–40. Association for Computational Linguistics.

David A. Jurgens, Peter D. Turney, Saif M. Mohammad, and Keith J. Holyoak. 2012. Semeval-2012 task 2: Measuring degrees of relational similarity. In *Proceedings of the First Joint Conference on Lexical and Computational Semantics-Volume 1: Proceedings of the main conference and the shared task, and Volume 2: Proceedings of the Sixth International Workshop on Semantic Evaluation*, pages 356–364. Association for Computational Linguistics.

Douwe Kiela and Stephen Clark. 2014. A systematic study of semantic vector space model parameters. In *Proceedings of the 2nd Workshop on Continuous Vector Space Models and their Compositionality (CVSC) at EACL*, pages 21–30.

Maximilian Köper, Christian Scheible, and Sabine Schulte im Walde. 2015. Multilingual reliability and semantic structure of continuous word spaces. In *Proceedings of the 11th International Conference on Computational Semantics 2015*, pages 40–45. Association for Computational Linguistics.

Siwei Lai, Kang Liu, Liheng Xu, and Jun Zhao. 2015. How to generate a good word embedding?

Gabriella Lapesa and Stefan Evert. 2014. A large scale evaluation of distributional semantic models: Parameters, interactions and model selection. 2:531–545.

Jean-Franois Lavallée and Philippe Langlais. 2010. Unsupervised morphological analysis by formal analogy. In *Multilingual Information Access Evaluation I. Text Retrieval Experiments*, pages 617–624. Springer.

Rmi Lebret and Ronan Collobert. 2015. Rehabilitation of count-based models for word vector representations. In *Computational Linguistics and Intelligent Text Processing*, pages 417–429. Springer.

Yves Lepage and Chooi-ling Goh. 2009. Towards automatic acquisition of linguistic features. In *Proceedings of the 17th Nordic Conference on Computational Linguistics (NODALIDA 2009), eds., Kristiina Jokinen and Eckard Bick*, pages 118–125.

Omer Levy and Yoav Goldberg. 2014a. Dependency-based word embeddings. In *ACL (2)*, pages 302–308.

Omer Levy and Yoav Goldberg. 2014b. Linguistic regularities in sparse and explicit word representations. In

Proceedings of the Eighteenth Conference on Computational Natural Language Learning, pages 171–180, Ann Arbor, Michigan, June. Association for Computational Linguistics.

Omer Levy, Yoav Goldberg, and Israel Ramat-Gan. 2014. Linguistic regularities in sparse and explicit word representations. In *CoNLL*, pages 171–180.

Omer Levy, Yoav Goldberg, and Ido Dagan. 2015. Improving distributional similarity with lessons learned from word embeddings. In *Transactions of the Association for Computational Linguistics*, volume 3, pages 211–225.

Tomas Mikolov, Kai Chen, Greg Corrado, and Jeffrey Dean. 2013a. Efficient estimation of word representations in vector space.

Tomas Mikolov, Wen tau Yih, and Geoffrey Zweig. 2013b. Linguistic regularities in continuous space word representations. In *Proceedings of the 2013 Conference of the North American Chapter of the Association for Computational Linguistics: Human Language Technologies (NAACL-HLT-2013)*, pages 746–751. Association for Computational Linguistics.

George Miller and Christiane Fellbaum. 1998. *Wordnet: An electronic lexical database*. MIT Press: Cambridge.

Jeffrey Pennington, Richard Socher, and Christopher D. Manning. 2014. Glove: Global vectors for word representation. In *Proceedings of the Empiricial Methods in Natural Language Processing (EMNLP 2014)*, volume 12, pages 1532–1543.

Enrico Santus, Frances Yung, Alessandro Lenci, and Chu-Ren Huang. 2015. EVALution 1.0: an evolving semantic dataset for training and evaluation of distributional semantic models. In *Proceedings of the 4th Workshop on Linked Data in Linguistics (LDL-2015)*, pages 64–69.

Radu Soricut and Franz Och. 2015. Unsupervised morphology induction using word embeddings. In *Human Language Technologies: The 2015 Annual Conference of the North American Chapter of the ACL*, pages 1627–1637.

Peter Turney, Michael Littman, Jeffrey Bigham, and Victor Shnayder. 2003. Combining independent modules to solve multiple-choice synonym and analogy problems. In *In Proceedings of the International Conference on Recent Advances in Natural Language Processing*, pages 482–489.

Peter D. Turney. 2008. A uniform approach to analogies, synonyms, antonyms, and associations. In *Proceedings of the 22nd International Conference on Computational Linguistics (Coling 2008)*, pages 905–912.

Ekaterina Vylomova, Laura Rimmel, Trevor Cohn, and Timothy Baldwin. 2015. Take and took, gaggle and goose, book and read: Evaluating the utility of vector differences for lexical relation learning.

Christian Wartena. 2014. On the effect of word frequency on distributional similarity. In *Proceedings of the 12th edition of the KONVENS conference - Hildesheim*, volume 1, pages 1–10.

Argument Identification in Chinese Editorials

Marisa Chow
Princeton University
1482 Frist Campus Ctr
Princeton, NJ 08544, USA
mlchow@princeton.edu

Abstract

In this paper, we develop and evaluate several techniques for identifying argumentative paragraphs in Chinese editorials. We first use three methods of evaluation to score a paragraph's argumentative nature: a relative word frequency approach; a method which targets known argumentative words in our corpus; and a combined approach which uses elements from the previous two. Then, we determine the best score thresholds for separating argumentative and non-argumentative paragraphs. The results of our experimentation show that our relative word frequency approach provides a reliable way to identify argumentative paragraphs with a F_1 score of 0.91, though challenges in accurate scoring invite improvement through context-aware means.

1 Introduction

Argumentation – the act of reasoning in support of an opinion or idea – frequently presents itself in all types of texts, from casual chat messages to online blogs. Argumentation mining aims to identify and determine a persuasive text's argumentative components, or the atomic units of its underlying structure. For example, an argumentation mining system might seek to locate and classify sections of claims and supporting evidence within an essay. More comprehensive mining might map the relations between different units, such as the support of evidence or the opposition of counterarguments to the thesis.

Argument identification offers a wide variety of practical applications. If argumentative text can be identified accurately, then the main arguments of large sets of data may be extracted. For example, argument identification could isolate arguments surrounding subjects like U.S. immigration law, or summarize the arguments in research papers. Recent efforts in argumentation mining have included applications such as automatic essay scoring (Song et al., 2014; Ong et al., 2014), online debates (Boltuzic and Šnajder, 2014), and arguments in specific domains such as online Greek social media sites (Sardianos et al., 2015). However, to our knowledge, no work in argumentation mining to date has been performed for Chinese, a large and rich domain for NLP work.

Here we focus on the first step of argumentation mining, locating argumentative units within a text. We develop and evaluate several methods of argument identification when performed upon a corpus of Chinese editorials, making the assumption that editorials are opinionated texts, although a single editorial may contain both opinionated and non-opinionated paragraphs.

Our work met with several challenges. Although newspaper editorials can be assumed to carry an opinion of some sort, the opinion is not always explicitly expressed at a word level, and methods of argumentation can vary widely from editorial to editorial. For example, one might exhibit a thesis followed by supporting evidence, but others might only state facts until the final paragraph. Furthermore, editorials commonly build arguments by citing facts. In our work, we not only had to define 'argumentative' and 'non-argumentative', but also limit the scope of an argument. In order to capture the larger argument structure, our work focuses on identifying arguments in paragraph units of no more than 200

Proceedings of NAACL-HLT 2016, pages 16–21,
San Diego, California, June 12-17, 2016. ©2016 Association for Computational Linguistics

characters (around 3-5 sentences), although we do not concatenate shorter paragraphs to ensure a minimum size.

Our task aims to label paragraphs such as the following as argumentative: "不幸的是，如今在深圳的各十字路口，绳子在显示作用，白线却无力地趴在地上。这是法规的悲哀。" ("Unfortunately, nowadays at Shenzhen's ten road intersections, cords are used to show that the white road lines lie uselessly on the ground. This legislation is tragic.")

The contributions of this paper are collecting and annotating a dataset of Chinese editorials; manually creating a list of argumentative words; and the comparison and analysis of three methods.

2 Data

2.1 Corpora

This work makes use of two corpora, one of Chinese editorials and one of Chinese reportage, both of which are subcorpora in the Lancaster Corpus of Mandarin Chinese (McEnery and Xiao, 2004). The LCMC, a member of the Brown family corpora, is a 1M balanced word corpus with seventeen subcorpora of various topics. We used the *Press: Reportage* and *Press: Editorials* subcorpora, containing 53K and 88K words respectively. Samples in both subcorpora were drawn from mainland Mandarin Chinese newspaper issues published between 1989 and 1993, which increases the likelihood that both articles and editorials discuss the same topics and use a similar vocabulary.

Our unit of text was the paragraph, which typically contains a single argument or thought. We decided to use paragraphs that were no more than 200 characters in our experimentation, assuming that longer paragraphs might hold multiple arguments. We split our raw data into two subsets: paragraphs 200 characters and below, and paragraphs larger than 200 characters. The small paragraphs were left in their original form, but we manually split the larger paragraphs into small sections under 200 characters, with individual paragraphs no smaller than 50 characters. We omitted large paragraphs which cannot reasonably be split up into sentences (for example, a long one-sentence paragraph).

2.2 Gold Standard Annotation

To evaluate our experiments, we employed workers through Amazon Mechanical Turk to tag our set of 719 editorial paragraphs. For each paragraph, the worker was asked, "Does the author of this paragraph express an argument?" In response, the worker categorized the paragraph by selecting "Makes argument," "Makes NO argument," or "Unsure". All text shown to the worker was written in both English and manually translated Mandarin. Instructions were screened by native speakers for clarity. Each paragraph was rated by three "Master Workers," distinguished as accurate AMT workers.

Though we provided clear instructions and examples for our categorization task, we found that the three workers for each task often did not all agree on an answer. Only 26% of paragraphs received an unambiguous consensus of "has argument" or "no argument" for the paragraph's argumentative nature. The rest of the paragraph results contain at least two different opinions about the paragraph. Since paragraphs receiving three different answers were likely unreliable for identification, we threw out those paragraphs, leaving 622 paragraphs for our methods. Around 78% of paragraphs were rated as argumentative, and 22% as non-argumentative.

Paragraph Consensus	Count	Percentage
Makes an argument	484	67.32%
Makes NO argument	138	19.19%
Unsure	43	5.98%
No consensus	54	7.51%
total	719	

Table 1: Breakdown of AMT paragraph results.

3 Models

We first score paragraphs according to the methods outlined below. Then, we determine the best score threshold for each method, and accordingly label paragraphs "argumentative" or "non-argumentative."

3.1 Method 1: Identification by Comparative Word Frequency

Our first method of evaluation is based on a process outlined by Kim and Hovy in a paper on identifying opinion-bearing words (Kim and Hovy, 2005). We first follow Kim and Hovy's process to construct a list of word-score pairs. Then, we use these scores to evaluate our paragraphs of editorial text.

Kim and Hovy postulate that words which appear more often in editorials than in non-editorial text could be opinion-bearing words. For a given word, we use the Reportage and Editorials subcorpora to find its unigram probabilities in both corpora, then compute a score that indicates its frequency bias toward editorial or reportage text. Words that are relatively more frequent in editorial text are more likely argumentative.

$$Score(W) = \frac{EditorialProb(W)}{ReportageProb(W)} \quad (1)$$

Kim and Hovy further specify a way to eliminate words which do not have a repeated bias toward editorial or reportage text. We divide the Reportage and Editorial corpora each into three subsets, creating three pairs of reportage and editorial subsets. Then, for each word, we compute word scores as specified above, but for each pair of reportage and editorial subsets. This creates $Score_1(W), Score_2(W), Score_3(W)$, which are essentially ratios between editorial or reportage appearances of a word. We only retain words whose scores are all greater than 1.0, or all below 1.0, since this indicates repeated bias toward either editorials or reportage (opinionated or non-opinionated) text.

After scoring individual words, we rate paragraphs by assigning a score based on the scores of the individual words which comprise them. If a paragraph P contains n opinion words with corresponding frequency $f_1, f_2, \ldots f_n$ and assigned scores $s_1, s_2, \ldots s_n$, then the score for the paragraph is calculated by following:

$$Score(P) = f_1 s_1 + f_2 s_2 + \ldots f_n s_n \quad (2)$$

From these scores and our tagged data, we determine a best score threshold by tuning on our tagged data, which produced a threshold of 40.0.

3.2 Method 2: Targeting Known Argumentative Words

Our second method involves creating a list of known argumentative words that appear in the Editorials

corpus and scoring paragraphs based on how many of these words appear in them. First, we constructed a list of the most frequent argumentative words that appear in the Editorials corpus. Then, we assigned each paragraph a score based on presence of these words.

We manually selected the most frequent argumentative words in the Editorials corpus by sorting a list of the words and their frequencies. Words were selected for their likelihood of indicating argumentation. Generally, the most common words which indicated opinion also possessed non-argumentative meanings. For example, the common word "要" can mean "to want" as well as "must" or "if."

Word	Translation	Count	%
我们	we	219	2.55
要	must	210	2.45
问题	problem	192	2.24
就	right away, at once	158	1.84
而	and so, yet, but	131	1.53
都	all, even (emphasis)	116	1.35
更	even more, further	87	1.01
但	but	86	1.00
还	still	84	0.98
好	good (adj)	76	0.89
人们	people	64	0.75
自己	self	61	0.71
却	however	57	0.66
人民	the people	53	0.62
必须	must	49	0.57
认为	believe	49	0.57
为了	in order to	48	0.56
我	I	47	0.55
重要	important	46	0.54
因此	consequently	46	0.54

Table 2: Constructed list of known argumentative words by frequency. Horizontal lines mark boundaries between 10-, 15-, and 20-word lists.

Scoring paragraphs based on this list was simple: we awarded a paragraph a point for each instance of any of the words on the list. We were interested in whether the presence of a few argumentative words could indicate argumentation in the entire paragraph. We determined the best word list size and the best threshold that returned the most accurate labels, a word list size of 15 words and a threshold of

1. For this model, a threshold of 1 means if the paragraph contains at least one word from the word list, it is labeled as argumentative.

3.3 Method 3: Combined Method

Our third method of identifying arguments combines the previous two methods. Similar to the second method, we scored paragraphs based on a list of argumentative words. However, instead of manually selecting argumentative words from a word frequency distribution, we created a list of opinionated words by picking a number of the highest-scoring words from the first method.

In structuring this combination method, we theorized that the highest-scoring words are those which are the most common opinionated words, since they have the highest probability of consistently appearing throughout the Editorials corpus and not the Reportage corpus. By using these words instead of manually-picked argumentative words, we scored paragraphs using a list of words based on the composition of the corpus itself, with the intent of creating a more relevant list of words.

Scoring remained similar to the second method, where we awarded a paragraph a point for each instance of any of the words on the list. Again, the threshold which produced the best results was 1. That is, if a paragraph contained at least one word from the list, it was labeled as argumentative.

4 Results

4.1 Method 1: Identification by Comparative Word Frequency

Method	Accuracy	Precision	Recall	F_1 score
1	0.841	0.847	0.971	0.905
2	0.801	0.826	0.942	0.880
3	0.371	0.850	0.233	0.366
1 = Relative Word Frequency Method (T=40)				
2 = Targeting Argument Words (T=1,W=15)				
3 = Combined Method (T=1,W=20)				
T = threshold, W = word list size				

Table 3: A comparison of the best metric scores of all three methods.

Our experiments produced the best performance under the relative word frequency method, achieving 84% accuracy and an F_1 score of 0.91. These scores were closely followed by the second method with 80% accuracy and an F_1 score of 0.88.

Despite these high scores, we were surprised to find that our relative word frequency system had scored many non-argumentative words very high. For example, the highest-scoring word was 自民党, "Liberal Democratic Party." When we eliminated words with non-argumentative POS tags (i.e. nouns and other noun forms), the highest-scoring word was 监测, "to monitor" (Table 4). These words were likely rare enough in the Reportage corpus that they were awarded high scores. Words indicative of arguments such as 必要, "necessary," scored high, but largely did not make up the highest-scoring words.

Word	Translation	Score
监测	to monitor	57.917
谈判	to negotiate	51.656
污染	to pollute	34.437
发展中国家	developing country	32.872
停火	to cease fire	29.741
整治	to rennovate, restore	28.176
腐败	to corrupt	26.610
北方	north	25.129
断	to break	25.129
匿	to hide	25.062

Table 4: Highest-scoring words from the Kim and Hovy scoring in the statistical method, words with non-argumentative POS tags removed.

As a result, our list of opinion-bearing words contained non-argumentative words along with argumentative identifiers, artificially raising paragraph scores. Paragraphs were more likely to score high, since our system labeled many non-argumentative paragraphs as argumentative. The inflated word scores are likely a result of mismatched editorial and reportage corpora, since a word that is relatively rare in the Reportage corpus and more common in the Editorials corpus will score high, regardless of its actual meaning. However, this approach still performed well, suggesting that these non-argumentative words, such as "to monitor," may be used to persuade in context (e.g. "The government monitors its people too closely").

4.2 Method 2: Targeting Known Argumentative Words

Our second method similarly performed well, with high accuracy and fewer false positives than the previous method, due to the list of words that clearly indicated argumentation. The best performance was given by a threshold of 1. That is, the system performed best when it marked a paragraph argumentative as long as it has at least one of the words from the list. Results did not significantly improve even if the list was expanded or the score threshold was raised, implying that adding words to the 10-word list, even if the new words had exclusively argumentative meanings, did not significantly improve performance. The more frequent semi-argumentative words like "而" ("and so," "yet") had a greater positive effect on accuracy than obviously argumentative words like "必须" ("must") which do not appear as often in the corpus.

4.3 Method 3: Combined Method

Since our combined method relied heavily upon the word scores generated by the relative word frequency approach, the results showed significant errors. Seeded with a word list that did not contain solely argumentative words (e.g. "to monitor" as well as "to pollute"), the combined method attempted to find argumentative paragraphs using words which did not exclusively indicate argumentation. Overall, the combined method rated many more argumentative paragraphs as non-argumentative than the reverse, and performed poorly overall with a F_1 score of 0.37.

5 Related Work

Prior work on argument identification has been largely domain-specific. Among them, Sardianos et al. (2015) produced work on argument extraction from news in Greek, and Boltûzic and Jan Ŝnajder (2015) worked on recognizing arguments in online discussions. Kiesel et al. have worked on a shared task for argument mining in newspaper editorials (Kiesel et al., 2015). They contributed a data set of tagged newspaper editorials and a method for modeling an editorial's argumentative structure.

Because argument mining is a relatively new field within the NLP community, there has been no argu-ment identification study performed on Chinese editorials, although there has been a significant amount of work on opinion identification. In particular, Bin Lu's work on opinion detection in Chinese news text (Lu, 2010) has produced a highest F-measure of 78.4 for opinion holders and 59.0 for opinion targets.

6 Conclusion and Future Work

In this study, we sought to computationally identify argumentative paragraphs in Chinese editorials through three methods: using relative word frequencies to score paragraphs; targeting known argumentative words in paragraphs; and combining the two methods. Our experiments produced the best performance under the relative word frequency method, achieving 84% accuracy and an F_1 score of 0.91.

Despite these high scores, we found our relative word frequency system scored many non-argumentative words very high. These words were likely rare enough in the Reportage corpus (but common enough in the Editorials corpus) that they were awarded high scores. As a result, our list of opinion-bearing words contained non-argumentative words along with argumentative identifiers, raising paragraph scores and producing false positives.

Future work could be done to improve upon Kim and Hovy's method in order to more accurately score words. In particular, it is necessary to avoid scoring non-argumentative words high, simply due to their presence in the Editorials corpus and absence in the Reportage corpus. In our experiment, we eliminated high-scoring non-argumentative words like "自民党" ("Liberal Democratic Party") by removing nouns from scoring. However, this also eliminates argumentative nouns like "问题," meaning "problem" or "issue." One solution to removing topic-specific nouns while keeping argumentative nouns is identifying the editorial topic and its domain-specific words, which would prevent the method from scoring rare but non-argumentative words high. Another benefit to determining word context is distinguishing between argumentative and non-argumentative senses of a word. For example, if the word "garbage" appears in an article discussing landfills, it is likely not argumentative. However, if it appears in an editorial discussing recent movies, it is more likely to be an argumentative word (e.g.

"That movie is garbage."). In our current system, we cannot distinguish between these two uses. If the word "garbage" appeared equally in news text as a neutral word (say, in an article discussing landfills) and in the editorials corpus as an argumentative word ("that's garbage!"), then the score of "garbage" would be low, and we would be unable to identify the argumentative nature of "garbage" in editorials. Another solution is to observe the context in which words appear. If the word "garbage" appears in proximity to words like "landfill" and "recycling," then we could guess that the usage of this word is non-argumentative.

By improving the list of opinionated words in the relative word frequency method, we could not only improve its scoring system, but perhaps even improve upon our combined method to produce even better, more accurate results than the first two methods used. We hope our research provides a benchmark or foundation for future research in the growing field of argument mining.

Acknowledgments

I would like to thank the Princeton University Department of Computer Science for their generous support in the funding of this project, without which this work would not be possible. I would also like to thank Professor Christiane Fellbaum for her invaluable guidance and advice throughout this project.

References

Filip Boltuzic and Jan Šnajder. 2014. Back up your stance: Recognizing arguments in online discussions. In *Proceedings of the First Workshop on Argumentation Mining*, pages 49–58. Citeseer.

Johannes Kiesel, Khalid Al-Khatib, Matthias Hagen, and Benno Stein. 2015. A shared task on argumentation mining in newspaper editorials. *NAACL HLT 2015*, page 35.

Soo-Min Kim and Eduard Hovy. 2005. Automatic detection of opinion bearing words and sentences. In *Companion Volume to the Proceedings of the International Joint Conference on Natural Language Processing (IJCNLP)*.

Bin Lu. 2010. Identifying opinion holders and targets with dependency parser in chinese news texts. In *Proceedings of the NAACL HLT 2010 Student Research Workshop*, pages 46–51.

Anthony McEnery and Zhonghua Xiao. 2004. The lancaster corpus of mandarin chinese: A corpus for monolingual and contrastive language study. *Religion*, 17:3–4.

Nathan Ong, Diane Litman, and Alexandra Brusilovsky. 2014. Ontology-based argument mining and automatic essay scoring. In *Proceedings of the First Workshop on Argumentation Mining*, pages 24–28.

Christos Sardianos, Ioannis Manousos Katakis, Georgios Petasis, and Vangelis Karkaletsis. 2015. Argument extraction from news. *NAACL HLT 2015*, page 56.

Yi Song, Michael Heilman, Beata Beigman, and Klebanov Paul Deane. 2014. Applying argumentation schemes for essay scoring.

Automatic tagging and retrieval of E-Commerce products based on visual features

Vasu Sharma and **Harish Karnick**
Dept. Of Computer Science and Engineering
Indian Institute of Technology, Kanpur
sharma.vasu55@gmail.com   hk@cse.iitk.ac.in

Abstract

This paper proposes an automatic tag assignment approach to various e-commerce products where tag allotment is done solely based on the visual features in the image. It then builds a tag based product retrieval system upon these allotted tags.

The explosive growth of e-commerce products being sold online has made manual annotation infeasible. Without such tags it's impossible for customers to be able to find these products. Hence a scalable approach catering to such large number of product images and allocating meaningful tags is essential and could be used to make an efficient tag based product retrieval system.

In this paper we propose one such approach based on feature extraction using Deep Convolutional Neural Networks to learn descriptive semantic features from product images. Then we use inverse distance weighted K-nearest neighbours classifiers along with several other multi-label classification approaches to assign appropriate tags to our images. We demonstrate the functioning of our algorithm for the Amazon product dataset for various categories of products like clothing and apparel, electronics, sports equipment etc.
Keywords: Content based image retrieval, Multi-Modal data embeddings and search, Automatic Image Annotation, E-commerce product categorization

1 Introduction

In the present day world of mass internet penetration and the advent of the e-commerce era the number of products being bought and sold online has increased exponentially in the past few years. In 2012, Business to Consumer (B2C) e-commerce sales grew 21.1% to top \$1 trillion for the first time[1]. This is expected to grow steadily at the rate of around 20% and is estimated to hit \$2.5 trillion by 2018 [2].

Given the explosive growth in the number of products being sold online and the relative heterogeneity in the categories these products could be allotted to, it has become physically impossible and infeasible to manually tag these products. Besides not everyone will tag the same images with the same tags. This leads to discrepancy in the kinds of tags allotted to the products. Search engines looking for products based on customers query heavily rely on these tags allotted to each image to return accurate and meaningful results to customers queries but mainly only the product images are available which is impossible for the search engine to make sense of. Besides the discrepancy in tagging leads to a lot of useful search results to get excluded.

An automatic tagging system can help take care of both of these problems and will be able to build an efficient product database querying system even if the database consists solely of visual information about the products. Such an automated systems will bring about tagging homogeneity so that similar products are tagged with the same tags. This will

---

[1] http://www.emarketer.com/Article/Ecommerce-Sales-Topped-1-Trillion-First-Time-2012/1009649
[2] http://www.emarketer.com/Article/Global-B2C-Ecommerce-Sales-Hit-15-Trillion-This-Year-Driven-by-Growth-Emerging-Markets/1010575

22

Proceedings of NAACL-HLT 2016, pages 22–28,
San Diego, California, June 12-17, 2016. ©2016 Association for Computational Linguistics

also eliminate the need for the laborious process of manually tagging such products.

The e-commerce marketplace is a truly multi-modal space with visual features co-existing with product descriptions and feature specifications. To be truly effective, such a marketplace must allow the user to be able to find products based on it's visual features as well as product descriptions. This paper proposes an efficient approach to create such a Multi-Modal visual feature based product information retrieval system.
This is achieved in a 2 step process:

1. (Image to Tags) Visual features are extracted from product images and are used to automatically annotate these product images with meaningful tags.

2. (Tags to Images) Now these tags are used to query a hash table indexed on these tags and used to retrieve all images corresponding to this tag.

The rest of the paper is organized as follows. Related literature is reviewed in Section 2. Section 3 presents our proposed approach along with details of techniques used. Sections 4 presents a detailed description of obtained results for various datasets. Section 5 and 6 present Conclusion and Future Work respectively.

2   Literature Review

The e-commerce boom we have seen in the past few years has created a lot of interest in this particular area of research as such a system which can automatically tag product images is of great commercial and economic value. We saw a lot of recent work on this suggesting that this a very active area of research and is quickly gaining popularity.
One of the best work in this field is from Zoghbi et al. (2016) who similar to us use visual features to assign textual descriptors to the image and use these descriptors for query based image retrieval. In this paper they use two latent variable models to bridge between textual and visual data: bilingual latent Dirichlet allocation and canonical correlation analysis. They report their results on a self created

image dataset and work only for apparel and do not generalise to other categories.
Another promising work on this problem was done by Mason et al (2013). In this work they use SIFT (Scale Invariant Feature Transform) features Lowe (2004), along with colour features, Gabor filters Fogel and Sagi (1989) and bag of HOG (Histogram of Gradient) features Dalal and Triggs (2005) as the visual features. Gibbs sampling is used to sample topic assignments for visual terms in the test image. Then they apply the technique of Latent Dirichlet Allocation (LDA) Blei et al. (2003) to generate probable captions for a given set of visual features.
Feng et al (2010), proposed a system called MixLDA which tried to automatically generate captions for news images which is similar to our task. Their model works with a bag-of-words representation and treats each article-image-caption tuple as a single document. LDA is then used to infer latent topics which generated these documents. It now uses the distribution over these latent topics to estimate the multimodal word distributions over topics for new images which in turn is used to estimate posterior of the topic proportions over visual documents. This is used to annotate the news images.
Style Finder Di et al. (2013), is another system which tries to identify visual features present in an image and uses those to build a visual feature vocabulary which could then be used for query based product retrieval. They use the women's coats dataset and extract SIFT, HoG and GIST features from these images and train binary linear SVM's to detect the presence or absence of each feature. We feel that such an approach would not be able to scale up to a very large number of labels as it tries to train a classifier for each label .
Another work by Zhan et al (2015) is also relevant to this problem. They try to automatically tag image features for shoe images by first identifying the viewpoint and then use view-specific part localization model based on the prior knowledge of the shoe structures under different viewpoints. Finally, they use a SVM classifier on low level features extracted from these localized shoe parts, which is ultimately used for attribute prediction.. Here their approach is restricted to only shoe images and cant scale to large number of images or to images of other product categories.

Whittlesearch approach Kovashka et al. (2015) was another interesting work where the authors try to cater to user queries based on relative strengths of visual attributes in a product image. First they learn a ranking function to predict the relative strength of certain visual attributes. This is achieved by casting estimation of such a ranking function as a large-margin formulation of Joachims Tsochantaridis et al. (2005) with suitable constraints, which could then easily be solved. The users can then query for products which have less or more of a certain attribute than a given image and are shown a ranked list of such products based on this ranking function. Based on the user feedback, they update their scoring function using what they call as the Relative Attribute Feedback approach.

Several other SVM based approaches on a variety of visual features like SIFT, HoG, SURF etc have also been proposed Rothe et al. (2015), Li (2010), Gangopadhyay (2001), Zeng et al. (2014), Tadse et al. (2014). However we note that none of these approaches attempt to generalize to the classification of all varieties of products and restrict themselves to certain product classes (mainly apparel and clothing). Besides, they do not operate on a multi label setting and hence need one-vs-all type classifiers to detect multiple labels which do not scale up for large number for possible tags. Our approach on the other hand is extremely adaptive and is able to identify tags for multiple categories of products. Besides we directly deal with tag annotation as a multi label problem allowing our approach to scale up to a large number of tag categories.

3 Approach

In this section we elaborate upon the approach we used to build the automatic annotation system and then how we use these tags to build an efficient tag based product retrieval system.

3.1 Dataset

Lack of open availability of a dataset is one of the biggest problems which hinders the development of effective automatic tagging systems for e-commerce products. Most of the data present on the web is highly unstructured and lacks proper labels and hence cant be effectively used. Even when the labels are there, they are extremely noisy and cant be relied upon. In our paper we present the results on the Amazon e-commerce product dataset McAuley et al. (2015b), McAuley et al. (2015a) which contains images of various product categories and their meta data which we parse to obtain the tags associated with each image. For this paper we demonstrate our approach for apparels and clothing, electronics and sports equipment categories and show that the approach scales up to large number of tags and performs well on a wide category of products. Images of these categories are tagged with a total of 1664, 886 and 2224 possible tags respectively.

3.2 Feature Extraction from Images

Researchers in the computer vision domain have frequently used Scale Invariant Feature Transform (SIFT) vectors, Histogram of Gradients (HoG) vectors, SURF vectors, Gabor filters etc. to extract useful features from images. However in our project we use features extracted from higher layers of a very Deep Convolutional Neural Network to serve as our visual features. Here we use the 19 layer deep VGG network Simonyan and Zisserman (2014) and it is trained on the Imagenet dataset first. We then use this trained network on the Imagenet dataset Russakovsky et al. (2015) and use the concept of 'Transfer Learning' Yosinski et al. (2014) to train it on our Amazon product dataset next. We also experiment with the VGG-16 and Googlenet networks, but VGG-19 features give us the best performance and hence we use them for our paper. The network structure is presented in Image 1.

It is observed that Deep Convolutional Neural networks have the ability to learn useful feature representations by non-linearly projecting the input images into a discriminative subspace where similar images tend to have similar intermediate feature representations while non-similar images are projected far from each other. This trend is independent of the dataset it is trained on and hence a network trained on Imagenet network too is able to learn useful feature representations for the Amazon product dataset when trained on it. Oquab et al. (2014), Bengio (2012)

Hence we could use VGG-19 models pre-trained on Imagenet and then adapt them for our dataset. This cuts down our training time tremendously as training

Deep CNN models from scratch is computationally very expensive. We use the 4096 Dimensional features from the last fully connected hidden layer of the VGG net as features to represent a given visual image.

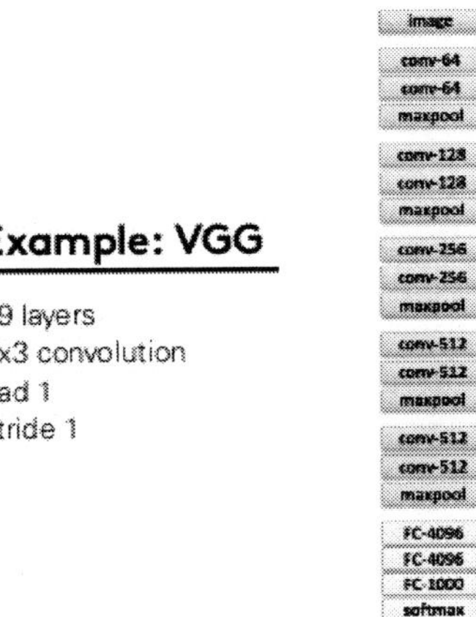

Figure 1: The VGG-19 Network
The conv layers represent convolution layers, Maxpool are Max Pooling layers and FC are Fully connected layers

3.3 Automatic tag assignment to images

After having obtained the extracted feature vectors for each images from the Deep CNN's, our next task to automatically assign all relevant tags to each image. This is essentially a multi label problem which is still a very active area of research till date. We avoid using one-vs-all classifiers like SVM's etc as such classifiers can't be scaled up for a very large number of tag categories which we observe in the case of e-commerce products. In this paper we use Weighted K-Nearest Neighbours approach with weights for each neighbour as inverse of the distance of the neighbour from the query point. For each query point we evaluate it's K nearest neighbours from the training set and evaluate the weighted average of the presence of each particular tag from among these K neighbours. Ultimately, we allot the D tags with the highest weighted average to the query image.

The 'presence score' of the occurrence of the tag t_i in the query image x could be calculated as:

$$S(t_i|x) = \sum_{j=1}^{K} \frac{I(i,j)}{d_{x,n_j}} / \sum_{j=1}^{K} \frac{1}{d_{x,n_j}}$$

Where d_{x,n_j} is the distance between query point and the jth neighbour, $I(i,j)$ is an indicator variable which is defined as follows:

$$I(i,j) = \begin{cases} 1 & \text{if } n_j \text{ has tag } t_i \\ 0 & \text{Otherwise} \end{cases}$$

This is how we do tag allocation to the various images. K-Nearest Neighbour approach is computationally very efficient and can be scaled up to a very large number of tags without a very large increase in computational complexity.

3.4 Querying product based on tagged visual features

Once we have a fully tagged dataset of product images we can easily store the tags and images which have been tagged with it in a hash table with the tag as the key. We also store the probability of the presence of this tag in each image. The image list corresponding to each tag is then sorted according to this probability score and stored and the value for the entry with the tag as the key.
Now when the user queries this database looking for products with a certain tagged feature, then the hash table is looked up for that tag and the images corresponding to those tags are returned in the order of higher probability score first. This helps us build a lightning fast retrieval system for tagged visual feature based queries for the various e-commerce products.

4 Results

4.1 Annotation Results

We present our results on 3 different categories of products i.e. apparel and clothing, electronics and sports equipment. The metrics we use to measure the performance of our method are Precision, Recall and F_1-score which are computed over all possible tag categories. These metric are defined as follows:

$$Precision = TP/(TP + FP)$$

(a) **Predicted tags:** Boots, Jacket, Western, Watches, Skirt, Jewelry Accessories
Actual Tags: Boots, Jacket, Western, Watches, Jewelry Accessories, Sunglasses, Handbags & Purses

(b) **Predicted Tags:** Baby Clothing, Jeans, Shoes, Sweater
Actual Tags: Baby Clothing, Jeans, Shoes, Sweater

(c) **Predicted Tags:** Hats, Skirt, Handbags & Purses, Floral Top
Actual Tags: Hats, Skirt, Handbags, Floral Top, Heels

Figure 2: Examples from Apparel category

(a) **Predicted tags:** LCD TV, Home Theater, Speakers, DVD player
Actual Tags: LCD TV, Home Theater, Speakers, DVD player, Amplifier

(b) **Predicted Tags:** Camera, Camera Lens, Memory card, USB drive, Camera Stand
Actual Tags: Camera, Camera Lens, Memory card, USB drive, Camera Stand, Stylus, USB cable, Camera Bag

(c) **Predicted Tags:** Mobile, Laptop, Mouse, Mike, Memory Card, Headphones, Monitor, MP3 Player
Actual Tags: Laptop, Mouse, Mike, Memory Card, Headphones, Monitor, MP3 Player, Calculator

Figure 3: Examples from Electronics category

(d) **Predicted tags:** Tennis Ball, Football, Rackets, Baseball equipment, Basketball, Rugby
Actual Tags: Tennis Ball, Football, Rackets, Baseball equipment, Basketball, Rugby, Glove

(e) **Predicted Tags:** Gym equipment, Treadmill, Fitness equipment
Actual Tags: Gym equipment, Treadmill, Fitness equipment

(f) **Predicted Tags:** Racket, Shuttlecock, Net, Tennis, Cage
Actual Tags: Racket, Shuttlecock, Net, Badminton equipment

Figure 3: Examples from Sports category

$$Recall = TP/(TP + FN)$$

$$F_1 Score = \frac{2 \cdot Precision \cdot Recall}{(Precision + Recall)}$$

Where TP stands for True positives, FP stands for False Positives and FN stands for False Negatives.

We present our results for 4 different values of K, applying the inverse distance weighed KNN in each case. Our results are shown in Table 1

Product Category	K	F_1 score	Precision	Recall
Apparel and Clothing	1	0.282	0.284	0.283
	3	0.343	0.536	**0.252**
	5	**0.345**	0.603	0.242
	7	0.340	**0.635**	0.232
Electronics	1	0.317	0.317	0.316
	3	0.396	0.621	**0.291**
	5	**0.407**	0.706	0.286
	7	0.406	**0.743**	0.280
Sports	1	0.251	0.252	0.250
	3	0.329	0.626	**0.223**
	5	**0.336**	0.765	0.215
	7	0.335	**0.819**	0.210

Table 1: Tag Annotation results

Some sample images and tags allotted to them for each category are shown in images 2, 3, 3. To the best of our knowledge, these results are the best on this given dataset. The tagged images clearly show that the approach works very well and is able to identify tags correctly despite the large amount of noise in the data and the large number of possible tags.

4.2 Retrieval Results

Once the Tag annotation was completed we set up the hash table based indexing system with the tags as keys and a list of images relevant to that tag sorted in order of 'presence score' of occurrence of that tag. We use this to perform our retrieval. We create a list of 1000 tag queries for each category and use this retrieval system to obtain the relevant images. The retrieval accuracy depends on the accuracy of tagging. We note that by retrieval times were blazingly fast with all 1000 queries for each product category. The retrieval times are presented in Table 2. Clearly the time complexity remains more or less constant for each of the categories despite the varying number of labels denoting that the retrieval times are constant with respect to increasing dataset size and number of labels.

Table 2: Performance of the Content Based Image Retrieval System for a list of 1000 query tags

Product Category	Retrieval Time(s)
Apparel and Clothing	0.083
Electronics	0.095
Sports	0.081

5 Conclusions

In this paper we proposed an Automatic tagging approach for e-commerce products by making use of it's visual features and using these tags to build an efficient query based product retrieval system. We demonstrated that the system performs extremely well and to the best of our knowledge, it outperforms all other systems for automatic e-commerce product tagging on this dataset. Besides the approach is highly scalable, catering to a very large number of tags and products and could easily generalize to multiple product categories and performs well on each category.

The retrieval system built on top of this is also extremely fast and is able to obtain meaningful results at lightning fast speeds.

6 Future Work

We plan to extend this work by incorporating better multi label algorithms which could provide even better performances. We are also exploring alternate feature representation techniques which could provide us with further semantic information. One such representation we plan to explore is to use the activation values from multiple layers of the VGG network as we know that each layer of the network learns a certain kind of distinguishing feature. A combination of such features might provide superlative performance over just using the features from a single layer.

References

[Bengio2012] Y. Bengio. 2012. Deep learning of representations for unsupervised and transfer learning. *JMLR: Workshop on Unsupervised and Transfer Learning*, 27:17–37.

[Blei et al.2003] D. Blei, A. Ng, and M. Jordan. 2003. Latent dirichlet allocation. *Journal of Machine Learning*, 3:993–1022.

[Dalal and Triggs2005] Navneet Dalal and Bill Triggs. 2005. Histograms of oriented gradients for human detection. pages 886–893.

[Di et al.2013] W. Di, C. Wah, A. Bhardwaj, R. Piramuthu, and N. Sundaresan. 2013. Style finder: Fine-grained clothing style detection and retrieval. pages 8–13.

[Feng and Lapata2010] Y. Feng and M. Lapata. 2010. How many words is a picture worth? automatic caption generation for news images. *Proceedings of the 48th Annual Meeting of the Association for Computational Linguistics*, pages 1239–1249.

[Fogel and Sagi1989] I. Fogel and D. Sagi. 1989. Gabor filters as texture discriminator. *Biological Cybernetics*, 61(1).

[Gangopadhyay2001] A. Gangopadhyay. 2001. An image-based system for electronic retailing. *Decision Support Systems*, 32.

[Kovashka et al.2015] A. Kovashka, D. Parikh, and K. Grauman. 2015. Whittlesearch: Interactive image search with relative attribute feedback. *Int. J. Comput. Vision*, 115(2):185–210.

[Li2010] Jing Li. 2010. The application of cbir-based system for the product in electronic retailing. *IEEE 11th International Conference on Computer-Aided Industrial Design Conceptual Design*, 2:1327–1330.

[Lowe2004] David Lowe. 2004. Distinctive image features from scale-invariant keypoints. *International Journal of Computer Vision*, 60:91–110.

[Mason and Charniak2013] Rebecca Mason and Eugene Charniak. 2013. Annotation of online shopping images without labeled training examples. *Proceedings of the NAACL HLT Workshop on Vision and Language (WVL 13)*, pages 1–9.

[McAuley et al.2015a] J. McAuley, R. Pandey, and J. Leskovec. 2015a. Inferring networks of substitutable and complementary products. *Knowledge Discovery and Data Mining*.

[McAuley et al.2015b] J. McAuley, C. Targett, J. Shi, and A. van den Hengel. 2015b. Image-based recommendations on styles and substitutes. *SIGIR*.

[Oquab et al.2014] M. Oquab, L. Bottou, I. Laptev, and J. Sivic. 2014. Learning and transferring mid-level image representations using convolutional neural networks. *Proceedings of the 2014 IEEE Conference on Computer Vision and Pattern Recognition*, pages 1717–1724.

[Rothe et al.2015] R. Rothe, M. Ristin, M. Dantone, and L. Van Gool. 2015. Discriminative learning of apparel features. pages 5–9.

[Russakovsky et al.2015] O. Russakovsky, J. Deng, H. Su, J. Krause, S. Satheesh, S. Ma, Z. Huang, A. Karpathy, A. Khosla, M. Bernstein, A. Berg, and Li Fei-Fei. 2015. Imagenet large scale visual recognition challenge. *International Journal of Computer Vision (IJCV)*, 115(3):211–252.

[Simonyan and Zisserman2014] K. Simonyan and A. Zisserman. 2014. Very deep convolutional networks for large-scale image recognition. *CoRR*, abs/1409.1556.

[Tadse et al.2014] R. Tadse, L. Patil, and C. Chauhan. 2014. Review on content based image retrieval for digital library using text document image. *International Journal of Computer Science and Mobile Computing*, 4:211–214.

[Tsochantaridis et al.2005] I. Tsochantaridis, T. Joachims, T. Hofmann, and Y. Altun. 2005. Large margin methods for structured and interdependent output variables. *J. Mach. Learn. Res.*, 6:1453–1484.

[Yosinski et al.2014] J. Yosinski, J. Clune, Y. Bengio, and H. Lipson. 2014. How transferable are features in deep neural networks? *CoRR*, abs/1411.1792.

[Zeng et al.2014] K. Zeng, N. Wu, and K. Yen. 2014. A color boosted local feature extraction method for mobile product search. *Int. J. on Recent Trends in Engineering and Technology*, 10.

[Zhan et al.2015] Huijing Zhan, Sheng Li, and A. C. Kot. 2015. Tagging the shoe images by semantic attributes. pages 892–895.

[Zoghbi et al.2016] Susana Zoghbi, Geert Heyman, Juan Carlos Gomez, and Marie-Francine Moens. 2016. Fashion meets computer vision and nlp and e-commerce search. *International Journal of Computer and Electrical Engineering*.

Combining syntactic patterns and Wikipedia's hierarchy of hyperlinks to extract meronym relations

Debela Tesfaye , Michael Zock and Solomon Teferra

ITPHD PROGRAM, Addis Ababa University, Addis Ababa, Ethiopia

LIF-CNRS, 163 Avenue de Luminy, 13288 Marseille, France

Addis Ababa University, Addis Ababa, Ethiopia

dabookoo@yahoo.com , michael.zock@lif.univ-mrs.fr, solomon_teferra_7@yahoo.com

Abstract

We present here two methods for extraction o, meronymic relation : (a) the first one relies solely on syntactic information. Unlike other approaches based on simple patterns, we determine their optimal combination to extract word pairs linked via a given semantic relation; (b) the second approach consists in combining syntactic patterns with the semantic information extracted from the Wikipedia hyperlink hierarchy (*WHH*) of the constituent words. By comparing our work with SemEval 2007 (Task 4 test set) and WordNet (WN) we found that our system clearly outperforms its competitors.

1 Introduction

The attempt to discover automatically semantic relations (*SR*) between words, or word pairs has attracted a number of researchers during the last decade which is understandable given the number of applications needing this kind of information. Question Answering, Information Retrieval and Text Summarization being examples in case (Turney and Littman, 2005; Girju et al., 2005).

SRs extraction approaches can be categorized on the basis of the kind of information used. For example, one can rely on syntactic patterns or semantic features of the constituent words. One may as well combine these two approaches.

The method using only syntactic information relies on the extraction of word-level, phrase-level, or sentence-level syntactic information. This approach has been introduced by Hearst (1992) who showed that by using a small set of lexico-syntactic patterns (*LSP*) one could extract with high precision hypernym noun pairs. Similar

methods have been used since then by (Auger and Barriere, 2008; Marshman and L'Homme, 2006). These authors reported results of high precision for some relations, for example hyponymy, noting poor recall which was low. Furthermore, the performance of this approach varies considerably depending on the type of relation considered (Ravichandran and Hovy, 2002, Girju et al., 2005.

An alternative to the *syntactic approach* is a method relying on the semantics features of a pair of words. Most researchers using this approach (Alicia, 2007; Hendrickx et.al, 2007) rely on information extracted from lexical resources like WN (Fellbaum, 1998). Alas, this method works only for languages having a resource equivalent to *WN*. Yet, even WN may pose a proble because of its low coverage across domains (tennis problem).

Hybrid approaches consist in the combination of syntactic patterns with the semantic features of the constituent words (Claudio, 2007; Girju et.al 2005). They tend to yield better results. However, their reliance on *WN* make them amenable to the same criticism as the ones just mentioned concerning *WN*. More recently Wikipedia based similarity measures have been proposed (Strube, et.al, 2006; Gabrilovich, and Markovitch, 2007). While this strategy produces excellent results, few attempts have been made to extract *SRs* (Nakayama et. al, 2007; Yulan et, al , 2007).

In this paper we propose two approaches to extract meronymic relations. In the first case we rely on the patterns learned from *LSPs*. Previous syntactic approaches aimed at finding stand-alone, unambiguous *LSPs*, for instance *X such as Y*, in order to extract a semantic relation like hyponymy. Yet, such unambiguous, stand-alone *LSPs* are very rare and yield low performance. Instead of using *LSPs* individually, which are often ambiguous, we try to combine them in such a way that they com-

Proceedings of NAACL-HLT 2016, pages 29–36,

San Diego, California, June 12-17, 2016. ©2016 Association for Computational Linguistics

plete each other. For instance, the ambiguity of the pattern "*NN$_1$ make of NN$_2$*" can be reduced via the pattern "*NN$_2$ to make NN$_1$*" in order to extract meronymy. *NN$_1$* and *NN$_2$* can stand for any pair of words. The second approach consists in disambiguating the word pairs extracted by *LSPs* via the information identified from the Wikipedia pages of the respective words.

Our contributions are twofold. First, we propose a novel technique for extracting and combining LSPs in order to extract SRs. Second, we propose an approach for disambiguating the syntactic patterns (say meronymic patterns like *NN$_1$-has-NN$_2$*) by building a hyperlink-hierarchy based on Wikipedia pages.

2   Our Approach in more detail

Previous work relies on unambiguous, stand alone *LSPs* to extract SRs. While this approach allows for high precision, it has been criticized for its low accuracy and its variability in terms of the SRs to be extracted. Not all SRs are equally well 'identified'. One of the main challenges and motivations for *LSP* mining lies in the disambiguation of *LSP* to allow for the extraction of SRs. To achieve this, we propose two methods:

— Determine an optimal combination of *LSPs* to represent the relation at hand (section 2.1).
— Combining *LSPs* with the semantic features of the constituent words extracted from the Wikipedia hyperlink-hierarchy (section 2.2).

2.1   Combination of syntactic patterns for relation extraction (CoSP-FRe)

The use of individual *LSP* for the extraction of word pairs linked via a given *SR* tends to produce poor results (Girju et al., 2005; Hearst, 1998). One reason for this lies in the fact that the majority of word pairs are linked via polysemous *LSPs* (Girju et.al , 2005). Hence, these patterns cannot be used alone, as they are ambiguous. At the same time they cannot be ignored as they have the potential to provide good clues concerning certain *SRs*. This being so we suggest to assign weights to the *LSPs* according to their relevance for a specific *SR*, and to optimally combine such weighted patterns for extracting word pairs linked via the SR at hand.

In order to determine the optimal combination of *LSPs* likely to extract *SRs*, we have harvested all *LSPs* encoding the relation at hand. We assigned weights to the patterns according to their relevance for the given *SRs*, and finally filtered the best combination of *LSPs*.

In order to extract such patterns linking word pairs via a certain *SR* , we selected seed-word pairs representative of the relation at hand. In order to balance the word pairs we followed standard taxonomies to group the relations and selected samples from each group (see Section 3.1.1). Sentences containing the word pairs were extracted and then identified their dependency structure. We identified dependency structure linking the word pairs using the shortest path *(ex. nsubj(have, aircraft)* and *dobj(have, engines*) from the *sentence aircrafts have engine)*. Having replaced the words by *NN$_1$* (whole) and *NN$_2$* (part) we obtained patterns like *NN$_1$ have NN$_2$*. We finally counted the frequency of the *LSPs* and ordered them according to their frequency and considering the top 50.

Determination of the optimal combination of LSPs encoding a given SR. To determine the optimal combination of LSPs, we identyfied the discrimination value (*DV*) for each pattern. The *DV* is a numerical value signaling the relevancy of a given *LSP* with respect to a given SR. We applied the following steps in order to identify the *DV* and to determine the optimal combination of the *LSPs*:

Step 1: For each extracted *LSP*, we extracted more connected word pairs from Wikipedia. We defined regular expression matching sentences linking word pairs via the *LSPs* and built then word pairs in a *LSPs* matrix (Matrix 1). Table 1 below shows sample word pairs connected by the patterns *NN$_1$ has NN$_2$* and *NN$_2$ of NN$_1$*. Next, we labeled the extracted word pairs with the SR type and built a matrix of word pairs by a specific *SR* type (Matrix 2). In Table 2 the word pairs from matrix 1 are labeled with their respective type of *SR*. We relied on WN to automatically label the word pairs. Starting with the first sense of the words occurring in *WN*, we traverse the hierarchies and identify the *SRs* encoded by the word pairs. Using the information from Matrix 1 and 2, we built a matrix of *SRs* to *LSPs* (Matrix 3). Table 3 shows sample Matrix 3. The rows of the matrix represent the SR type, while columns represent the

LSPs' encoding. The cells are populated by the number of word pairs linked by the *LSP* encoding the *SR*. The *DV* of *LSP* for a given *SR* is given by the following formula:

$$DV = \frac{FPR}{FP} * \log\left(\frac{TNR}{TRE}\right) \qquad (1)$$

FP represents the total number of word pairs connected by the *LSP* (from Matrix 1). *FPR* stands for the number of word pairs connected by the given *SR* (from Matrix 2), while *TNR* and *TRE* represent respectively the total number of *SRs* (from Matrix 3) and the total number of SRs encoded by the pattern (from Matrix 3).

Word Pairs	LSP
Car Engine	NN$_1$ has NN$_2$
Girl Car	NN$_1$ has NN$_2$
Door Car	NN$_2$ of NN$_1$
Aircraft Engine	NN$_1$' NN$_2$

Table 1: Sample Matrix 1.

Word Pairs	SR Type
Car Engine	Meronymy
Girl Car	Possession
Door Car	Meronymy
Aircraft Engine	Meronymy

Table 2: Sample Matrix 2.

SR Type	NN$_1$ has NN$_2$	NN$_2$ of NN$_1$	NN$_1$' NN$_2$
Meronymy	1	1	1
Possession	1	0	0

Table 3: Sample Matrix 3.

Step 2: Identify the optimal combination of *LSP* to represent a given relation. First, we build a matrix combining *LSPs* encoding the respective *SRs* (Matrix 4) from matrix 3. The *LSPs* in Matrix 3 are combined until no other combination is possible. The cells of the Matrix 4 are populated by the number of word pairs linked via the respective combination of *LSPs*. Next we calculated the discrimination value (*DV-g*) for the combined *LSPs*, the *DV-g* being calculated for each combination of *LSP* corresponding to a given SR. We then selected the combination of *LSPs* with maximum *DV-g* for each SR. The *DV-g* for the combined LSPs corresponding to a given SR is given by the following formula:

$$DV - g = \frac{FPR - g}{FP - g} * \log\left(\frac{TNR}{TRE - g}\right) \qquad (2)$$

FP-g expresses the total number of word pairs connected by the group of patterns. It is determined by taking the intersection of word pairs connected via the combined *LSPs* (from Matrix 4), where *FPR-g* represents the number of word pairs connected by the combined *LSPs* for a given *SR*. This value is determined by taking the intersection of positive word pairs connected by the combined *LSP* for a given *SR* (from Matrix 4). Finally, *TNR* and *TRE* represent respectively the total number of *SRs* (from Matrix 4) and the total number of SRs encoded by the combination of the *LSP*.

SR Type	NN$_1$ has NN$_2$+ NN$_2$ of NN$_1$	NN$_2$ of NN$_1$+ NN$_1$' NN$_2$
Meronymy	2	2
Possession	0	0

Table 4: Sample Matrix 4.

As can be seen from table 3, the pattern "*NN$_1$ has NN$_2$*" when used independently encodes both a meronymic and a non-meronymic word pair. From table 4 above there are two meronymic word pairs linked by the combination of patterns "*NN$_1$ has NN$_2$ + NN$_2$ of NN$_1$*" while there are no non-meronymic word pairs. Hence the non-meronymic word pair retrieved via the pattern "*NN$_1$ has NN$_2$*" is filtered out as a result of having combined it with the pattern "*NN$_2$ of NN$_1$*".

2.2 Wikipedia hyperlink hierarchies for *SR* extraction (WHH-Fsre): the case of meronymy extraction

We used here the hyperlink-hierarchies built on the basis of a selected set of sentences of Wikipedia pages containing the respective word pairs in order to disambiguate *LSPs* encoding them. The basic motivations behind this approach are as follows:

1. Words linked to the Wikipedia page title (*WPT*) via *LSP* encoding *SR* are more reliable than word pairs linked in arbitrary sentences.
2. Word pairs encoding a given SR are not always directly connected via *LSPs*. SRs encoded by a given word pair can also be encoded by their respective higher/lower order conceptual terms. For instance, the following two sentences "germ is an embryo of seed" and "grain is a seed" yield relations like hyponymy (*germ, embryo,* and *grain, seed*), meronymy (*embryo, seed,* and *germ, grain*), the latter (*germ, grain*) being inferred via the relation of their higher order terms (*embryo* and *seed*).

The candidate meronymic word pairs extracted via meronymic *LSPs* are further refined by using the patterns learned from their conceptual hierarchies built on the basis of semantic links, namely, *'hypernymic-link'* (*HL*), and the *'meronymic-link'* (*ML*). We extracted the hyperlinks connected to the Wikipedia pages of the respective meronymic candidates by using hypernymic and meronymic *LSP*. The hyperlink hierarchies were built by considering only important sentences (1 and 2 below) from the Wikipedia pages of the pair of terms: (1) definition sentences and (2) sentences linking hyperlinks to the *WPT* using meronymic *LSPs*. Since the meronymic *LSP* vary according to the nature of the arguments, the patterns used to extract hyperlinks for building the hierarchies were learned by taking the nature of the meronymic relations into account (section 2.1). The definition sentences are used to extract *hypernymic-hyperlink*[1], and the sentences linking hyperlinks to the *WPT* using meronymic *LSPs* are used to extract *meronymic-hyperlink*[2]. Using the hierarchy constructed for the candidate word pairs, this approach determines whether the pairs are meronyms or not based on the following assumptions:

(a) The hyperlink hierarchies of hierarchical meronymys constructed form their respective *HL* have a common ancestor in the hierarchy. Figure 1 shows the component-Integral meronyms *'car engine'* sharing the parent *'machine'* in their hyperlink-hierarchy constructed from their respective Wikipedia page definitions.

(b) The hyperlink hierarchies of both hierarchical and non-hierarchical-meronyms constructed from their respective *ML* and/or *HL* converge along the path in the hierarchy.

Extraction of the hyperlinks. To extract the hyperlinks, we performed the following operations:
Step 1: For simple meronymic pairs we identified the respective Wikipedia pages aligning the word pairs with the *WPT* based on the overlap of the

surface word form. The word pairs were selected based on standard categories used for describing meronymic taxonomy (Winston et al. 1987, see also section 3.1.1). We first cleaned Wikipedia articles and extracted Wikipedia definitions and sentences linking *WPT* with hyperlinks using meronymic *LSPs*.
Step 2: Annotations. We manually annotated both kinds of sentences using two kinds of information: *WPT* and the hyperlinks. The hyperlink either links the term to its meronyms or hypernyms.
Step 3: Extract *LSPs* linking the *WPT* with the hyperlinks. We assigned *DV* (section 2.1) for the patterns and considered the most frequent *LSPs*. The hyperlinks broadly fall in either of two categories: (a) *hypernymic-hyperlink*. They are extracted by the patterns linking the tuple *(hyperlink, wpt)*, for instance, *is-a (hyperlink, Wikipedia page title)* as in the example (b,c); (b) *meronymic-hyperlinks*. They are extracted via *LSPs* linking the tuple *(hyperlink, wpt)*, for instance, *made-from (hyperlink, wpt)*.

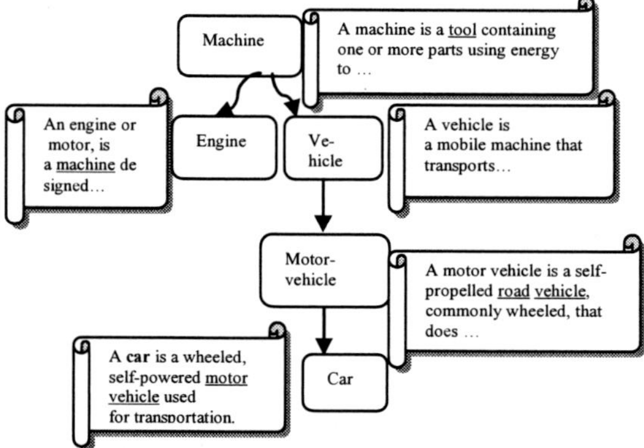

Fig. 1. Wikipedia definitions and the resulting *hypernymic-hyperlink* hierarchies for the meronyms *'car engine'*

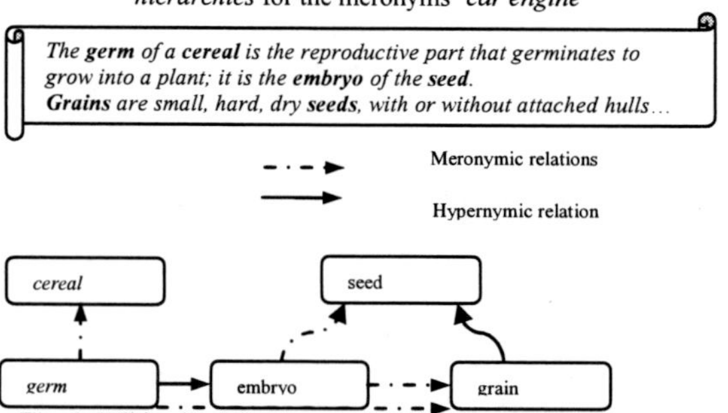

Fig. 2. Wikipedia definitions and the *hyponymic* and *meronymic* hyperlink-hierarchies of the meronym *'grain germ'*

Constructing the hierarchy. For a given pair of terms, we identified the respective Wikipedia

---

[1] *The hypernymic-hyperlink is a word defining a term via its higher-order concept, providing in addition a hyperlink to oth-er Wikipedia pages for further reading. The hypernymic-hyperlinks are underlined on figure 1.*

[2] *Meronymic-hyperlink is a word describing a term using its whole concept and providing a hyperlink to other Wikipedia pages for further reading.*

pages, by aligning the pairs with the *wpt* and by using word form overlap to extract their associated initial *hypernymic* and *meronymic hyperlinks (hl$_i$)* based on the patterns learned in step 2.2.1. We further identified the respective Wikipedia pages for the *hypernymic* and *meronymic-hyperlink* (hl$_i$) identified before and extracted the associated *hypernymic* and *meronymic hyperlinks* (hl$_{i+1}$). Next we connected *(hl$_i$)* with *(hl$_{i+1}$)* to form a hierarchy (hypernyms are connected to each other and to meronyms and vice versa). The hyperlinks are extracted until the hierarchies converge, or until the *hypernymic-hierarchy* reaches seven layers (most word pairs converge earlier than that).

Decide on the meronymic status of words. The *hypernymic or meronymic-hyperlink* of one of the words of the pair is searched in the *hierarchy* of the other, and if this link occurs we consider the word pairs as meronyms. Figure 2 shows that the meronymic word pair *'germ grain'* converges at *'seed'* in the *hierarchies* built from their respective Wikipedia pages.

3 Experiment

To show the validity of our line of reasoning we carried out three experiments:

I. Extract the optimal combination of *LSPs* encoding meronymic relation only.

II. Evaluate *CoSP-FRe* for meronymy extraction.

III. Evaluate *WHH-Fre* for extracting meronymy.

3.1 Extract the optimal combination of LSPs encoding meronymy

Training data set. Two sets of data are required: (a) the initial meronymic word pairs used to train our system (b) the corpus from which the *LSPs* were selected. To select the representative list of meronymic pairs, we used a standard taxonomy. Indeed, several scholars have proposed taxonomies of meronyms (Winston et al., 1987; Pribbenow, 1995; Keet & Artale, 2008). We followed Winston's classical proposal:

component – integral-object (cio)	handle– cup
member – collection (mc)	tree – forest
portion – mass (pm)	grain – salt
stuff – object (so)	steel – bike
feature–activity (fa)	paying–shopping
place-area (pa)	oasis–desert

For the training we used the part-whole training set of SemEval-2007 task 4 (Girju et al. 2007) .

Experimental setup. To determine the optimal combination of LSPs encoding meronyms we identified *LSPs* encoding meronymy according to the procedures described in section 2.1. Since most of these patterns are rare we considered only those with a frequency of 100 and above. For individual *LSP* extraction, we identified the *DVs* associated with the meronymic relation by using the formula 1 followed by the *DV-gs* for every combination of *LSPs* by using the second formula. The combined *LSPs* are sorted based on their *DV*. Finally we selected the LSP with the highest *DV* as representatives of the respective meronymic types.

Sno	Pattern	DV-g
1	NN$_1$ make of NN$_2$+ NN$_2$ to make NN$_1$ + NN$_2$ used NN$_1$ + NN$_1$ NN$_2$	83.6%
2	NN$_1$ make from NN$_2$+ NN$_2$ to make NN$_1$ + NN$_2$ used NN$_1$ + NN$_1$ NN$_2$	81%

Table 5. Part of the optimal combination of patterns for staff object meronymic relations

As can be seen from Table 5 the *DV-g* of staff object meronymic relations patterns is 83.6. The discrimination values for the *LSP* in the group when used individually is below 50%.

Evaluation . The goal is to evaluate the degree of correspondance between the meronyms extracted by *CoSP-FRe* and *WHH-FRe* on one hand and the one by human annotators on the other.

Test data set. We used two data sets: (a) the part-whole test set of the SemEval-2007 task 4 (Girju et al. 2007) which contains 72 examples (26 positive and 46 negative) and some meronymic word pairs gleaned from WN.

Comparison with other systems. We have compared our work against three approaches that achieved the best performance on SemEval-2007 task 4, and two other approaches. We categorized these approaches as (a) *WN*-based: CMU-AT (Alicia, 2007) & ILK (Hendrickx et.al, 2007), (b) syntactic and (c) hybrid approaches: FBK-IRST (Claudio, 2007) & Girjus et.al (2005). We used the individual *LSPs* (*ILSP*) extracted in Sections 2.1 & the *LSPs* extracted by Girju, et.al (2005) as syntactic approach. The *LSPs* extracted by Girju, et.al (2005) are the subset of the LSPs extracted in Sections 2.1.

Results. We computed precision, recall and F-measures as the performance metric. *Precision* is defined as the ratio of the number of correct meronyms extracted and by the total number of extracted word pairs. *Recall* is defined as the ratio between the number of correct meronyms extracted and the total number of meronyms in the test set.

Approaches	P	R	F
CoSP-FRe	76%	88%	81.5%
WHH-FRe	88%	90%	88.9%
ILSP	41.6%	87%	56.2%
CMU-AT	57.7%	45.5%	50.8%
FBK-IRST	65.5%	73.1%	69.1%
ILK	48.4 %	57.7%	52.6%

Table 6. Recall (r), Precision (p) and F-Measure (f) of our approach and related works in the SemEval 2007 test set

We have also extracted meronymic word pairs from random Wikipedia pages of 100 articles and added 85% of the word pairs encoded in *WN*.

Discussions. The results for both approaches are discussed here below:

CoSP-FRe. The precision of *CoSP-FRe* is improved over syntactic approach as the ambiguity of the individual LSP's is reduced when patterns are combined. Recall is improved as a result of using ambiguous *LSPs* for extracting word pairs. This contrasts with all the other syntactic approaches which relied only on unambiguous *LSPs*. In our approach, ambiguous *LSPs* are also used in combination with other *LSPs*. Hence the coverage is significantly improved.

WHH-FRe. Several kinds of hierarchies were formed. Some of them are made of hypernymic or meronymic links, while others are a combination of both links. *WHH-FRe* outperforms significantly previous approaches both with respect to recall and precision as it combines two important features. First *LSPs* are used to extract lists of candidate pairs. Second semantic features of the constituent words extracted from Wikipedia hyperlink-hierarchy is used to further refine. Precision is improved for several reasons: relations encoding *LSPs* which link hyperlinks and *WPT* are more reliable than word pairs connected via arbitrary sentences. The features learned from the Wikipedia hyperlink-hierarchy further cleaned the word pairs extracted by *LSPs*. Recall is also improved since word pairs indirectly linked via their respective higher/lower order hierarchy were also extracted.

4   Related Works

4.1   Syntactic approaches

The work of (Turney, 2005, 2006; Turney and Littman, 2005; Chklovski and Pantel, 2004) is closely related to our work (CoSP-Fre) as it also relies on the use of the distribution of syntactic patterns. However, their goals, algorithms and tasks are different. The work of (Turney, 2005, 2006; and Turney and Littma, 2005) is aimed at measuring relational similarity and is applied to the classification of word pairs (ex. *quart: volume* vs *mile: distance*) while we are aimed at extracting SRs.

4.2   Hybrid approaches

The work of Girju et.al (2005) is more related to our *WHH-FRe* in that they combined *LSPs* with the semantic analysis of the constituent words to disambiguate the *LSPs*. They used *WN* to get the semantics of the constituent words. Alicia (2007) converts word pairs of the positive examples into a semantic graph mapping the pairs to the *WN* hypernym hierarchy. Claudio (2007) combines information from syntactic processing and semantic information of the constituent words from *WN*. Wikipedia-based approaches mainly focused on the identification of similarity (Nakayama et. al, 2007; Yulan et, al , 2007). Also, there is hardly any recent work concerning the extraction of meronyms. Many researchers are working on the identification of semantic similarity achieving excellent result by using standard datasets (Camacho-Collados, Taher and Navigli, 2015; Taher and Navigli , 2015). Yet, most of this work dates back to 2010 and before.

5   Conclusions

We presented here two novel approaches for extracting *SRs*: *CoSP-FRe* and *WHH-FRe*. The strength of *CoSP-FRe* is its capacity to determine an optimal combination of *LSPs* in order to extract *SRs*. The approach yielded high precision and recall compared to other syntactic approaches. *WHH-FRe* perform significantly better than previous approaches both with respect to recall and precision as our approach combines *LSP* and the lexical semantics of the constituted words gleaned from their respective Wikipedia pages.

References

Alain A. and Caroline B. (2008). *Pattern-based approaches to semantic relation extraction: A state-of-the-art.* Terminology Journal, 14(1):1–19

Alicia T. and Scott E. Fahlman (2007). *CMU-AT: Semantic Distance and Background Knowledge for Identifying Semantic Relations.* Proceedings of the 4th International Workshop on Semantic Evaluations (SemEval-2007), pages 121–124, Prague.

Chklovski, T., and Pantel, P. (2004). *VerbOcean: Mining the Web for fine-grained semantic verb relations.* In Proceedings of Conference on Empirical Methods in Natural Language Processing (EMNLP-04). pp. 33-40. Barcelona, Spain.

Claudio G, Alberto L., Daniele P. and Lorenza R. (2007). *FBK-IRST: Kernel Methods for Semantic Relation Extraction.* Proceedings of the 4th International Workshop on Semantic Evaluations (SemEval-2007), pages 121–124, Prague.

Fellbaum, C. editor. (1998). *WordNet: An electronic lexical database and some of its applications.* MIT Press.

Gabrilovich, E., Markovitch, S. (2007). *Computing semantic relatedness using wikipedia-based explicit semantic analysis.* In: International Joint Conference on Artificial Intelligence, pp. 12-20.

Girju R., Moldovan D., Tatu, M. & Antohe, D. (2005). *Automatic discovery of Part–Whole relations.* ACM 32(1)

Girju, R., Nakov, P., Nastase, V., Szpakowicz, S., Turney, P., & Yuret, D. (2007). *Semeval- 2007 task 04: Classification of semantic relations between nominals.* In Proceedings of the Fourth International Workshop on Semantic Evaluations (SemEval 2007), pp. 13–18, Prague, Czech Republic.

Hearst, M. (1998). WordNet: *An electronic lexical database and some of its applications.* In Fellbaum, C., editor, Automated Discovery of WordNet Relations. MIT Press.

Hearst, M. A. (1992). *Automatic acquisition of hyponyms from large text corpora.* In Proceedings of the 14th International Conference on Computational Linguistics, pages 539–545.

Hendrickx I., Morante R., Sporleder C., Antal v. d. Bosch (2002). ILK: Machine learning of semantic relations with shallow features and almost no data. Proceedings of the 4th International Workshop on Semantic Evaluations (SemEval-2007), pages 121–124, Prague, June 2007

Jose Camacho-Collados, Mohammad Taher Pilehvar and Roberto Navigli (205). *NASARI: a Novel Approach to a Semantically-Aware Representation of Items, Human Language Technologies.* The 2015 Annual Conference of the North American Chapter of the ACL, pp 567–577, Denver, Colorado,USA.

Keet, C.M. and Artale, A. (2008*). Representing and Reasoning over a Taxonomy of Part-Whole Relations.* Applied Ontology, 2008, 3(1-2): 91-110

Marneffe M., MacCartney B. and Christopher D. Manning. (2006). *Generating Typed Dependency Parses from Phrase Structure Parses.* In LREC 2006.

Marshman, E. and M.-C. L' Homme. (2006*).Disambiguation of lexical markers of cause and effect" In Picht, H. (ed.). Modern Approaches to Terminological Theories and Applications.* Proceedings of the 15th European Symposium on Language for Special Purposes, LSP 2005. 261-285. Bern: Peter Lang.

Moldovan D., Badulescu A., Tatu M., Antohe D., and Girju R. (2004). *Models for the semantic classification of noun phrases.* In Proc. of the HLT-NAACL 2004 Workshop on Computational Lexical Semantics, pages 60– 67, Boston, USA.

Nakayama, K., Hara, T., and Nishio S. (2007). *Wikipedia Mining for an Association Web Thesaurus Construction.* In: Web Information Systems Engineering – WISE, Lecture Notes in Computer Science, Springer Berlin / Heidelberg, 322-334

Nakayama K., Hara T. and Nishio S. (2008). *Wikipedia Link Structure and Text Mining for Semantic Relation Extraction.* SemSearch 2008, CEUR Workshop Proceedings, ISSN 1613-0073, online at CEUR-WS.org/Vol-334/

Peter D. Turney and Michael L. Littman. (2005). *Corpusbased learning of analogies and semantic rela-tions.* Machine Learning, in press.

Peter D. Turney and Michael L. Littman. (2005). Corpus based learning of analogies and semantic relations. Machine Learning, 60(1–3):251–278

Peter D. Turney. (2006). *Expressing implicit semantic relations without supervision.* In Proceedings of ACL-2006.

Pribbenow, S. (1995). *Parts and Wholes and their Relations.* Habel, C. & Rickheit, G. (eds.): Mental Models in Discourse Processing and Problem Solving. John Benjamins Publishing Company, Amsterdam

Strube, M., and Ponzetto, S.P. (2006). *WikiRelate! Computing semantic relatedness using Wikipedia.* In: Proceedings of the National Conference on Artificial Intelligence, pp. 1419- 1429

Taher M. and Navigli R. (2015). *Align, Disambiguate and Walk: A Unified Approach for Measuring Semantic Similarity.* Proceedings of the 51st Annual Meeting of the Association for Computational Linguistics, , Sofia, Bulgaria, 1341–1351,

Winston, M., Chaffin, R. & Hermann, D. (1987). *Taxonomy of part-whole relations*. Cognitive Science, 11(4), 417–444.

Yan Y., Matsuo Y. , Ishizuka M. (2009). *An Integrated Approach for Relation Extraction from Wikipedia Texts* . CAW2.0 2009, Madrid, Spain.

Data-driven Paraphrasing and Stylistic Harmonization

Gerold Hintz
Research Training Group AIPHES / Language Technology
Department of Computer Science, Technische Universität Darmstadt
`hintz@aiphes.tu-darmstadt.de`

Abstract

This thesis proposal outlines the use of unsupervised data-driven methods for paraphrasing tasks. We motivate the development of knowledge-free methods at the guiding use case of multi-document summarization, which requires a domain-adaptable system for both the *detection* and *generation* of sentential paraphrases. First, we define a number of guiding research questions that will be addressed in the scope of this thesis. We continue to present ongoing work in unsupervised lexical substitution. An existing supervised approach is first adapted to a new language and dataset. We observe that supervised lexical substitution relies heavily on lexical semantic resources, and present an approach to overcome this dependency. We describe a method for unsupervised relation extraction, which we aim to leverage in lexical substitution as a replacement for knowledge-based resources.

1 Introduction

One of the key research questions in semantic understanding of natural language is bridging the lexical gap; i.e. in absence of lexical overlap between a pair of text segments, judging their semantic content with respect to semantic similarity, entailment, or equivalence. The term *paraphrase* is used to describe semantic equivalence between pairs of units of text, and can be loosely defined as being *interchangeable* (Dras, 1999). Being able to decide if two text units are paraphrases of each other, as well as the reverse direction - generating a paraphrase for a given phrase, are ongoing efforts. Both components are useful in a number of downstream tasks. One guiding use case for the methods developed in the scope of this thesis is their applicability to automatic summarization (Nenkova et al., 2011). In *extractive summarization*, a good summary should select a subset of sentences while avoiding redundancy. This requires detecting semantic equivalences between sentences. *Abstractive summarization* requires a system to further rephrase the summary, to match space constraints, achieve fluency, or unify stylistic differences in multiple source documents. Here, a paraphrasing component can modify the extracted source sentences to meet such external requirements. The primary focus of this work will be the development of novel methods for both *detecting* and *generating* paraphrases of natural language text. In the wider setting of this thesis, we are particularly interested in multi-document summarization (MDS). To scale to the requirements of multi-domain content, our main interest is in knowledge-free and unsupervised methods for these tasks.

The remainder of this paper is structured as follows. In Section 2 we will briefly cover related work in different subareas pertaining to paraphrasing. In Section 3 we will define a number of research questions, which are central to the thesis. Section 4 will then present some ongoing work in lexical substitution and first steps to move towards a knowledge-free unsupervised approach. Finally, Section 5 will give a conclusion and an outlook to future work being addressed in the thesis.

37

Proceedings of NAACL-HLT 2016, pages 37–44,
San Diego, California, June 12-17, 2016. ©2016 Association for Computational Linguistics

2 Related work

Paraphrase-related research can roughly be categorized into three areas: 1. *Paraphrase identification* - deciding or ranking the degree of how paraphrastic two given elements are; 2. *Paraphrase generation* - given a text element, generate a meaning-preserving reformulation; and 3. *Paraphrase extraction* - given an input corpus, extract meaningful pairs of paraphrastic elements. We will cover each area briefly; an extensive, high-level summary can be found in (Androutsopoulos and Malakasiotis, 2010).

2.1 Paraphrase Identification

The task of paraphrase identification is strongly related to *Semantic Textual Similarity* (STS) and *Recognizing Textual Entailment* (RTE) tasks. STS has most recently been addressed as a shared task at *SemEval-2015* (Agirre et al., 2015), which gives a good overview of current state-of-the art methods. For the specific task of identifying pairs of paraphrases, the use of discriminative word embeddings (Yin and Schütze, 2015) have recently been shown to be effective.

2.2 Paraphrase Generation

Paraphrase generation, being an open generation task, is difficult to evaluate. However, as a preliminary stage to full paraphrasing a number of *lexical substitution* tasks have become popular for evaluating context-sensitive lexical inference since the *SemEval-2007: lexsub* task (McCarthy and Navigli, 2007). A lexical substitution system aims to predict substitutes for a target word instance within a sentence context. This implicitly addresses the problem of resolving the ambiguity of polysemous terms. Over the course of a decade, a large variety of supervised (Biemann, 2013) and unsupervised (Erk and Padó, 2008; Moon and Erk, 2013; Melamud et al., 2015a) approaches have been proposed for this task.

2.3 Paraphrase Extraction

One of the earlier highly successful approaches to paraphrase extraction was shown by Lin and Pantel (2001). The main idea is an extension of the distributional hypothesis from words sharing similar context to similar paths between pairs of words sharing the same substituting words. Thus, a set of similar paths are obtained which can be regarded as prototypical paraphrases. A notable later method to extract a large database of paraphrases makes use of parallel bilingual corpora. The bilingual pivoting method (Bannard and Callison-Burch, 2005) aligns two fragments within a source language based on an overlap in their translation to a "pivoting" language. The paraphrase database, PPDB (Ganitkevitch et al., 2013) was obtained by applying this approach to large corpora.

3 Research Questions

We define a number of research questions (RQ), which have been partially addressed, and shall also provide a guiding theme to be followed in future work.

RQ 1: How can the lexical substitution task be solved without prior linguistic knowledge? Existing approaches to lexical substitution rely frequently on linguistic knowledge. A lexical resource, such as *WordNet* (Fellbaum, 1998), is used to obtain a list of candidate substitutes, and focus is then shifted towards a ranking-only task. State-of-the-art unsupervised systems can still be improved by leveraging lexical resources as candidate selection filters[1]. We argue that this is related mostly to *semantic word relations*. Whereas some semantic relations (synonymy, hypernymy) are well suited for substitution, other relations (antonymy, opposition) are indicators for bad substitutes. Unsupervised distributed methods are susceptible to not recognizing these different word relations, as they still share similar contexts. As part of this research question, we investigate how knowledge-free approaches can be used to overcome this lack of semantic information. We elaborate on this RQ in Section 4.2.

RQ 2: What is the gap between lexical substitution and full paraphrasing? We aim to further examine the remaining gap to a full paraphrasing system that is not restricted to single words. As

---

[1] We have experimentally confirmed that a fully unsupervised approach (Melamud et al., 2015b) can be improved by restricting substitution candidates to those obtained from *WordNet*

a first step, we extend lexical substitution to multi-word expressions (MWE). As most existing research considers only the restricted case of single words, the adaptation of existing features and methods to nominal phrases, and more complex MWEs, will be investigated in detail. Furthermore, the lexical substitution task is conventionally only defined as providing a ranked list of lemmas as target substitutes. In general, directly replacing the target word in the existing context results in a syntactically incorrect sentence. This is is the case for languages with inflection, but also for words with discontinuous expressions, which may require restructuring the sentence. As a next step we plan on leveraging morphological tagging (Schmid and Laws, 2008) to apply syntactic reformulation, by adapting a rule-based transformation framework (Ruppert et al., 2015).

RQ 3: How can a paraphrasing system be employed for stylistic harmonization? In multi-document summarization, source documents frequently originate from different text genres. E.g. a news document employs a different writing style than a blog post or a tweet. Detecting such *stylistic variation* across genres has received some attention (Brooke and Hirst, 2013). Recently, stylistic information has successfully induced for paraphrases within PPDB (Pavlick and Nenkova, 2015). Using a simple log ratio of observation probability of a given phrase across distinct domains, the *style* of the phrase could be mapped in a spectrum for multiple dimensions, such as *formal / casual* or *simple / complex*. When generating a summary containing such different genres, fluency and coherence of the resulting document have to be considered. To improve summaries, a system could perform the following steps

1. Given an input corpus, *identifying* different styles and given a document *detecting* its style

2. Given an input sentence and its *source style*, paraphrasing it to match a desired *target style*

We can achieve this by considering the difference of distributional expansions across multiple domains. For example, the trigram context "four _ passengers" might frequently be expanded with "aircraft" in a news-domain corpus, whereas a tweet domain more frequently uses "airplane", with both expansions being distributionally similar. We can thus learn that "aircraft" could be a substitution to adapt towards news-style language and selectively perform such replacements.

RQ 4: Can we exploit structure in monolingual corpora to extract paraphrase pairs? Paraphrase databases, such as PPDB (Ganitkevitch et al., 2013), are constructed from bilingual parallel corpora. Here an assumption is used that equivalent text segments frequently align to the same segment in a different "pivoting" language. The center of this RQ is the goal to extract paraphrase pairs, similar to PPDB, from *monolingual* corpora by exploiting different structure. One such structure can be seen in news corpora. When given a document timestamp, it is possible to exploit the notion of *burstiness* to find out if two documents are related to the same or different events. We aim to adapt techniques aimed at summarization to extract pairs of paraphrases (Christensen, 2015).

4   Ongoing Work and Preliminary Results

4.1   Delexicalized lexical substitution

In a first work we address RQ 1 and perform lexical substitution in a previously unexplored language. With *GermEval-2015* (Miller et al., 2015), the lexical substitution challenge was posed for the first time using German language data. It was shown that an existing supervised approach for English (Szarvas et al., 2013) can be adopted to German (Hintz and Biemann, 2015). Although the wider focus of the thesis will be the use of fully unsupervised methods, in this first step lexical semantic resources are utilized both for obtaining substitution candidates as well as extracting semantic relation features between words. The suitability of various resources, *GermaNet* (Hamp and Feldweg, 1997), *Wiktionary*[2], and further resources crawled from the web, are evaluated with respect to the *GermEval* task. It was found that no other resource matches the results obtained from *GermaNet*, although its coverage is still the primary bottleneck for this system. As lexical substitution data is now available in at least three languages (English, German, and Italian), we also explore language transfer learning for lexical substi-

---

[2]*Wiktionary*: https://www.wiktionary.org/

tution. Experimental results suggest that *delexicalized features* can be extended to not only generalize across lexical items, but can further train a model across languages, suggesting the model to be language independent. For this, we adapt existing features from (Szarvas et al., 2013) and extend the feature space based on more recent approaches. We follow a state-of-the-art unsupervised model (Melamud et al., 2015b) to further define features in a syntactic word embedding space. As a preliminary result, feature ablation tests show that the strongest features for lexical substitution are semantic relations from multiple aggregated lexical resources. This insight motivates the next step towards a knowledge-free system.

4.2 Unsupervised semantic relation extraction

Semantic relations have been identified a strong features for lexical substitution (Sinha and Mihalcea, 2009); selecting candidates based on aggregated information of multiple resources usually results in good performance. Consequently, when obtaining substitution candidates from different sources, such as a distributional thesaurus (DT), a key challenge lies in overcoming a high amount of *related* but not substitutable words. Prime examples are *antonyms*, which are usually distributionally similar but no valid lexical substitutions (replacing "hot" with "cold" alters the meaning of a sentence). Figure 1 illustrates this challenge at the example of an instance obtained from the SemEval-2007 data. Here, candidates from a DT are compared against candidates obtained from *WordNet*. Both resources yield related words (e.g. "task", "wage", "computer science" are all related to the target "job") - however, for lexical resources we can leverage semantic relations as a much more fine-grained selection filter beyond relatedness (in the example, entries such as "computer science" can be excluded by discarding the *topic* relation). On the other hand, obtaining candidates only from a lexical resource necessarily limits the system to its coverage. Whereas *WordNet* is a high-quality resource with good coverage, alternatives for other languages may be of inferior quality or are lacking altogether. To quantify this, we have evaluated the overlap of semantic relations present in *GermaNet* (Hamp and Feldweg, 1997) with the gold substitutes in the *GermEval-*

His **job** was unpaid, but he was working just to keep fit.
  work (4)
  employment (2)
  post (1)

DT entries	WordNet entries	(label)
job#NN	business	synset
task#NN	occupation	synset
employment#NN	task	co-hyponym
position#NN	chore	co-hyponym
worker#NN	activity	hypernym
post#NN	**work**	hyponym
employee#NN	**employment**	hyponym
acre#NN	**post**	hyponym
foot#NN	obligation	hypernym
wage#NN	computer science	topic
work#NN	computing	topic

Figure 1: Comparison of substitution candidates obtained from a DT (most similar words) and a lexical resource (WordNet), for a given example sentence from SemEval-2007. Bold items denote overlap with gold substitutes.

2015 lexsub task. Figure 2 illustrates this overlap and further shows the stages at which the resource fails. Whereas all target words are contained in GermaNet, only 85% of the substitutes are contained as lexical items. When considering only *synonyms*, *hyponyms* and *hypernyms* as relations, only 20% of all gold substitutes can be retrieved. This number constitutes an upper bound for the recall of a lexical substitution system. If, instead, candidates are obtained based on distributional similarity, we can obtain a much higher upper bound on recall of substitution candidates. Figure 3 shows the recall of the top-k similar words, based on a distributional thesaurus computed from a 70M sentence newspaper corpus (Biemann et al., 2007). Even when considering only the top-50 most similar words, a recall of 29% can be achieved, whereas this value plateaus at about 45% - improving over the lexical resource baseline more than twofold. In summary, we make two observations:

1. Similarity-based approaches, such as distributional similarity, have better coverage for substitution candidates, at the cost of higher noise

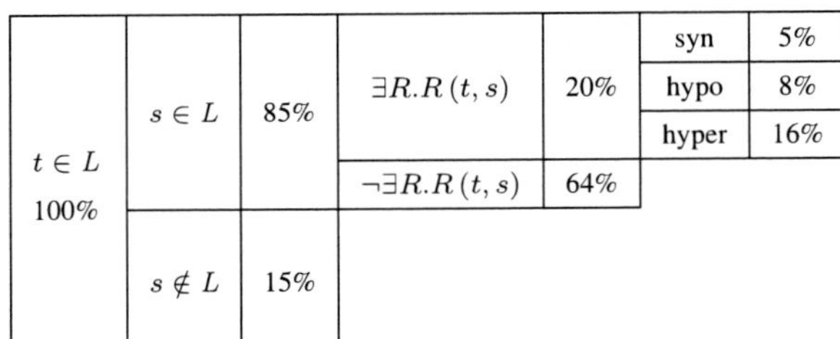

						syn	5%
$t \in L$ 100%	$s \in L$	85%	$\exists R.R\,(t,s)$	20%		hypo	8%
						hyper	16%
			$\neg\exists R.R\,(t,s)$	64%			
	$s \notin L$	15%					

Figure 2: Presence of lexical substitution gold pairs in a lexical resource L. $t \in L$ denotes that a target is present in L. $\exists R.R\,(t,s)$ denotes the fraction within those pairs for which a semantic relation existed. We used GermaNet as a lexical resource L and compare to gold substitutes from *GermEval-2015*

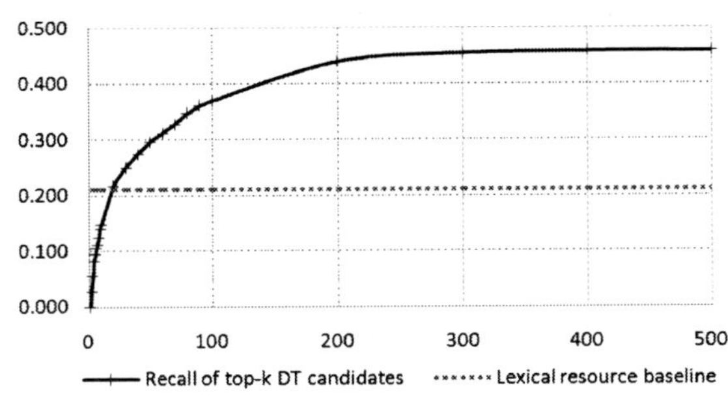

Figure 3: Recall of lexical substitution candidates as top-k similar DT entries, compared to lexical resource baseline (using synonyms, hyponyms and hypernyms)

2. The *semantic relation* between target and substitute is a strong indicator for substitutability

These observations motivate a similarity-based selection of substitution candidates, which does not rely on knowledge-based resources. We argue that the second key component to lexical substitution is an unsupervised extraction of semantic relations. For this we follow (Herger, 2014), who leverages the *extended distributional hypothesis*, stating that "if two *paths* tend to occur in similar context, the meanings of the *paths* tend to be similar" (Lin and Pantel, 2001). The original motivation for this is obtaining inference rules, or equivalences between paths. For example, it can be discovered that *"X is author of Y"* $\approx$ *"X wrote Y"*. In reverse however, we can also discover pairs of words (X, Y), which tend to be connected with the same paths. We can thus compute a DT on pairs of words rather than single words, using their path as context features. Our al-

$\downarrow$ extract pairs

(bubble, burst)

(price, demand)

$\downarrow$ compute path features

(price, demand) $\rightarrow$ `X plunged and Y`

(price, demand) $\rightarrow$ `X-cc_plunge_Y`

(price, demand) $\rightarrow$ `X-cc_#VB_Y`

Figure 4: Extraction of pairs and path context features. Context features shown here are token substring, lemmatized syntactic dependency edges, and POS-normalized dependency edges

gorithm for semantic relation extraction can thus be described as follows:

1. Extract pairs of words from background corpus, based on distributional similarity

2. Compute context features for each pair based on their connecting path

3. Compute the similarity between pairs of pairs, based on shared context features

4. Cluster pairs of words based on their similarity

For step 1, we experimented with different filtering strategies, based on word frequency, sentence length, token distance, and POS tags. As context features we aggregate multiple variants to generalize a path: we replace the occurrence of the pair (X, Y) with the literal strings "X" and "Y" and then extract the token substring, as well paths defined by syntactic dependency edges. Steps 1 and 2 are visualized in Figure 4. For steps 3 and 4, we adapt the DT computation from (Biemann and Riedl, 2013) and obtain similarity scores based on the overlap of the most salient context features, i.e. generalized paths. At this stage, we obtain a distributional similarity between pairs of words, e.g. the pair (*famine, epidemic*) is distributionally similar to (*problem, crisis*). This resembles the notion of word analogies, which can be obtained in embedding spaces (Levy et al., 2014), however our model results in discrete notions of relations as opposed to non-interpretable vectors. For this, we cluster word pairs by applying Chinese Whispers (Biemann, 2006). Table 1 shows the final output of the semantic relation clustering exemplified for four resulting clusters. Although the data is not perfectly consistent, clusters tend to

Cluster 1	**Cluster 2**
painter::designer	sailboat::boat
welder::electrician	trawler::boat
architect::engineer	ship::boat
sailor::pilot	helicopter::boat
poet::artist	helicopter::vessel
pull::push	coat::dress
consultant::specialist	plane::vessel
distributor::producer	soldier::policeman
decorator::gardener	driver::passenger

Cluster 3	**Cluster 4**
rain::drought	glaucoma::blindness
heat::cold	exposure::illness
legroom::mobility	famine::malnutrition
concern::anger	traffic::pollution
exercise::eating	humans::stress
vengeance::forgiveness	obesity::illness
competitiveness::efficiency	overwork::depression
respect::contempt	hurricane::flooding
hipness::authenticity	inflammation::pain
supervision::management	drought::crisis

Table 1: Exemplary output of semantic relation clustering (cluster subsets)

represent a similar relation between each respective pairs of words. These relations often correspond to those found in lexical resources, such as hyponymy or antonymy. However, the relations are frequently fragmented into smaller, domain-specific clusters. In the above example, Cluster 1 and Cluster 2 both correspond to a relation resembling *hypernymy* - however, in Cluster 1 this relation is mostly clustered for professions (e.g. a "welder" is-a-kind of "electrician"), whereas Cluster 2 corresponds roughly to vehicles or items (a "sailboat" is-a-kind-of "boat"). Cluster 3 can be reasonably considered as containing antonymous terms ("rain" is-opposite-of "drought"). In some cases, clusters contain relations of words not generally found in semantic resources. Cluster 4 contains word pairs having a causation relation (e.g. "glaucoma" *causes* "blindness"); it is further interesting to observe that items in this cluster contain exclusively negative outcomes ("illness", "stress", "flooding", etc.). Previous work has conventionally evaluated semantic relation extraction intrinsically with respect to a lexical resource as a gold stan-

dard (Panchenko and Morozova, 2012). However, we are interested in utilizing semantic relations for paraphrasing tasks and will therefore follow up with an extrinsic evaluation in a lexical substitution system. Our goal is to leverage unsupervised clusters, e.g. as feature input, to overcome the need for lexical semantic resources.

5   Conclusion and Outlook

In this paper we have outlined the guiding theme of a thesis exploring data-driven methods for paraphrasing and defined a set of research questions to sketch a path for future work. We addressed the first step of lexical substitution. We showed that a supervised, delexicalized framework (Szarvas et al., 2013) can be successfully applied to a previously unexplored language. We make a number of observations on multiple language lexsub tasks: Obtaining substitution candidates from lexical resources achieves best system performance, despite incurring a very low upper bound on substitution recall. Obtaining candidates in an unsupervised manner by considering distributionally similar words increases this upper bound more than twofold, at the cost of more noise. We further observe that the strongest features in this setting are semantic relations between target and substitute, obtained from the aggregated lexical resources. Hence, we conclude that obtaining semantic relations in an unsupervised way is a key step towards knowledge-free lexical substitution. We continue to present an unsupervised method for obtaining clusters of semantic relations, and show preliminary results. As a next step we aim at integrating such relation clusters into a lexical substitution system. We also plan on extending lexical substitution towards a full paraphrasing system, by moving from single-word replacements to longer multiword expressions, as well as applying syntactic transformations as a post-processing step to the substitution output. In related branches of this thesis we will also explore methods for extracting paraphrases from structured corpora, and ultimately apply a two-way paraphrasing system to a multi-document summarization system, supporting both selection of non-redundant sentences as well as sentence rephrasing to perform harmonization of language style.

Acknowledgments

This work has been supported by the German Research Foundation as part of the Research Training Group "Adaptive Preparation of Information from Heterogeneous Sources" (AIPHES) under grant No. GRK 1994/1.

References

Eneko Agirre, Carmen Banea, et al. 2015. Semeval-2015 task 2: Semantic textual similarity, English, Spanish and pilot on interpretability. In *Proceedings of the 9th International Workshop on Semantic Evaluation (SemEval 2015)*, Denver, CO, USA.

Ion Androutsopoulos and Prodromos Malakasiotis. 2010. A survey of paraphrasing and textual entailment methods. *Journal of Artificial Intelligence Research*, 38:135–187.

Colin Bannard and Chris Callison-Burch. 2005. Paraphrasing with bilingual parallel corpora. In *Proceedings of the 43rd Annual Meeting on Association for Computational Linguistics*, pages 597–604, Ann Arbor, MI, USA.

Chris Biemann and Martin Riedl. 2013. Text: Now in 2D! a framework for lexical expansion with contextual similarity. *Journal of Language Modelling*, 1(1):55–95.

Chris Biemann, Gerhard Heyer, Uwe Quasthoff, and Matthias Richter. 2007. The leipzig corpora collection: monolingual corpora of standard size. In *Proceedings of Corpus Linguistics*, Birmingham, UK.

Chris Biemann. 2006. Chinese whispers: an efficient graph clustering algorithm and its application to natural language processing problems. In *Proceedings of the first workshop on graph based methods for natural language processing*, pages 73–80, New York, NY, USA.

Chris Biemann. 2013. Creating a system for lexical substitutions from scratch using crowdsourcing. *Language Resources and Evaluation*, 47(1):97–122.

Julian Brooke and Graeme Hirst. 2013. A multidimensional bayesian approach to lexical style. In *Proceedings of the 2013 Conference of the North American Chapter of the Association for Computational*, pages 673–679.

Janara Maria Christensen. 2015. *Towards Large Scale Summarization*. Ph.D. thesis, University of Washington.

Mark Dras. 1999. *Tree Adjoining Grammar and the Reluctant Paraphrasing of Text*. Ph.D. thesis, Macquarie University.

Katrin Erk and Sebastian Padó. 2008. A structured vector space model for word meaning in context. In *Proceedings of the Conference on Empirical Methods in Natural Language Processing*, pages 897–906, Waikiki, HI, USA.

Christiane Fellbaum. 1998. *WordNet*. Wiley Online Library.

Juri Ganitkevitch, Benjamin Van Durme, and Chris Callison-Burch. 2013. PPDB: The paraphrase database. In *HLT-NAACL*, pages 758–764, Atlanta, GA, USA.

Birgit Hamp and Helmut Feldweg. 1997. GermaNet - a lexical-semantic net for German. In *In Proceedings of ACL workshop Automatic Information Extraction and Building of Lexical Semantic Resources for NLP Applications*, pages 9–15.

Priska Herger. 2014. Learning semantic relations with distributional similarity. Master's thesis, TU Berlin.

Gerold Hintz and Chris Biemann. 2015. Delexicalized supervised German lexical substitution. In *Proceedings of GermEval 2015: LexSub*, pages 11–16, Essen, Germany.

Omer Levy, Yoav Goldberg, and Israel Ramat-Gan. 2014. Linguistic regularities in sparse and explicit word representations. In *Proceedings of the 52nd Annual Meeting of the Association for Computational Linguistics*, pages 171–180, Baltimore, MD, USA.

Dekang Lin and Patrick Pantel. 2001. DIRT - discovery of inference rules from text. In *Proceedings of the seventh ACM SIGKDD international conference on Knowledge discovery and data mining*, pages 323–328, San Francisco, CA, USA.

Diana McCarthy and Roberto Navigli. 2007. SemEval-2007 task 10: English lexical substitution task. In *Proceedings of the 4th International Workshop on Semantic Evaluations*, pages 48–53, Prague, Czech Rep.

Oren Melamud, Ido Dagan, and Jacob Goldberger. 2015a. Modeling word meaning in context with substitute vectors. In *Proceedings of the 2015 Conference of the North American Chapter of the Association for Computational Linguistics*, pages 472–482, Denver, CO, USA.

Oren Melamud, Omer Levy, Ido Dagan, and Israel Ramat-Gan. 2015b. A simple word embedding model for lexical substitution. *VSM Workshop*. Denver, CO, USA.

Tristan Miller, Darina Benikova, and Sallam Abualhaija. 2015. GermEval 2015: LexSub – A shared task for German-language lexical substitution. In *Proceedings of GermEval 2015: LexSub*, pages 1–9, Essen, Germany.

Taesun Moon and Katrin Erk. 2013. An inference-based model of word meaning in context as a paraphrase distribution. *ACM Transactions on Intelligent Systems and Technology (TIST)*, 4(3):42.

Ani Nenkova, Sameer Maskey, and Yang Liu. 2011. Automatic summarization. In *Proceedings of the 49th Annual Meeting of the Association for Computational Linguistics: Tutorial Abstracts of ACL 2011*, page 3, Portland, OR, USA.

Alexander Panchenko and Olga Morozova. 2012. A study of hybrid similarity measures for semantic relation extraction. In *Proceedings of the Workshop on Innovative Hybrid Approaches to the Processing of Textual Data*, pages 10–18, Jeju, South Korea.

Ellie Pavlick and Ani Nenkova. 2015. Inducing lexical style properties for paraphrase and genre differentiation. In *Proceedings of the 2015 Annual Conference of the North American Chapter of the Association for Computational Linguistics, NAACL*, pages 218–224, Denver, CO, USA.

Eugen Ruppert, Jonas Klesy, Martin Riedl, and Chris Biemann. 2015. Rule-based dependency parse collapsing and propagation for German and English. In *Proceedings of the German Society for Computational Linguistics & Language Technology 2015*, pages 58–66, Essen, Germany.

Helmut Schmid and Florian Laws. 2008. Estimation of conditional probabilities with decision trees and an application to fine-grained pos tagging. In *Proceedings of the 22nd International Conference on Computational Linguistics*, volume 1, pages 777–784, Manchester, UK.

Ravi Sinha and Rada Mihalcea. 2009. Combining lexical resources for contextual synonym expansion. In *Proceedings of the Conference in Recent Advances in Natural Language Processing*, pages 404–410, Borovets, Bulgaria.

György Szarvas, Chris Biemann, Iryna Gurevych, et al. 2013. Supervised all-words lexical substitution using delexicalized features. In *Proceedings of the 2013 Conference of the North American Chapter of the Association for Computational Linguistics: Human Language Technologies*, pages 1131–1141, Atlanta, GA, USA.

Wenpeng Yin and Hinrich Schütze. 2015. Discriminative phrase embedding for paraphrase identification. In *Proceedings of the 2015 Conference of the North American Chapter of the Association for Computational Linguistics: Human Language Technologies*, pages 1368–1373, Denver, CO, USA.

Detecting "Smart" Spammers On Social Network:
A Topic Model Approach

Linqing Liu,[1] Yao Lu,[1] Ye Luo[1,*], Renxian Zhang[2,*], Laurent Itti[1,3] and Jianwei Lu[1,4,*]

[1] iLab Tongji, School of Software Engineering, Tongji University
[2] Dept. of Computer Science and Technology, Tongji University
[3] Dept. of Computer Science and Neuroscience Program, University of Southern California
[4] Institute of Translational Medicine, Tongji University
`likicode@gmail.com, {95luyao,rxzhang}@tongji.edu.cn,`
`{kennyluo2008,jwlu33}@hotmail.com, itti@usc.edu`

Abstract

Spammer detection on social network is a challenging problem. The rigid anti-spam rules have resulted in emergence of "smart" spammers. They resemble legitimate users who are difficult to identify. In this paper, we present a novel spammer classification approach based on Latent Dirichlet Allocation (LDA), a topic model. Our approach extracts both the local and the global information of topic distribution patterns, which capture the essence of spamming. Tested on one benchmark dataset and one self-collected dataset, our proposed method outperforms other state-of-the-art methods in terms of averaged F1-score.

1 Introduction

Microblogging such as Twitter and Weibo is a popular social networking service, which allows users to post messages up to 140 characters. There are millions of active users on the platform who stay connected with friends. Unfortunately, spammers also use it as a tool to post malicious links, send unsolicited messages to legitimate users, etc. A certain amount of spammers could sway the public opinion and cause distrust of the social platform. Despite the use of rigid anti-spam rules, human-like spammers whose homepages having photos, detailed profiles etc. have emerged. Unlike previous "simple" spammers, whose tweets contain only malicious links, those "smart" spammers are more difficult to distinguish from legitimate users via content-based features alone (Ferrara et al., 2014).

---

*Corresponding Author

There is a considerable amount of previous work on spammer detection on social platforms. Researcher from Twitter Inc. (Chu et al., 2010) collect bot accounts and perform analysis on the user behavior and user profile features. Lee et al. (2011) use the so-called social honeypot by alluring social spammers' retweet to build a benchmark dataset, which has been extensively explored in our paper. Some researchers focus on the clustering of urls in tweets and network graph of social spammers (Yang et al., 2012; Wang et al., 2015; Wang, 2010; Yang et al., 2011), showing the power of social relationship features.As for content information modeling, (Hu et al., 2013) apply improved sparse learning methods. However, few studies have adopted topic-based features. Some researchers (Liu et al., 2014) discuss topic characteristics of spamming posts, indicating that spammers are highly likely to dwell on some certain topics such as promotion. But this may not be applicable to the current scenario of smart spammers.

In this paper, we propose an efficient feature extraction method. In this method, two new topic-based features are extracted and used to discriminate human-like spammers from legitimate users. We consider the historical tweets of each user as a document and use the Latent Dirichlet Allocation (LDA) model to compute the topic distribution for each user. Based on the calculated topic probability, two topic-based features, the Local Outlier Standard Score (LOSS) which captures the users interests on different topics and the Global Outlier Standard Score (GOSS) which reveals the users interests on specific topic in comparison with other users, are

Proceedings of NAACL-HLT 2016, pages 45–50,
San Diego, California, June 12-17, 2016. ©2016 Association for Computational Linguistics

extracted. The two features contain both local and global information, and the combination of them can distinguish human-like spammers effectively.

To the best of our knowledge, it is the first time that features based on topic distributions are used in spammer classification. Experimental results on one public dataset and one self-collected dataset further validate that the two sets of extracted topic-based features get excellent performance on human-like spammer classification problem compared with other state-of-the-art methods. In addition, we build a Weibo dataset, which contains both legitimate users and spammers.

To summarize, our major contributions are twofold:

- We extract topic-based features (GOSS and LOSS) for spammer detection, which outperform state-of-the-art methods.
- We build a dataset of Chinese microblogs for spammer detection.

In the following sections, we first propose the topic-based features extraction method in Section 2, and then introduce the two datasets in Section 3. Experimental results are discussed in Section 4, and we conclude the paper in Section 5. Future work is presented in Section 6.

2 Methodology

In this section, we first provide some observations we obtained after carefully exploring the social network, then the LDA model is introduced. Based on the LDA model, the ways to obtain the topic probability vector for each user and the two topic-based features are provided.

2.1 Observation

After exploring the homepages of a substantial number of spammers, we have two observations. 1) social spammers can be divided into two categories. One is content polluters, and their tweets are all about certain kinds of advertisement and campaign. The other is fake accounts, and their tweets resemble legitimate users but it seems they are simply random copies of others to avoid being detected by anti-spam rules. 2) For legitimate users, content polluters and fake accounts, they show different patterns on topics which interest them.

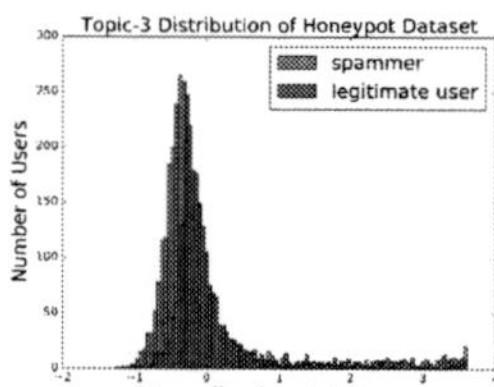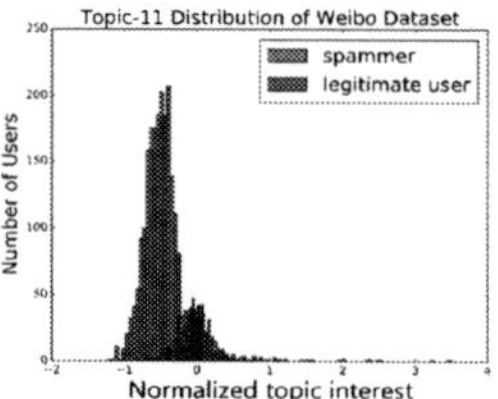

Figure 1: The topic distribution of legitimate users and social spammers on Honeypot dataset (left) and on Weibo dataset (right), respectively.

- Legitimate users mainly focus on limited topics which interest him. They seldom post contents unrelated to their concern.
- Content polluters concentrate on certain topics.
- Fake accounts focus on a wide range of topics due to random copying and retweeting of other users tweets.
- Spammers and legitimate users show different interests on some topics e.g. commercial, weather, etc.

To better illustrate our observation, Figure. 1 shows the topic distribution of spammers and legitimate users in two employed datasets(the Honeypot dataset and Weibo dataset). We can see that on both topics (topic-3 and topic-11) there exists obvious difference between the red bars and green bars, representing spammers and legitimate users. On the Honeypot dataset, spammers have a narrower shape of distribution (the outliers on the red bar tail are not counted) than that of legitimate users. This is because there are more content polluters than fake accounts. In other word, spammers in this dataset tend to concentrate on limited topics. While on the Weibo dataset, fake accounts who are interested in different topics take large proportion of spammers. Their distribution is more flat (i.e. red bars) than that of the legitimate users. Therefore we can detect spammers by means of the difference of their topic distribution patterns.

2.2 LDA model

Blei et al.(2003) first presented Latent Dirichlet Allocation(LDA) as an example of topic model.

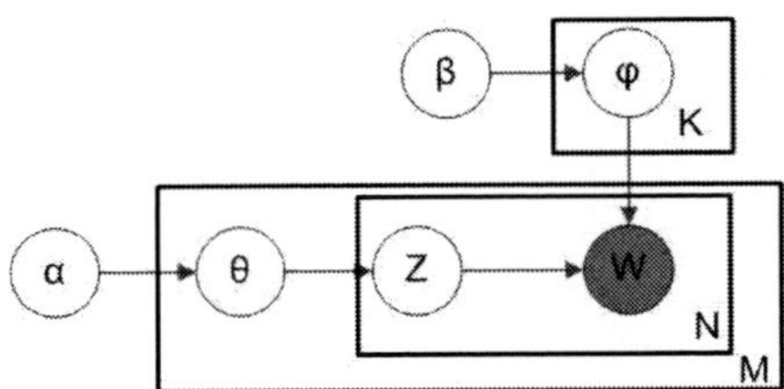

Figure 2: The generative model of LDA

Each document i is deemed as a bag of words $W = \{w_{i1}, w_{i2}, ..., w_{iM}\}$ and M is the number of words. Each word is attributable to one of the document's topics $Z = \{z_{i1}, z_{i2}, ..., z_{iK}\}$ and K is the number of topics. ψ_k is a multinomial distribution over words for topic k. θ_i is another multinomial distribution over topics for document i. The smoothed generative model is illustrated in Figure. 2. α and β are hyper parameter that affect scarcity of the document-topic and topic-word distributions. In this paper, α, β and K are empirically set to 0.3, 0.01 and 15. The entire content of each Twitter user is regarded as one document. We adopt Gibbs Sampling (Griffiths and Steyvers, 2004) to speed up the inference of LDA. Based on LDA, we can get the topic probabilities for all users in the employed dataset as: $X = [X_i; X_2; \cdots ; X_n] \in R^{n \times K}$, where n is the number of users. Each element $X_i = [p(z_1) p(z_2) \cdots p(z_K)] \in R^{1 \times K}$ is a topic probability vector for the ith document. X_i is the raw topic probability vector and our features are developed on top of it.

2.3 Topic-based Features

Using the LDA model, each person in the dataset is with a topic probability vector X_i. Assume $x_{ik} \in X_i$ denotes the likelihood that the ith tweet account favors k^{th} topic in the dataset. Our topic based features can be calculated as below.

Global Outlier Standard Score measures the degree that a user's tweet content is related to a certain topic compared to the other users. Specifically, the "GOSS" score of user i on topic k can be calculated as Eq.(1):

$$\mu(x_k) = \frac{\sum_{i=1}^{n} x_{ik}}{n},$$
$$GOSS(x_{ik}) = \frac{x_{ik} - \mu(x_k)}{\sqrt{\sum_i (x_{ik} - \mu(x_k))^2}}. \quad (1)$$

The value of $GOSS(x_{ik})$ indicates the interest-

ing degree of this person to the kth topic. Specifically, if $GOSS(x_{ik}) > GOSS(x_{jk})$, it means that the ith person has more interest in topic k than the jth person. If the value $GOSS(x_{ik})$ is extremely high or low, the ith person showing extreme interest or no interest on topic k which will probably be a distinctive pattern in the fowllowing classfication. Therefore, the topics interested or disliked by the ith person can be manifested by $f^i_{GOSS} = [GOSS(x_{i1}) \cdots GOSS(x_{iK})]$, from which the pattern of the interested topics with regarding to this person is found. Denote $f^i_{GOSS} = [GOSS(x_{i1}) \cdots GOSS(x_{iK})]$ our first topic-based feature, and it hopefully can get good performance on spammer detection.

Local Outlier Standard Score measures the degree of interest someone shows to a certain topic by considering his own homepage content only. For instance, the "LOSS" score of account i on topic k can be calculated as Eq.(2):

$$\mu(x_i) = \frac{\sum_{k=1}^{K} x_{ik}}{K},$$
$$LOSS(x_{ik}) = \frac{x_{ik} - \mu(x_i)}{\sqrt{\sum_k (x_{ik} - \mu(x_i))^2}}. \quad (2)$$

$\mu(x_i)$ represents the averaged interesting degree for all topics with regarding to i^{th} user and his tweet content. Similarly to $GOSS$, the topics interested or disliked by the ith person via considering his single post information can be manifested by $f^i_{LOSS} = [LOSS(x_{i1}) \cdots LOSS(x_{iK})]$, and $LOSS$ becomes our second topic-based features for the ith person.

3 Dataset

We use one public dataset Social Honeypot dataset and one self-collected dataset Weibo dataset to validate the effectiveness of our proposed features.

Social Honeypot Dataset: Lee et al. (2010) created and deployed 60 seed social accounts on Twitter to attract spammers by reporting back what accounts interact with them. They collected 19,276 legitimate users and 22,223 spammers in their datasets along with their tweet content in 7 months. This is our first test dataset.

Our Weibo Dataset: Sina Weibo is one of the most famous social platforms in China. It has implemented many features from Twitter. The 2197 legitimate user accounts in this dataset are provided

Feature	Method	Weibo Dataset			Honeypot Dataset		
		Precision	Recall	F1-score	Precision	Recall	F1-score
GOSS	SVM	0.974	0.956	0.965	0.884	0.986	0.932
	Adaboost	0.936	0.929	0.932	0.874	**0.990**	0.928
	RandomForest	0.982	0.956	0.969	0.880	0.969	0.922
LOSS	SVM	0.982	0.958	0.97	0.887	0.983	0.932
	Adaboost	0.941	0.929	0.935	0.878	0.976	0.924
	RandomForest	0.986	0.956	0.971	0.882	0.965	0.922
GOSS+LOSS	SVM	0.986	0.958	0.972	0.890	0.988	**0.934**
	Adaboost	0.938	0.931	0.934	0.881	0.976	0.926
	RandomForest	**0.988**	**0.958**	**0.978**	**0.895**	0.951	0.922

Table 1: Performance comparisons for our features with three baseline classifiers

by the *Tianchi Competition*[1] held by Sina Weibo. The spammers are all purchased commercially from multiple vendors on the Internet. We checked them manually and collected 802 suitable "smart" spammers accounts.

Preprocessing: Before directly performing the experiments on the employed datasets, we first delete some accounts with few posts in the two employed since the number of tweets is highly indicative of spammers. For the English Honeypot dataset, we remove stopwords, punctuations, non-ASCII words and apply stemming. For the Chinese Weibo dataset, we perform segmentation with "Jieba"[2], a Chinese text segmentation tool. After preprocessing steps, the Weibo dataset contains 2197 legitimate users and 802 spammers, and the honeypot dataset contains 2218 legitimate users and 2947 spammers. It is worth mentioning that the Honeypot dataset has been slashed because most of the Twitter accounts only have limited number of posts, which are not enough to show their interest inclination.

		Predicted	
		Polluter	Legitimate
Actual	Polluter	TP	FN
	Legitimate	FP	TN

Table 2: Confusion matrix

4 Experiment

4.1 Evaluation Metrics

The evaluating indicators in our model are show in Table 2 . We calculate precision, recall and F1-score (i.e. F1 score) as in Eq. (3). Precision is the ratio of selected accounts that are spammers. Recall is the ratio of spammers that are detected so. F1-score is the harmonic mean of precision and recall.

$$precision = \frac{TP}{TP + FP}, recall = \frac{TP}{TP + FN}$$
$$F1 - score = \frac{2 \times precision \times recall}{precision + recall} \quad (3)$$

4.2 Performance Comparisons with Baseline

Three baseline classification methods: Support Vector Machines (SVM), Adaboost, and Random Forests are adopted to evaluate our extracted features. We test each classification algorithm with scikit-learn (Pedregosa et al., 2011) and run a 10-fold cross validation. On each dataset, the employed classifiers are trained with individual feature first, and then with the combination of the two features. From Table 1, we can see that GOSS+LOSS achieves the best performance on F1-score among all others. Besides, the classification by combination of LOSS and GOSS can increase accuracy by more than 3% compared with raw topic distribution probability.

4.3 Comparison with Other Features

To compare our extracted features with previously used features for spammer detection, we use three

---

[1]Tianchi Site http://tianchi.aliyun.com
[2]Jieba Project Page https://github.com/fxsjy/jieba

Features	SVM			Adaboost		
	Precision	Recall	F1-score	Precision	Recall	F1-score
UFN	0.846	0.919	0.881	0.902	0.934	0.918
UC	0.855	0.904	0.879	0.854	0.901	0.877
UH	0.906	0.8	0.85	0.869	0.901	0.885
UFN+UC+UH	0.895	0.893	0.894	0.925	0.920	0.923
LOSS+GOSS	0.890	0.988	0.934	0.881	**0.976**	0.926
UFN+UC+UF+LOSS+GOSS	0.925	0.920	0.923	**0.952**	0.946	**0.949**

Table 3: Comparisons of our features and Lee et al.'s features

Feature	Description
UFN	standard deviation of following
	standard deviation of followers
	the number of following
	following and followers ratio
UC	|links| per tweet
	|@username| in tweets / |tweets|
	|unique @username| in tweets / |tweets|
	|unique links| per tweet
UH	the change rate of number of following

Table 4: Honeypot Feature Groups

most discriminative feature sets according to Lee et al. (2011)(Table 4). Two classifiers (Adaboost and SVM) are selected to conduct feature performance comparisons. Using Adaboost, our LOSS+GOSS features outperform all other features except for UFN which is 2% higher than ours with regard to precision on the Honeypot dataset. It is caused by the incorrectly classified spammers who are mostly news source after our manual check. They keep posting all kinds of news pieces covering diverse topics, which is similar to the behavior of fake accounts. However, UFN based on friendship networks is more useful for public accounts who possess large number of followers. The best recall value of our LOSS+GOSS features using SVM is up to 6% higher than the results by other feature groups. Regarding F1-score, our features outperform all other features. To further show the advantages of our proposed features, we compare our combined LOSS+GOSS with the combination of all the features from Lee et al. (2011) (UFN+UC+UH). It's obvious that LOSS+GOSS have a great advantage over UFN+UC+UH in terms of recall and F1-score. Moreover, by combining our LOSS+GOSS

features and UFN+UC+UH features together, we obtained another 7.1% and 2.3% performance gain with regard to precision and F1-score by Adaboost. Though there is a slight decline in terms of recall. By SVM, we get comparative results on recall and F1-score but about 3.5% improvement on precision.

5 Conclusion

In this paper, we propose a novel feature extraction method to effectively detect "smart" spammers who post seemingly legitimate tweets and are thus difficult to identify by existing spammer classification methods. Using the LDA model, we obtain the topic probability for each Twitter user. By utilizing the topic probability result, we extract our two topic-based features: GOSS and LOSS which represent the account with global and local information. Experimental results on a public dataset and a self-built Chinese microblog dataset validate the effectiveness of the proposed features.

6 Future Work

In future work, the combination method of local and global information can be further improved to maximize their individual strengths. We will also apply decision theory to enhancing the performance of our proposed features. Moreover, larger datasets on both Twitter and Weibo will be built to further validate our method.

References

David M Blei, Andrew Y Ng, and Michael I Jordan. 2003. Latent dirichlet allocation. *the Journal of machine Learning research*, 3:993–1022.

Zi Chu, Steven Gianvecchio, Haining Wang, and Sushil Jajodia. 2010. Who is tweeting on twitter: human, bot, or cyborg? In *Proceedings of the 26th annual computer security applications conference*, pages 21–30. ACM.

Emilio Ferrara, Onur Varol, Clayton A. Davis, Filippo Menczer, and Alessandro Flammini. 2014. The rise of social bots. *CoRR*, abs/1407.5225.

Thomas L Griffiths and Mark Steyvers. 2004. Finding scientific topics. *Proceedings of the National Academy of Sciences*, 101(suppl 1):5228–5235.

Xia Hu, Jiliang Tang, Yanchao Zhang, and Huan Liu. 2013. Social spammer detection in microblogging. In *Proceedings of the Twenty-Third international joint conference on Artificial Intelligence*, pages 2633–2639. AAAI Press.

Kyumin Lee, Brian David Eoff, and James Caverlee. 2010. Devils, angels, and robots: Tempting destructive users in social media. In *ICWSM*.

Kyumin Lee, Brian David Eoff, and James Caverlee. 2011. Seven months with the devils: A long-term study of content polluters on twitter. In *ICWSM*. Citeseer.

Yu Liu, Bin Wu, Bai Wang, and Guanchen Li. 2014. Sdhm: A hybrid model for spammer detection in weibo. In *Advances in Social Networks Analysis and Mining (ASONAM), 2014 IEEE/ACM International Conference on*, pages 942–947. IEEE.

F. Pedregosa, G. Varoquaux, A. Gramfort, V. Michel, B. Thirion, O. Grisel, M. Blondel, P. Prettenhofer, R. Weiss, V. Dubourg, J. Vanderplas, A. Passos, D. Cournapeau, M. Brucher, M. Perrot, and E. Duchesnay. 2011. Scikit-learn: Machine learning in Python. *Journal of Machine Learning Research*, 12:2825–2830.

Bo Wang, Arkaitz Zubiaga, Maria Liakata, and Rob Procter. 2015. Making the most of tweet-inherent features for social spam detection on twitter. *arXiv preprint arXiv:1503.07405*.

Alex Hai Wang. 2010. Don't follow me: Spam detection in twitter. In *Security and Cryptography (SECRYPT), Proceedings of the 2010 International Conference on*, pages 1–10. IEEE.

Chao Yang, Robert Chandler Harkreader, and Guofei Gu. 2011. Die free or live hard? empirical evaluation and new design for fighting evolving twitter spammers. In *Recent Advances in Intrusion Detection*, pages 318–337. Springer.

Chao Yang, Robert Harkreader, Jialong Zhang, Seungwon Shin, and Guofei Gu. 2012. Analyzing spammers' social networks for fun and profit: a case study of cyber criminal ecosystem on twitter. In *Proceedings of the 21st international conference on World Wide Web*, pages 71–80. ACM.

Developing language technology tools and resources for a resource-poor language: Sindhi

Raveesh Motlani
FC Kohli Center on Intelligent Systems (KCIS)
International Institute of Information Technology, Hyderabad
`raveesh.motlani@gmail.com`

Abstract

Sindhi, an Indo-Aryan language with more than 75 million native speakers[1] is a resource-poor language in terms of the availability of language technology tools and resources. In this thesis, we discuss the approaches taken to develop resources and tools for a resource-poor language with special focus on Sindhi. The major contributions of this work include raw and annotated datasets, a POS Tagger, a Morphological Analyser, a Transliteration and a Machine Translation System.

1 Introduction

Language technology tools are vital resources that ensure digital existence of a language for a long time. Such tools and resources are necessary for natural language processing and have aplenty applications in the digital era. For instance, cross-lingual technologies such as machine translation help people across the world communicate with each other using their native languages and access information present in a language they do not know. Similarly, automatic speech recognition helps people interact with machines using natural languages. There are many more such applications where a better understanding of natural languages by machines could be helpful in various ways. Language technology tools facilitate the understanding of natural languages by computers. A lot of popular languages in the world are equipped with such tools and applications but a larger set of languages in this world lack these basic tools. It is important to protect such languages from being digitally endangered.

Our work is based on one such resource-poor language, Sindhi. Our aim is to develop some basic resources, language processing tools and an application which will help Sindhi in its digital existence.

2 About the Sindhi language

Sindhi is an Indo-Aryan language spoken by more than 75 million speakers in the world. The majority of this population resides in India and Pakistan.[2] Historically, Sindhi was written using several writing systems (Landa, Khojki, Waranki, Khudawadi, Gurumukhi, Perso-Arabic and Devanagari), many of which are extinct now. Currently, Devanagari and Perso-Arabic scripts are primarily used to write in Sindhi. Both these scripts are official scripts of Sindhi in India, whereas only Perso-Arabic is the official script of Sindhi in Pakistan.

During the colonial rule, the British chose Perso-Arabic as the standard script, which led to creation of large amount of literature in this script. There are many news websites and blogs in Sindhi (Perso-Arabic) published from Pakistan.[3] This may be because Sindhi speakers are more in Pakistan than India and also have a geographical state called 'Sindh'. In contrast, literature in Sindhi (Devanagari) on the web is very small. In India, Sindhi is an official language but not of a particular geographical state and therefore it does not enjoy the support that other state-official languages do.

---

[1]https://en.wikipedia.org/wiki/Sindhi_language

[2]Sindhi is an official language in India and Pakistan.
[3]http://www.abyznewslinks.com/pakis.htm

Proceedings of NAACL-HLT 2016, pages 51–58,
San Diego, California, June 12-17, 2016. ©2016 Association for Computational Linguistics

3   Related Work

Sindhi is written using two writing forms, the Devanagari script and the Perso-Arabic script. Previously, some research on Sindhi has been done with Perso-Arabic as the preferred script. An account of this research is given below.

A rule-based POS Tagger was developed by Mahar et al. (2010) using a lexicon of 26,355 entries and 67 tags. Its accuracy was reported to be 96.28%. A finite-state machine for capturing noun inflections in Sindhi was developed by Rahman et al. (2010). Zeeshan et al. (2015) have worked on developing a spell checker. Unfortunately, the above described tools are not publicly available. Therefore we could not evaluate and compare them or use them for developing resources for Sindhi (Devanagari).

A computational grammar library for Sindhi (Perso-Arabic) in Grammatical Framework[4] (Ranta, 2009) was developed by Jherna Devi Oad (2012). This library has 44 categories, 190 functions and 360 lexical entries. It was referred to during the development of our Sindhi (Perso-Arabic) morphological analyser.

4   Developing Datasets

A dataset is the most important requirement for building language technology tools and resources for any language. The following section describes how we collected and developed the datasets for both the scripts of Sindhi. A summary of the datasets and tools developed by us or other researchers for both scripts of Sindhi is provided in Table 1.

4.1   Sindhi (Devanagari) Datasets

The amount of raw texts available on the web for Sindhi (Devanagari) is very small. Initially we contacted various publishers and news agencies to source raw data, but the problem was further compounded as many publishers on the web have not yet moved to Unicode standards.

Raw Textual Data: We collected several short stories, books, articles, etc. and manually created data for Devanagari. Through this manual process, we were able to handle certain issues such as usage of correct Unicode encoding, normalization,

script and grammar. Later, we developed a Unicode Converter[5] for legacy fonts, which helped us collect more data. We currently have a raw corpus of 326813 words, with average sentence length of 9.35 words and a vocabulary (unique words) of 22300 words.

Part-of-Speech Annotated Data: Since Sindhi did not have a POS Tagset, we adapted the BIS Tagset[6] which is comprehensive and designed to be extensible to any Indian Language. We annotated the data using this tagset and help from two annotators. We obtained a κ score (Cohen, 1960) of 0.96 when evaluated for Inter-Annotator Agreement on 793 words. Currently, we have tagged corpus of 44692 words. This data was subsequently used to build an automatic Part-of-Speech Tagger (discussed in Section 5.1).

4.2   Sindhi (Perso-Arabic) Datasets

As previously mentioned, large amount of content exists on the web for Sindhi in Perso-Arabic script, which can be used to source raw textual data.

Raw Textual Data: We collected textual data from Sindhi Wikipedia dump[7], news websites and blogs[8]. We currently have a corpus of about 1 million tokens.

Parallel Data: A sentence-aligned parallel corpora is an indispensable resource for any language pair. Many languages across the world are not fortunate enough to have such a parallel corpora available, including Sindhi. We have developed a small parallel corpus between Urdu and Sindhi, which are closely related languages. We initiated the development process by collecting some sentences from the Urdu Treebank (Bhat and Sharma, 2012), general conversations, news articles and essays and translating them to Sindhi manually. We now have a parallel corpus of 1400 sentences and it is being used for various purposes (Section 6), including automatic generation of more parallel data (see 6.3).

---

[4]http://www.grammaticalframework.org/lib/src/sindhi

[5]http://goo.gl/d5a8X2

[6]http://goo.gl/AZxk7x

[7]https://dumps.wikimedia.org/sdwiki/sdwiki-20150826-pages-articles.xml.bz2

[8]http://tinyurl.com/Sindhi-URLs

Data, Tools & Applications	Sindhi Devanagari	Sindhi Perso-Arabic
POS Annotated Data	**Yes**	Yes*
Chunk Annotated Data	No	No
Dependency Annotated Data	No	No
Parallel Data (Urdu-Sindhi)	No	**Yes**
POS Tagger	**Yes**	Yes*
Morphological Analyser	No	**Yes**
Spell-Checker	No	Yes*
Transliteration	**Yes**	**Yes**
Machine Translation (Urdu-Sindhi)	No	**Yes**

Table 1: The status of various resources developed for each script of Sindhi. * Resources developed by other researchers.

5 Developing Tools

After developing the datasets, we used them in creation of certain language technology tools which we describe below. Table 1 summarizes some tools developed for Sindhi by us and other researchers.

5.1 Part-of-Speech Tagger

Part-of-Speech (POS) tagging is the task of assigning an appropriate part-of-speech label to each word in a sentence, based on both its definition as well as its context. POS tagging is a fundamentally important task, as it gives information about words, their neighbors and the syntactic structure around them. This information is useful in syntactic parsing and other applications such as named-entity recognition, information retrieval, speech processing, etc.

The data that we annotated with POS tags was used to build an automatic POS Tagger[9] for Sindhi (Devanagari) (Motlani et al., 2015) using Conditional Random Fields[10] (Lafferty et al., 2001). We employed 10-fold cross validation to train and test the tagger. We experimented with several models by using various set of features, including linguistically motivated features such as *affixes* (which capture the morphological properties of the language) and *context* (which capture the syntactic structure of the language).

The current best performing model gives an average accuracy of 92.6% , which is 11% better than

baseline[11] tagger. This tagger is being used to generate more POS annotated data through bootstrapping and post-editing methods.

5.2 Morphological Analyser

The morphological analysis of a word involves capturing its inherent properties such as gender, number, person, case, etc. Morphological features also help in improving the performance of other NLP tools such as, pos tagger, spell-checker, parsers, machine translation, etc. Thus, morphological analysis is a fundamental and crucial task.

We used Apertium's lttoolbox (Forcada et al., 2011) to develop a paradigm based finite-state morphological analyser for Sindhi (Perso-Arabic) (Motlani et al., 2016). This morphological analyser currently has about 3500 entries and a coverage of more than 81% on Sindhi Wikipedia dump consisting of 341.5k tokens. This analyser is publicly available on Apertium[12].

Sindhi is a morphologically rich language (Rahman and Bhatti, 2010). It uses suffixes for constructing derivational and inflectional morphemes. A major challenge for us is to incorporate the vast morphology. We currently have 72 paradigms in the analyser and are expanding them to cover all possible inflections. This, along with adding more entries to the lexicon, would help increase the coverage further. Another challenge is processing partially or fully diacritised input. The analyser can handle usual Sindhi texts which lack in diacritics but it tends to

---

[9]https://github.com/kindleton/sindhi_pos_tagger

[10]We used CRF++, an open source implementation of CRFs. https://taku910.github.io/crfpp/

[11]The baseline model assigns most frequent tag corresponding to a word, based on word-tag frequencies in training data.

[12]http://tinyurl.com/SindhiMorphAnalyser

make errors for other kinds of input because it is difficult to lookup in the lexicon and disambiguate.

5.3 Transliteration System

A transliteration system is a much needed tool to bridge the gap between content in Perso-Arabic and Devanagari scripts. Moreover, such a system could also facilitate sharing of resources developed in either scripts. Although a transliteration system would be very useful but there are various challenges that we face. Some of them are :

1. **Unavailability of Transliteration Pairs** : Transliteration pairs is a key resource for learning a transliteration model. In cases where a seed set is not available, transliteration pairs can be easily mined from a parallel data between the source and target language pair. We do not have any parallel data between Sindhi (Perso-Arabic) and Sindhi (Devanagari).

2. **Missing Diacritics** : Many Perso-Arabic script based languages do not use diacritics marks in their texts. This further leads to semantic and syntactic ambiguities, because a word can have multiple interpretations. An example: 'چپ' *cp* can be either *capa* 'lips' or *cupa* 'silent'.

3. **Differences in Character-Sets** : The alphabets in Sindhi (Perso-Arabic) are a variant of the Persian script. It is composed of 52 letters, including Persian letters, digraphs and eighteen other letters (illustrated in Table 2) to capture the sounds particular to Sindhi and other Indo-Aryan languages. The alphabets in Sindhi Devanagari are composed of 65 characters, including, short-vowels and 4 special characters representing Sindhi implosives. A one-to-one mapping cannot be developed between them.

5.3.1 Unsupervised Transliteration Pairs Mining

There is a lot of literature on automatic extraction of transliteration pairs using seed data and parallel corpora (Sajjad et al., 2012; Durrani et al., 2014; Jiampojamarn et al., 2010; Kumaran et al., 2010). Since our scenario is resource-poor, we designed

گؕ	[ŋ]	ج	[ɲ]	ٻ	[ɓ]
ڳ	[ɠ]	ڇ	[ʃ]	ڀ	[bʱ]
ڪ	[k]	ڄ	[cʰ]	ڌ	[dʱ]
ڱ	[ŋ]	ٿ	[tʰ]	ڏ	[ɗ]
ڦ	[pʰ]	ت	[t]	ڊ	[ɖ]
ڙ	[ɽ]	ٺ	[tʰ]	ڍ	[ɖʱ]

Table 2: The characters found in the alphabet of Sindhi (Perso-Arabic) script which are not present in the Persian alphabet and their phonetic representation.

and used an unsupervised approach for transliteration pair mining that prescinds from prior knowledge of seed corpus and parallel data.

In this approach, a discriminative transliteration detection engine takes three inputs: a limited character mapping[13] and unique word-list in source and target language.

These lists are iterated over to obtain a list of candidate word pairs. These candidate word pairs are then discriminated based on orthographic similarity. The orthographic similarity is measured by converting the characters of source and target word into an intermediate representation using the character mapping and calculating the edit-distance between them normalized by their word-length. The candidate pairs with larger edit-distance are pruned out and the remaining are treated as possible transliteration pairs.

5.3.2 Preliminary Results

The transliteration problem can be posed as a phrase-based SMT problem, where sentences are analogous to words and words are analogous to characters. We used the MOSES (Koehn et al., 2003) toolkit to train transliteration models by treating each transliteration pair (space separated sequence of characters) as the parallel data.

We had mined 112434 possible transliteration pairs from our raw datasets and trained a transliteration model. We evaluated it on a short story of 3247 words and obtained the following results shown in Table 3. We have also demonstrated an example in

---

[13]In our experiments we used a mapping of only those consonants and vowels which can be mapped one-to-one or many-to-one. Diacritics, most vowels and other ambiguous characters were not mapped. The bash command 'uconv' can be used to develop a mapping between various scripts.

Top-k	k=1	k=5	k=10	k=25
Precision (%)	60.14	83.27	87.12	90.08

Table 3: Results of preliminary experiments on transliteration. Top-k refers to first k candidates output by the system.

Table 4, where words of a source sentence in Sindhi (Perso-Arabic) are transliterated to Sindhi (Devanagari).

5.3.3 Context Aware Transliteration

The systems developed using previous approach can produce transliteration candidates for a given input word (as shown in Table 4), but there are various challenges in case of Sindhi (described in Section 5.3) because of which the precision of best output (top-1) is low. We believe this system can be improved using context in selecting the correct transliteration from candidate transliterations (top-k) of an input word. Currently, we are experimenting with context-based transliteration using Viterbi decoding and Language Model re-ranking.[14]

6 Statistical Machine Translation for Sindhi

Development of fundamental tools and resources discussed in the previous sections are important for larger NLP applications on Sindhi. An important application that can be developed without using these tools is an SMT system. Although phrase-based SMT requires only parallel data, rule-based and factored based machine translation systems depend on these fundamental tools.

In this section we shall discuss our ongoing work on developing a Sindhi-Urdu SMT system.

6.1 The Language Pair: Urdu and Sindhi

Sindhi and Urdu are spoken by a large number of native speakers (75 million and 159 million[15] around the world). These languages belong to Indo-Aryan language family and have evolved in the same geographical region for many years. Thus, they have many syntactic and semantic similarities. For instance, they share vocabulary, typography and sen-

Source Word	Translit. (Top-3)	Ref. Word	Pos.
سندس	संदसि संदस संदनि	संदसि	1
جيب	जी जीब जीबु	जेब	4
مان	मां मानु में	मां	1
کو	को कयो कवि	को	1
موبائيل	मोबाइल मोबाइलु मोबाईल	मोबाईल	3
کڍي	कढी कढ़ी कढीग	कढी	1
ويو	वयो वियो वयोसि	व्यो	6
هئس	हुयस हिकु हास	हुउसि	None

Table 4: This table shows words of source sentence, their top-3 transliteration outputs given by the system, the reference word and the position at which an output matches the reference. This sentence is taken from test data, in English it means *'Someone had taken out mobile (phone) from his pocket (and left)'*.

tence structures (for example, both follow subject-object-verb word-order). These similarities are major reasons behind choosing this language pair for the purpose of developing parallel data (Section 4.2) and subsequently a SMT system.

In our opinion, Sindhi would benefit a lot from Sindhi-Urdu parallel data, as Urdu is comparatively resource rich language and techniques like projection (Yarowsky et al., 2001; Das and Petrov, 2011; Täckström et al., 2012) can be employed to leverage several resources for Sindhi.

6.2 Development

When we started working on SMT for Sindhi-Urdu, we only had about 1200 parallel sentences, a baseline

---

[14]Re-ranking the top-k transliteration candidates for ambiguous words in a particular context window

[15]https://en.wikipedia.org/wiki/Urdu

SMT system[16] was created using them.

This baseline system was evaluated on 70 held-out test sentences. The output sentences were given to a translator evaluation by rating each sentence on a scale of 1-5 (where, 1-very bad and 5-very good). The average rating obtained was 2.65 points. We also calculated other popular metrics for evaluation of MT system. BLEU (Papineni et al., 2002) score was 38.62, METEOR (Banerjee and Lavie, 2005) score was 77.97 and TER (Translation Error Rate) (Snover et al., 2006) was 38.28 . Note that, BLEU and METEOR scores are high due to small size of training data and vocabulary. Results of TER and human-evaluation are a better reflection of baseline system's performance.

6.3 Improvement

We manually analysed the errors made by the baseline SMT system and found that too many out-of-vocabulary (OOV) words. Other than those, words which were incorrectly translated were either due to presence in very low frequency in training data or due to ambiguity created by multiple possible translations.

Thus, we need to employ various techniques in order to significantly improve over baseline performance and develop a reasonably good translation system. One such technique is bootstrapping more parallel data using the baseline SMT system. Although, creating parallel data is faster in this process but it is still a time consuming and laborious task. Therefore, we also need to use certain automatic techniques. Some of them are described below

6.3.1 Bootstrapping more Parallel Data

The performance of a SMT system depends largely on the amount of parallel data used for training the system, which is very less in our case. Therefore, we are trying to generate more parallel data by using the baseline SMT system to bootstrap more parallel corpus. We source new sentences from the web (news articles, essays, short stories, etc.), translate it and then provide it to translators for post-editing.

6.3.2 Bilingual Lexicon Extraction from Comparable Corpora

Bilingual lexicon extraction is an automatic way to extract parallel data from non-parallel texts. Research in this area has been active for past several years and various approaches with promising results have been proposed (Rapp, 1995; Haghighi et al., 2008; Laroche and Langlais, 2010; Vulić et al., 2011; Irvine and Callison-Burch, 2013). The process involves finding possible translation candidates for a source word in target data using several features like orthographic, temporal, topical and contextual similarity. Presence of seed lexicon further benefits this process. Since Urdu and Sindhi are closely related languages and we have small parallel data, we can compute these features to induce lexicon of Urdu in Sindhi and obtain possible translation pairs.

We are exploring these different techniques on comparable data sourced from Wikipedia pages inter-lingually linked between Sindhi and Urdu and some news articles[17] published in these languages. The extracted parallel data will be supplemented to the phrase-table learned by Moses (Klementiev et al., 2012). This parallel data shall improve the coverage of the SMT system, although its impact on the SMT system's performance is yet to be evaluated.

6.3.3 Rule-Based Transliteration

The Sindhi (Perso-Arabic) and Urdu alphabets share many characters with very few differences. This typographic similarity can also be used to reduce OOV errors, specially for named entities. Therefore, we are developing a rule-based transliteration system by mapping the different characters in their scripts.

7 Conclusion

My thesis aims at developing some fundamental tools and resources and an application for a resource-poor and multi-script language, Sindhi. The main contribution of my work includes collection and creation of raw and annotated datasets, constructing NLP tools such as POS tagger, morphological analyser, building a transliteration system without parallel data in an unsupervised fashion and developing

---

[16]The baseline is a phrase-based SMT system, trained using Moses toolkit (Koehn et al., 2003) with word-alignments extracted from GIZA++ (Och and Ney, 2000) and using 3-gram language models created using KenLm (Heafield et al., 2013)

[17]Sindhi : http://www.onlineindusnews.com/
Urdu : http://www.onlineindusnews.net/

a SMT system for Sindhi-Urdu and improving it using various techniques. While my work shall supplement development of NLP applications for Sindhi, it shall also motivate research on languages surviving in similar resource-poor setting.

Acknowledgments

The research presented in this paper was done in collaboration with my advisors, Prof. Dipti M. Sharma and Dr. Manish Shrivastava. The Part-of-Speech annotation was done in collaboration with Dr. Pinkey Nainwani and Harsh Lalwani. I would like to acknowledge the people who have helped me various tasks like collecting the data, translations and understanding Sindhi better such as, Mehtab Ahmed Solangi, Mr. Bhagwan Babani and Mr. Chunnilaal Wadhwani. I would like to thank Nehal J. Wani, Arnav Sharma, Himanshu Sharma and Dr. Francis M. Tyers for their constant motivation and support. Lastly, I am thankful to the anonymous reviewers for their invaluable feedback and suggestions. This publication reflects the authors views only.

References

Satanjeev Banerjee and Alon Lavie. 2005. Meteor: An automatic metric for mt evaluation with improved correlation with human judgments. In *Proceedings of the acl workshop on intrinsic and extrinsic evaluation measures for machine translation and/or summarization*, volume 29, pages 65–72.

Riyaz Ahmad Bhat and Dipti Misra Sharma. 2012. A dependency treebank of urdu and its evaluation. In *Proceedings of the Sixth Linguistic Annotation Workshop*, pages 157–165. Association for Computational Linguistics.

Zeeshan Bhatti, Imdad Ali Ismaili, Waseem Javid Soomro, et al. 2015. Phonetic-based sindhi spellchecker system using a hybrid model. *Digital Scholarship in the Humanities*.

Jacob Cohen. 1960. A coefficient of agreement for nominal scales. *Educational and Psychological Measurement*.

Dipanjan Das and Slav Petrov. 2011. Unsupervised part-of-speech tagging with bilingual graph-based projections. In *Proceedings of the 49th Annual Meeting of the Association for Computational Linguistics (ACL '11)*, page Best Paper Award.

Nadir Durrani, Hassan Sajjad, Hieu Hoang, and Philipp Koehn. 2014. Integrating an unsupervised translit-eration model into statistical machine translation. In *EACL*, pages 148–153.

M. L. Forcada, M. Ginestí-Rosell, J. Nordfalk, J. O'Regan, S. Ortiz-Rojas, J. A. Pérez-Ortiz, F. Sánchez-Martínez, G. Ramírez-Sánchez, and F. M. Tyers. 2011. Apertium: a free/open-source platform for rule-based machine translation. *Machine Translation*, 25(2):127–144.

Aria Haghighi, Percy Liang, Taylor Berg-Kirkpatrick, and Dan Klein. 2008. Learning bilingual lexicons from monolingual corpora.

Kenneth Heafield, Ivan Pouzyrevsky, Jonathan H. Clark, and Philipp Koehn. 2013. Scalable modified Kneser-Ney language model estimation. In *Proceedings of the 51st Annual Meeting of the Association for Computational Linguistics*, pages 690–696, Sofia, Bulgaria, August.

Ann Irvine and Chris Callison-Burch. 2013. Combining bilingual and comparable corpora for low resource machine translation. In *Proceedings of the Eighth Workshop on Statistical Machine Translation*, pages 262–270.

Sittichai Jiampojamarn, Kenneth Dwyer, Shane Bergsma, Aditya Bhargava, Qing Dou, Mi-Young Kim, and Grzegorz Kondrak. 2010. Transliteration generation and mining with limited training resources. In *Proceedings of the 2010 Named Entities Workshop*, pages 39–47. Association for Computational Linguistics.

Alexandre Klementiev, Ann Irvine, Chris Callison-Burch, and David Yarowsky. 2012. Toward statistical machine translation without parallel corpora. In *Proceedings of the 13th Conference of the European Chapter of the Association for Computational Linguistics*, pages 130–140. Association for Computational Linguistics.

Philipp Koehn, Franz Josef Och, and Daniel Marcu. 2003. Statistical phrase-based translation. In *Proceedings of the 2003 Conference of the North American Chapter of the Association for Computational Linguistics on Human Language Technology-Volume 1*, pages 48–54. Association for Computational Linguistics.

A Kumaran, Mitesh M Khapra, and Haizhou Li. 2010. Report of news 2010 transliteration mining shared task. In *Proceedings of the 2010 Named Entities Workshop*, pages 21–28. Association for Computational Linguistics.

John D. Lafferty, Andrew McCallum, and Fernando C. N. Pereira. 2001. Conditional random fields: Probabilistic models for segmenting and labeling sequence data. In *Proceedings of the Eighteenth International Conference on Machine Learning*, pages 282–289, San Francisco, CA, USA. Morgan Kaufmann Publishers Inc.

Audrey Laroche and Philippe Langlais. 2010. Revisiting context-based projection methods for term-translation spotting in comparable corpora. In *Proceedings of the 23rd international conference on computational linguistics*, pages 617–625. Association for Computational Linguistics.

Javed Ahmed Mahar and Ghulam Qadir Memon. 2010. Rule based part of speech tagging of sindhi language. In *Proceedings of the 2010 International Conference on Signal Acquisition and Processing*, ICSAP '10, pages 101–106, Washington, DC, USA. IEEE Computer Society.

Raveesh Motlani, Harsh Lalwani, Manish Shrivastava, and Dipti Misra Sharma. 2015. Developing part-of-speech tagger for a resource poor language: Sindhi. In *Proceedings of the 7th Language and Technology Conference (LTC 2015), Poznan, Poland.*

Raveesh Motlani, Francis M. Tyers, and Dipti M. Sharma. 2016. A finite-state morphological analyser for sindhi. In *Proceedings of the Tenth International Conference on Language Resources and Evaluation (LREC'16)*. European Language Resources Association (ELRA), May.

Jherna Devi Oad. 2012. *Implementing GF Resource Grammar for Sindhi language*. Msc. thesis, Chalmers University of Technology, Gothenburg, Sweden.

Franz Josef Och and Hermann Ney. 2000. Improved statistical alignment models. In *Proceedings of the 38th Annual Meeting on Association for Computational Linguistics*, pages 440–447. Association for Computational Linguistics.

Kishore Papineni, Salim Roukos, Todd Ward, and Wei-Jing Zhu. 2002. Bleu: a method for automatic evaluation of machine translation. In *Proceedings of the 40th annual meeting on association for computational linguistics*, pages 311–318. Association for Computational Linguistics.

Mutee U Rahman and Mohammad Iqbal Bhatti. 2010. Finite state morphology and Sindhi noun inflections. *In Proceedings of the 24th Pacific Asia Conference on Language, Information and Computation, PACLIC 24, Tohoku University, Japan*, 134:669–676.

Aarne Ranta. 2009. Gf: A multilingual grammar formalism. *Language and Linguistics Compass*, 3.

Reinhard Rapp. 1995. Identifying word translations in non-parallel texts. In *Proceedings of the 33rd Annual Meeting on Association for Computational Linguistics*, ACL '95, pages 320–322, Stroudsburg, PA, USA. Association for Computational Linguistics.

Hassan Sajjad, Alexander Fraser, and Helmut Schmid. 2012. A statistical model for unsupervised and semi-supervised transliteration mining. In *Proceedings of the 50th Annual Meeting of the Association for Computational Linguistics: Long Papers-Volume 1*, pages 469–477. Association for Computational Linguistics.

Matthew Snover, Bonnie Dorr, Richard Schwartz, Linnea Micciulla, and John Makhoul. 2006. A study of translation edit rate with targeted human annotation. In *Proceedings of association for machine translation in the Americas*, pages 223–231.

Oscar Täckström, Ryan McDonald, and Jakob Uszkoreit. 2012. Cross-lingual word clusters for direct transfer of linguistic structure. In *Proceedings of the 2012 Conference of the North American Chapter of the Association for Computational Linguistics: Human Language Technologies*, NAACL HLT '12, pages 477–487, Stroudsburg, PA, USA. Association for Computational Linguistics.

Ivan Vulić, Wim De Smet, and Marie-Francine Moens. 2011. Identifying word translations from comparable corpora using latent topic models. In *Proceedings of the 49th Annual Meeting of the Association for Computational Linguistics: Human Language Technologies: Short Papers - Volume 2*, HLT '11, pages 479–484, Stroudsburg, PA, USA. Association for Computational Linguistics.

David Yarowsky, Grace Ngai, and Richard Wicentowski. 2001. Inducing multilingual text analysis tools via robust projection across aligned corpora. In *Proceedings of the First International Conference on Human Language Technology Research*, HLT '01, pages 1–8, Stroudsburg, PA, USA. Association for Computational Linguistics.

Effects of Communicative Pressures on
Novice L2 Learners' Use of Optional Formal Devices

Yoav Binoun, Francesca Delogu, Clayton Greenberg,
Mindaugas Mozuraitis, and **Matthew W. Crocker**
Department of Computational Linguistics
Saarland University
66123 Saarbrücken, Germany
{ybinoun,delogu,claytong,mindauga,crocker}@coli.uni-saarland.de

Abstract

We conducted an Artificial Language Learning experiment to examine the production behavior of language learners in a dynamic communicative setting. Participants were exposed to a miniature language with two optional formal devices and were then asked to use the acquired language to transfer information in a cooperative game. The results showed that language learners optimize their use of the optional formal devices to transfer information efficiently and that they avoid the production of ambiguous information. These results could be used within the context of a language model such that the model can more accurately reflect the production behavior of human language learners.

1 Introduction

According to the Uniform Information Density hypothesis (Jaeger, 2010), language users optimize their production behavior to transfer information efficiently. More specifically, language users distribute information evenly across an utterance, avoiding peaks and troughs in information density (see Jaeger, 2010; Mahowald et al., 2013; Frank and Jaeger, 2008; Jaeger and Levy, 2006). Additionally, according to Grice's (1975) second Maxim of Quantity, language users avoid the use of redundant or ambiguous information in cooperative situations, although previous work suggests redundant utterances are sometimes preferred (see Arts, 2011; Engelhardt et al., 2006).

Previous work using the artificial grammar learning paradigm (AGL) has suggested that language

learners diverge from the statistical properties of the input language data to make the language more efficient (Fedzechkina et al., 2012). In that study, language learners optimized the use of optional case marking in sentences where animacy and constituent order (SOV vs. OSV) created ambiguity. We conducted a novel study, within the AGL paradigm, to explore whether this behavior extends to a dynamic communicative setting involving a cooperative game. We investigated whether, in this setting, language learners preserve the statistical properties of the input language data or whether they adjust to dynamic communicative pressures (conditions) that arise at production time. Three options were considered:

1. Language users prefer the most efficient structures for information transfer, regardless of the communicative setting and the learning process.

2. Language users are sensitive to the learning process and strictly follow (during production) the frequency of patterns to which they were initially exposed (during learning).

3. Language users consider the communicative setting and dynamically adjust their language production behavior according to changes in the communicative conditions, such as acoustic noise or ambiguities against the visual context.

To provide language users with controlled, yet variable structures, we presented participants with an artificial language with optional overt subjects (OS) and optional agreement affixes (AA) on the

Proceedings of NAACL-HLT 2016, pages 59–65,
San Diego, California, June 12-17, 2016. ©2016 Association for Computational Linguistics

verb. We examined the distribution of usage of these optional devices within the cooperative game.

2 Experiment

Our AGL experiment consisted of two parts. The first part, roughly 25 minutes long, was the learning part (*learning phase*); in this part, participants learned and were tested on an miniature artificial language. The learning phase was divided further into a noun exposure section and a verb exposure section. The second part, roughly 20 minutes long, was the game part (*game phase*); in this part, participants had to describe a target video to a confederate using the language they had learned, while a competitor video was also present. We recorded and transcribed utterances produced by participants during the game phase for the analysis.

The artificial language included two optional formal devices, namely optional overt subjects (OS) and optional agreement affixes (AA) on the verb (see Section 2.1.2 for examples). We manipulated three factors (one acoustic and two visual) during the interaction with the confederate throughout the game phase. The acoustic factor was a recording of coffee shop background noise in two levels of volume, high and low. The hypothesis was that with a higher level of acoustic noise, participants would include more of the optional formal devices in their utterances. The visual factors were determined by the potential overlap between the target and the competitor videos. More specifically, the two videos could have 1) same or different subject and 2) same or different verb. Thus, the experiment used a $2 \times 2 \times 2$ design crossing subject overlap, verb overlap and level of noise. We hypothesized that language learners would change their behavior online and prefer to include the optional formal devices of the input language in their utterances when the subject/verb overlap created ambiguity or when the acoustic noise level was high.

2.1 Method

2.1.1 Participants

Twenty nine Saarland University students (between ages 18-33) participated in the experiment and were monetarily compensated upon completion of participation. Since the optional formal devices of the artificial language were borrowed from Hebrew, we ensured that all of the participants had no prior knowledge of Semitic languages. Rather, all participants were native speakers of German. Out of the twenty nine participants, three participants were removed from the data due to repeating errors in the artificial language production and two were removed from the data due to recording errors.

2.1.2 Materials

Artificial language stimuli During the learning phase, participants were exposed to 8 nouns: 4 subjects (man, woman, men and women) and 4 objects (apple, cheese, carrot and cake) in still images and text as well as to 2 verbs (eat and drop) in videos and text. All nouns were accompanied by the same determiner ("ha"). All sentences in the artificial language had SVO constituent order. Zero, one, or two optional devices could be present, therefore the translation for the sentence

"(The man) [eats]-<SG. MASC.> ⟨the apple⟩"

could be produced in the following four ways:

(OS)	Verb + (AA)	Object	Exposure
(ha dini)	[akal]-<ini>	⟨ha tapu⟩	25%
	[akal]-<ini>	⟨ha tapu⟩	25%
(ha dini)	[akal]	⟨ha tapu⟩	25%
	[akal]	⟨ha tapu⟩	25%

Table 1: Sentence type exposure during learning

The overt subjects in () and the agreement affixes on the verb in <>, could be dropped. During learning all four possibilities were equally probable, as shown in Table 1.

Visual stimuli The visual stimuli during the noun exposure part of the learning phase consisted of images of the nouns accompanied by written (and acoustic) descriptions in the artificial language. Each subject was presented one time, while objects were presented two times: one time with the object appearing alone in the screen (e.g. one apple) and one time with two images of the object on the screen (e.g. two apples). This was done in order to clarify that objects did not take a plural form (similar to "sheep" in English, for example). In total, 12 images were presented in the noun learning phase: 4

subjects, 4 objects (appearing alone on the screen) and 4 objects (appearing two times on the screen).

During the verb exposure part, video representations of simple transitive verbs between these nouns were played, also accompanied by their descriptions in text and audio form. Each verb was presented 32 times: 4 times per subject, across 4 different subjects and 2 objects. All images were created in Adobe Illustrator CS6, and the videos were created in Adobe Flash CS6 using these images.

The visual stimuli during the game phase consisted of videos showing the same representations of verbs performed by the same subjects and objects, but in different combinations than in the learning phase. For example, since in the learning phase the man was shown eating the cake and the carrot, in the game phase the man was only shown eating the cheese and the apple. Each target video was paired with a competitor video to create four different combinations:

same subject	same verb	diff. object
same subject	diff. verb	same object
diff. subject	same verb	same object
diff. subject	diff. verb	same object

Table 2: List of the visual communicative conditions.

Note that the game required some difference between the target and competitor videos, so it was necessary to have a distinction in the object for the same subject and same verb condition. An arrow indicated on every screen which video was the target. In total 64 screens were played during the game phase in 4 blocks. Each block was balanced for noise and visual communicative conditions.

Audio stimuli During the learning phase, audio and written descriptions in the artificial language accompanied the visual stimuli. Audio stimuli consisted of whole sentence recordings during the verb exposure part, and the nouns during the noun exposure. The audio stimuli were recorded by a male speaker of Hebrew, in a soundproof recording booth using Praat (Version 5.3).

During the game phase, acoustic noise was introduced in two levels, high and low. The noise was a 10 seconds long recording from a local coffee shop, with no intelligible speech in it. The noise at the low level condition was set to 40 dB and at the high level condition was set to 70 dB.

Procedure The learning phase of the experiment was implemented in Microsoft PowerPoint 2013 and run on a laptop. During the noun exposure, participants were exposed to all the nouns from the artificial language vocabulary in picture, text and audio form. After the audio description ended, the text disappeared and participants had to repeat what they have heard and read, in order to facilitate learning. At the end of the noun exposure, a short noun testing part was played. Participants were presented with the same images and four text choices of nouns from the artificial language vocabulary. Participants had to choose the correct option. After choosing one of the possibilities, the correct choice was presented to the participants for personal feedback.

During the verb exposure part, participants watched videos showing the subjects performing actions denoted by simple transitive verbs ("eat" and "put down") on the objects in different combinations. Each video was consequently shown four times, each time accompanied by the description in a different sentence type. Participants were allowed to repeat the description during all screens and all except for 3 did so. Following the verb learning, a verb testing part was played. During this part, 34 test screens were played for the participants. On each screen, two videos were shown to the participant and only an audio description of one of them was played. After the description ended, participants had to indicate which of the videos was described. After making their choices, an arrow showed which option was the correct one providing feedback for the answers. At the end of the learning phase, a production test took place. Participants were shown 8 videos which they had to describe using the language they had learned. After production, all four possible sentences for the video were presented, and the experimenter indicated which option the participant had produced, thus hinting that all four options are equally usable in the language.

During the game phase, participants were introduced to a confederate, supposedly a well-trained speaker of the artificial language. The game phase was implemented and run in E-prime (Psychology Software Tools, Inc.) on two desktop computers in two opposite rooms, one computer for the participant and another for the confederate. The participants had to play a cooperative game with the confederate as follows: In each turn, the participant was shown two videos and had to describe one of them to the confederate, who in turn, selected the described video from the same set. The supposed goal of the game was for the confederate to correctly identify as many videos as possible. Thus, the participants were motivated to be understandable and efficient.

In total, 64 rounds of the game were played. Two short practice sessions were played before the game started. In the first practice sessions, the participant was playing the confederate's role, in order to understand the game from both sides. Four practice rounds were played and the confederate described the target video of each round using a different sentence type. The second practice session consisted of 8 additional rounds in which the participant could ask questions about the game.

2.2 Results

The raw counts of the occurrences of each sentence type by visual communication condition are presented in Table 3.

Sentence types production				
Condition	$-OS$ $-AA$	$+OS$ $-AA$	$-OS$ $+AA$	$+OS$ $+AA$
DSDV	73	106	18	132
DSSV	26	136	30	206
SSDV	115	86	23	153
SSSV	118	88	25	166

Table 3: Sentence type production. Condition: DSDV-Different Subject Different Verb, DSSV-Different Subject Same Verb, SSDV-Same Subject Different Verb, SSSV-Same Subject Same Verb.

The table suggests that visual communicative condition had an effect on use of the optional formal devices. Namely, participants diverged from the input language in the following ways:

1) Participants dropped the subjects more often when the competitor video showed the same subject as the target video. 2) participants preferred redundant utterances, mainly when the competitor video showed a different subject and the same verb (DSSV) as the target video. 3) Participants avoided

using the $-OS + AA$ sentence type, showing a possible bias towards the syntactic feature over the morphological one. Table 4 gives the raw counts of the occurrences of each sentence type by acoustic noise level.

Sentence types production				
Noise	$-OS$ $-AA$	$+OS$ $-AA$	$-OS$ $+AA$	$+OS$ $+AA$
H	73	106	18	132
L	26	136	30	206

Table 4: Sentence type production. Noise: H - High noise level, L - Low noise level.

The data was analyzed with linear mixed effects models constructed using the glmer() function of the "lme4" package in R (see Bates et al., 2015; R Core Team, 2015). We trained one model to predict use of OS, given in Table 5, and one model to predict use of AA, given in Table 6.

Fixed effects table $-$ OS model			
	Estimate	Std. Err.	P-Value
Intercept	2.36	0.66	
SO	-1.33	0.16	**< 0.001**
VO	0.63	0.15	**< 0.001**
AN	-0.05	0.16	0.75
SO:VO	-1.22	0.3	**< 0.001**
SO:AN	-0.11	0.31	0.72
VO:AN	-0.33	0.31	0.28
SO:VO:AN	0.8	0.61	0.19

Table 5: LME model. $OS \sim$ SO∗VO∗AN $+(1|$ participant$)$ $+(1|$ item$)$

Fixed effects table $-$ AA model			
	Estimate	Std. Err.	P-Value
Intercept	0.2	0.92	
SO	-0.46	0.16	**< 0.01**
VO	0.54	0.15	**< 0.001**
AN	-0.01	0.16	0.96
SO:VO	-0.87	0.3	**< 0.01**
SO:AN	-0.4	0.3	0.18
VO:AN	0.06	0.3	0.85
SO:VO:AN	-0.48	0.61	0.43

Table 6: LME model. $AA \sim$ SO∗VO∗AN $+(1|$ participant$)$ $+(1|$ item$)$

Each model included the effects of Subject Overlap (SO, same subject vs. different subject in the two videos), Verb Overlap (VO, same verb vs. different verb), Acoustic Noise (AN, high vs. low) and all possible interactions. We also included a by-item and a by-participant random intercept.

Both models revealed significant effects of Subject Overlap, Verb Overlap as well as an interaction between these two factors. Specifically, as predicted, participants used more often the OS or the AA to disambiguate the target video when the competitor video had a different subject performing the verb. Also, when the verb was the same in both videos, participants preferred to include the subject or the affix to better disambiguate the target, since the verb did not. The interactions between the Subject Overlap and Verb Overlap factors are shown in Figure 1 and in Figure 2. The graphs show that when the competitor video displayed the same subject, the formal devices did not help to disambiguate the target video. So, it is reasonable that in this case, the Verb Overlap factor did not have an effect on the production of the optional devices. On the other hand, when the competitor video displayed a different subject, the formal devices could help to disambiguate the target video. So, it is also reasonable that in this case, the Verb Overlap factor had a significant effect. In particular, participants produced more optional devices in the same verb condition, because the verb was not available for disambiguation.

2.3 Discussion and Conclusions

Three options of communicative behavior after recent exposure to the input language data were considered: 1) language learners favor efficient language use regardless of the learning process and the communicative setting, 2) the production behavior of language learners preserves the statistical properties of the input, 3) language learners are sensitive to dynamic communicative conditions and alter language use accordingly. The experimental data support the third option, since visual context affected production of optional formal devices. Acoustic noise, however, did not have an effect. It is possible that the acoustic noise levels were not different enough to provoke changes in behavior. Additionally, the data suggested that the use of the syntactic formal device (OS) was slightly preferred over the morphological one (AA). A possible explanation for

this is that since the affix attaches to the verb, the Verb Overlap factor was more salient. A possible systematic bias in favor of syntactic formal devices over morphological ones could be explored in future work.

The strong tendency of our participants to avoid global ambiguity (which occurred in the $-OS - AA$ condition) is fully consistent with the "make your contribution as informative as is required" part of the Gricean Maxim of Quantity. However, the most popular sentence type among our participants ($+OS + AA$) was redundant in nature, which does not strictly conform to the "do not make your contribution more informative than is required" part of the Gricean Maxim of Quantity.

Since the participants in this study optimized their usage of optional devices according to the presumed shared knowledge between the producer and comprehender, our experiment is quite consistent with models of language production that include Audience Design, such as the Uniform Information Density Hypothesis. Had we found an effect of acoustic noise, we could have made a stronger link to this hypothesis, but we remain hopeful that such information density-sensitive producer manipulations can be captured in future work.

The confirmed bias towards redundant structures, sensitive to assumptions about the knowledge of the comprehender, could be a useful behavior to exploit in both models of sentence processing and applied language models for technological applications. In particular, our results are informative about when language learners use these specific optional devices. Therefore, it would be reasonable for computers to leverage those expectations when processing human input, and to conform to the same expectations when producing linguistic output.

Acknowledgments

We thank Oded Bengigi and Asaf Meidan for creation of the visual stimuli, to Philipp Wettmann for acting as the confederate during experiments and to the anonymous reviewers whose valuable ideas contributed to this paper. This research was supported by the German Research Foundation (DFG) as part of the SFB 1102: "Information Density and Linguistic Encoding".

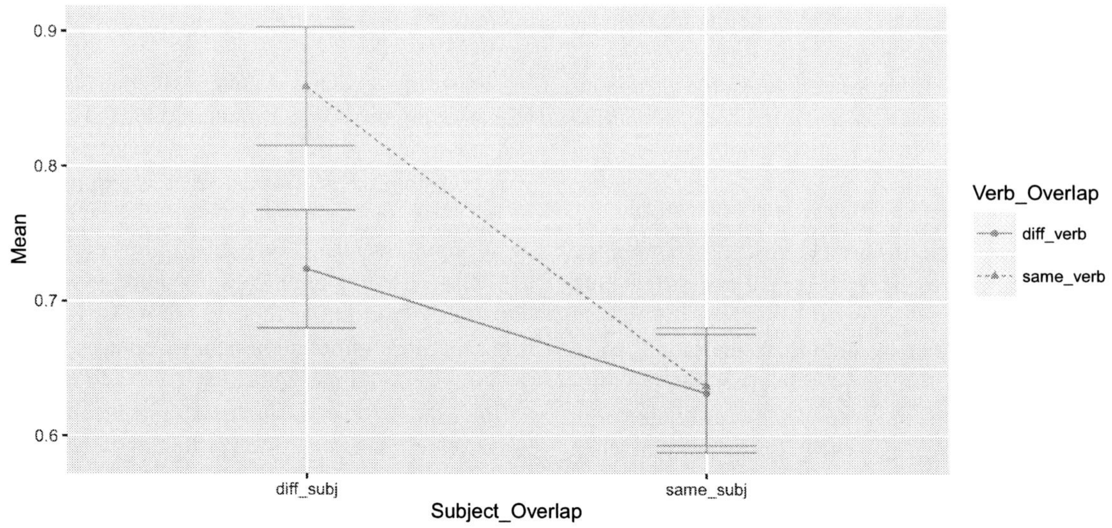

Figure 1: SO:VO interaction plot for the $OS \sim$ SO∗VO∗AN $+(1|$ participant$) +(1|$ item$)$ model

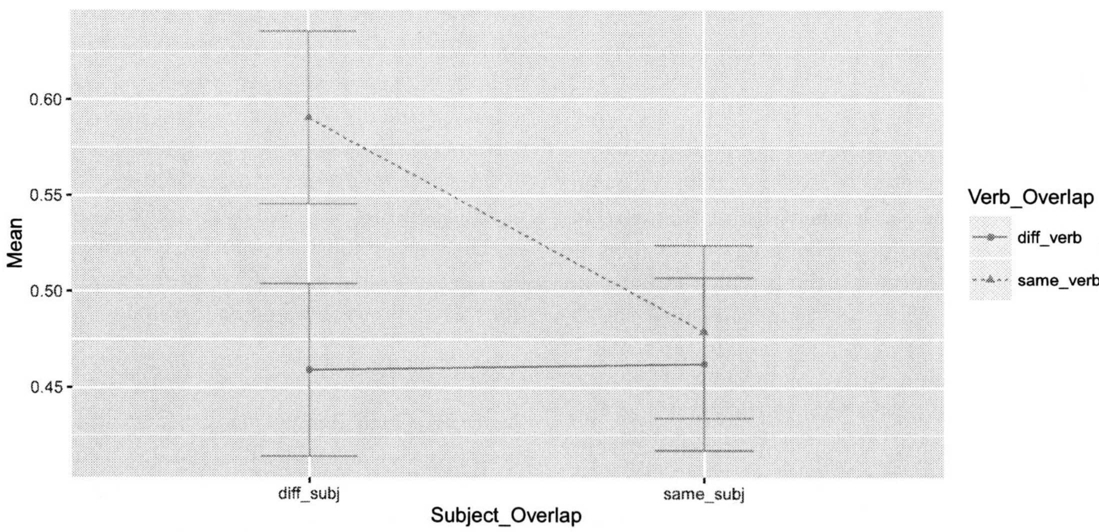

Figure 2: SO:VO interaction plot for the $AA \sim$ SO∗VO∗AN $+(1|$ participant$) +(1|$ item$)$ model

References

Arts, A. (2011). Overspecification facilitates object identification. *Journal of Pragmatics*, pages 361–374.

Bates, D., Mächler, M., Bolker, B., and Walker, S. (2015). Fitting linear mixed-effects models using lme4. *Journal of Statistical Software*, 67(1):1–48.

Engelhardt, P. E., Bailey, K. G., and Ferreira, F. (2006). Do speakers and listeners observe the gricean maxim of quantity? *Journal of Memory and Language*, 54(4):554–573.

Fedzechkina, M., Jaeger, T. F., and Newport, E. L. (2012). Language learners restructure their input to facilitate efficient communication. *Proceedings of the National Academy of Sciences*, 109(44):17897–17902.

Frank, A. and Jaeger, T. F. (2008). Speaking rationally: Uniform information density as an optimal strategy for language production. In *Proceedings of the 30th annual meeting of the cognitive science society*, pages 933–938. Cognitive Science Society Washington, DC.

Grice, H. P. (1975). *Logic and conversation*. Academic Press, University of California, Berkeley.

Jaeger, T. and Levy, R. P. (2006). Speakers optimize information density through syntactic reduction. In *Advances in neural information processing systems*, pages 849–856.

Jaeger, T. F. (2010). Redundancy and reduction: Speakers manage syntactic information density. *Cognitive psychology*, 61(1):23–62.

Mahowald, K., Fedorenko, E., Piantadosi, S. T., and Gibson, E. (2013). Info/information theory: Speakers choose shorter words in predictive contexts. *Cognition*, 126(2):313–318.

R Core Team (2015). *R: A Language and Environment for Statistical Computing*. R Foundation for Statistical Computing, Vienna, Austria.

Explicit Argument Identification for Discourse Parsing In Hindi: A Hybrid Pipeline

Rohit Jain and **Dipti Misra Sharma**
Language Technologies Research Center (LTRC), IIIT-H
Hyderabad,
Telangana, India

Abstract

Shallow discourse parsing enables us to study discourse as a coherent piece of information rather than a sequence of clauses, sentences and paragraphs. In this paper, we identify arguments of explicit discourse relations in Hindi. This is the first such work carried out for Hindi. Building upon previous work carried out on discourse connective identification in Hindi, we propose a hybrid pipeline which makes use of both sub-tree extraction and linear tagging approaches. We report state-of-the-art performance for this task.

1 Introduction

Units within a piece of text are not meant to be understood independently but understood by linking them with other units in the text. These units may be clauses, sentences or even complete paragraphs. Establishing relations between units present in a text allows the text to be semantically well structured and understandable. Understanding the internal structure of text and the identification of discourse relations is called discourse analysis.

A fully automated shallow discourse parser would greatly aid in discourse analysis and improve the performance of Text summarization and Question answering systems. Given a text, a shallow discourse parser would identify discourse relations, consisting of two spans of text exhibiting some kind of relationship between each other. Discourse relations whose presence is marked explicitly by discourse connectives are called Explicit discourse relations and those which are not are called Implicit discourse relations.

At present, complete shallow discourse parsers are only available for English (Lin et al., 2014; Wang and Lan, 2015; Ali and Bayer, 2015). The ongoing CoNLL 2016 shared task on Shallow Discourse Parsing has included Chinese as well. Work towards a complete shallow discourse parser in Hindi has also begun. Jain et al. (2016) reported state-of-the-art results for discourse connective identification in Hindi. Our work focuses on the next part towards a shallow discourse parser for Hindi i.e. argument identification for Explicit discourse relations.

In this paper, we discuss current approaches for this task and also propose a hybrid pipeline incorporating many of these approaches. We report high accuracies of 93.28% for Arg2 identification, 71.09% for Arg1 identification and 66.3% for Arg1-Arg2 identification.

The rest of the paper is organized as follows. Section 2 briefly introduces the Hindi Discourse Relations Bank(HDRB). Related work carried out in English is discussed in Section 3. In section 4, we describe in detail our approach to argument identification of Explicit discourse relations. Section 5 discusses the performance of the proposed pipeline and we conclude in Section 6.

2 Hindi Discourse Relations Bank(HDRB)

The Hindi Discourse Relation Bank(HDRB) was created broadly following the lines of Penn Discourse TreeBank(PDTB) (Miltsakaki et al., 2004; Prasad et al., 2008)'s lexically grounded approach along with a modified annotation workflow, additional grammatical categories for explicit connectives, semantically driven Arg1/Arg2 labelling and

Proceedings of NAACL-HLT 2016, pages 66–72,
San Diego, California, June 12-17, 2016. ©2016 Association for Computational Linguistics

modified sense hierarchies.(Oza et al., 2009; Kolachina et al., 2012)

HDRB was annotated on a subset of the Hindi TreeBank (Begum et al., 2008) which includes part-of-speech, chunk and dependency parse tree annotations. HDRB contains 1865 sentences and a word count of 42K. Furthermore HDRB contains 650 explicit discourse relations and 1200 implicit discourse relations.

In HDRB, one of the arguments occurs after the discourse connective and the other occurs before the connective. Discourse relations not adhering to this rarely occur in the corpus. However, due to the semantic labelling of Arg1 and Arg2, Arg2 does not always occur after the connective. For example:

- चंदीगढ में बृहस्पतिवार की सुभह भारी वर्शा की वजह से इसके आसपास और निचले इलाकों में बाढ़ की स्थिति पैदा हो गई और कई सद्कों, विशेष कर दक्सीणी सेकटरों मेइ स्थिती काफी बिगड गई है ।

- *Heavy rains have occurred in Chandigarh* because of which **there is possibility of floods in nearby and lower areas and the condition of roads, especially in the southern sectors, has worsened.**

The relation sense is "Contingency cause relation", where the situation described in Arg2 (italicized) is the cause of the the situation described in Arg1 (bolded). Due to this fact, Arg2 occurs before Arg1. However, for the purpose of argument identification we refer to the argument occurring before the connective as Arg1 and the argument occurring after the connective as Arg2. We believe changing the labels later on during sense identification to be the simpler approach.

In the corpus, Arg1 can occur in the same sentence as the connective (**SS**) or in the sentence preceding that of the connective (**PS**) with proportions of 46% and 54% respectively, whereas Arg2 only occurs in the same sentence as the connective.

Arg1 can cover 1,2,3 or even more than 4 sentences with proportions of 89.2%, 5.4%, 2.6% and 2.8% respectively. As such in this paper, we only consider the sentence containing the connective and the sentence immediately preceding it for Arg1 identification.

3 Related Work

Argument identification for Hindi has not been explored before, therefore we discuss some of the approaches adopted for English.

Ghosh et al. (2011) proposed a linear tagging approach for argument identification using Conditional random fields and n-best results.

Lin et al. (2014) proposed a sub-tree extraction approach for argument identification. Firstly an argument position classifier was employed to decide the location of Arg1(PS/SS). In the case of PS, Arg1 was labelled as the entire preceding sentence. For tagging Arg1(SS) and Arg2, a argument node identifier was employed to decide which nodes were part of Arg1(SS) or Arg2. Next sub-tree extraction was used to extract Arg1(SS) and Arg2. However, since it is not necessary that arguments may be dominated entirely by a single node as pointed out by Dinesh et al. (2005), this method has inherent shortcomings.

Kong et al. (2014) proposed a constituent based approach where, similar to Lin, an argument identifier is employed to decide which constituents are Arg1 and Arg2. Previous sentence was considered as a special constituent to handle Arg1(PS). A constituent pruner was also employed to reduce the number of candidate constituents considered for Arg1 and Arg2. In addition, Integer Linear Programming(ILP) with language specific constraints, was employed to ensure the argument identifier made legitimate global predictions.

Approaches in English can be summed up as two sub-tasks: (1) Considering the possible constituents/nodes/words to be identified as Arg1 or Arg2 by use of subtree extraction (Lin et al., 2014), constituent pruning (Kong et al., 2014) or simple baseline (Ghosh et al., 2011) approaches. (2) Classification of selected constituents/nodes/words as Arg1/Arg2/None by use of CRF(Ghosh et al., 2011) or classifier(Lin et al., 2014; Kong et al., 2014) based approaches.

4 A Hybrid Pipeline to Argument Identification

We base our pipeline on the two sub tasks discussed in the previous section. We use a method similar to subtree extraction to extract possible candidates for Arg1/Arg2 and use CRF tagging to further refine the extent of the extracted arguments.

We approach the task of Arg1 and Arg2 identification seperately since tagging Arg1 is inherently more difficult. We first discuss Arg2 identification and then Arg1 identification. Features used are listed in Table 1.

4.1 Arg2 Identification

Doing a simple analysis on HDRB, we find that Arg2 largely lies in two positions in the dependency tree. Arg2 can either occur in the subtree of the connective node(Conn-SubTree) or in the subtree of the first verb group node occurring as parent to the connective node(Parent-VG-SubTree) as shown in Image 1.

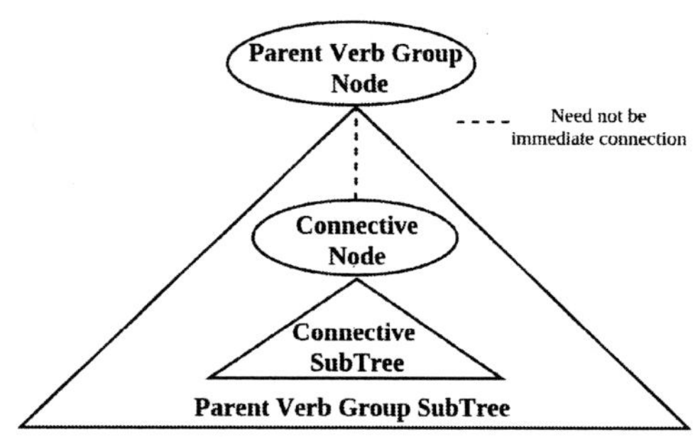

Figure 1: Arg2 Sub Tree Positions

To decide the position of Arg2, we make use of a classifier with *Conn-Str*, *Conn-Pos-Sentence*, *Is-Leaf-Node*, *VG-In-SubTree*, *VG-In-Parent-SubTree* and *Right-Word-Location* as features. Once we have the position of Arg2, all the nodes present in the subtree are extracted as Arg2. Henceforth, we refer to this step as ***SubTree-Extraction***.

Although Arg2 lies in either in "Conn-SubTree" or "Parent-VG-SubTree", it does not necessarily cover the entire subtree. Thus we need to refine the extent of Arg2 extracted from the *SubTree-Extraction* . We approach this as a linear tagging task, allowing us to capture the local dependency between nodes. We use *Conn-Rel-Pos*, *Node-Tag*, *Clause-End*, *Is-Conn* and *Part-of-Conn-Sub-Tree* as features. Henceforth, we refer to this step as ***Partial-SubTree***.

We find that Arg2 sometimes extends further up into the dependency tree. For example:

- इसके अलावा , उन्होंने रैली भी निकाली और

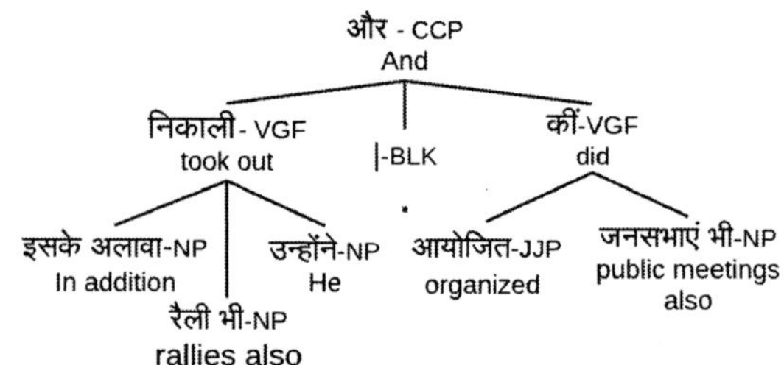

Figure 2: Arg2 Extended example dependency tree

जनसभाएं भी आयोजित कीं ।

- In addition, he also took out rallies and also organized public meetings.

इसके अलावा (In addition)'s Arg2 lies in "Parent-VG-SubTree". However, the presence of *and* indicates some kind of correlation between "he also took out rallies" and "also organized rallies". This correlation is also indicated in the dependency tree where both VG groups are children of *and*. To handle these and other similar cases we employ a classifier to decide whether extension beyond the current node is necessary. The current node is either connective node or the parent VG node of the connective node depending upon the decision made in the *SubTree-Extraction* step. We use *Conn-Str*, *Node-Tag* of current node, *Node-Tag* of parent of current node, *Conn-Rel-Pos* for parent of current node as features for this step. Henceforth we refer to this step as ***SubTree-Extension***.

SubTree-Extraction, *Partial-SubTree* and *SubTree-Extention* complete the pipeline for Arg 2 identification.

4.2 Arg1 Identification

Following the approach adopted for English (Kong et al., 2014; Lin et al., 2014; Wang and Lan, 2015), we approach Arg1 as two distinct problems: Arg1(SS) and Arg1(PS) identification. We employ a classifier to decide the position of Arg1. We use *Conn-Str*, *Node-Tag* of connective, *Conn-Pos-Sentence*, *Chunk-Before-Conn* as features for this step. Henceforth we refer to this step as ***Arg1 Pos Identification***.

The position of Arg1(SS) in the dependency tree, similar to Arg2, shows strong correlation with the position of the connective in the dependency

Feature Name	Feature Description	Used In
Conn-Str	Connective String	A2 (SE1,SE2), A1(PI) A1-SS(PI,SE1,SE2)
Conn-Pos	Connective part-of-speech tag	
Node-Tag	Chunk tag of the node	A2 (PS,SE2), A1(PI) A1-SS(SE1,PS,SE2)
Conn-Pos Sentence	Connective position in the sentence (Start/Middle)	A2(SE1), A1(PI), A1-SS(SE1)
Is-Leaf-Node	Connective node is a leaf node in the dependency tree	A2(SE1), A1-SS(SE1)
VG-In SubTree	Presence of VG node in sub tree of node	A2(SE1), A1-SS(SE1)
VG-In-Parent SubTree	Presence of VG node in parent of node	A2(SE1), A1-SS(SE1)
Right-Word Location	Location of word immediately after connective in the dependency tree w.r.t connective node	A2(SE1), A1-SS(SE1)
Conn-Rel Pos	Position of chunk w.r.t connective in sentence. (Before/After)	A2(PS,SE2), A1(PS,SE2)
Clause-End	Indicates presence of clause boundary	A2(PS), A1(PS)
Is-Conn	Node is part of a discourse connective or not	A2(PS), A1-SS(PS)
Part-Conn SubTree	Indicates whether node is part of discourse connective subtree, other than the connective in question	A2(PS) A1-SS(PS)
Chunk-Before Conn	Number of chunks before discourse connective	A1(P1)
Arg2-Pos	Position of Arg2 in dependency tree	A1-SS(SE1)
Conn-Two Clause	Indicates the presence of two verb groups as children to connective node. Captures possible coordination of two verb groups by connective	A1-SS(SE1)
Verb-Group	Verb group string & POS tag sequence	A1-PS(VSL)
Verb-Group Compact	Verb group string and POS tag sequence consisting of main main and its corresponding auxiliary verbs	A1-PS(VSL)
Verb-Root Inflection	Root and Inflection of main and auxiliary verbs	A1-PS(VSL)

A1:Arg1,A2:Arg2,A1-SS:Arg1 Same Sentence, A1-PS: Arg1 Previous Sentence

SE1:SubTree Extraction, PS:Partial SubTree, SE2:SubTree Extension, PI:Position Identifier, VSL: VG SubTree Labelling

Table 1: List of features used for Argument Identification

tree. In addition to *Conn-SubTree* and *Parent-VG-SubTree*, Arg1(SS) also lies in the subtree of the first verb group node occurring as parent to *Parent-VG* (pParent-VG-SubTree). This happens when Arg2 lies in the *Parent-VG-SubTree*.

To identify Arg1(SS), we use the same pipeline used for Arg2 identification, with certain differences in choice of features. *SubTree-Extraction* uses *Conn-Str, Is-Leaf-Node, Arg2-Pos, Node-Tag* of parent node of connective, *Node-Tag* of parent of parent node of connective, *Conn-Two-Clause* as features. Both *Patial-SubTree* and *SubTree-Extension* use the same set of features used for Arg2 identification.

SubTree-Extraction, Partial-SubTree and *SubTree*

- *Extention* complete the pipeline for Arg 1 (SS) identification.

A similar pipeline for Arg1(PS) identification cannot be used, since both Arg2 and Arg1(SS) showed a strong correlation to the connective node in the dependency tree. No such anchor node exists for Arg1(PS).

We divide the dependency tree of previous sentence into smaller verb group subtrees(VG SubTree). We consider each of them as candidates to be labelled as Arg1(SS). In the case of nested verb group sub trees, we treat them as two separate verb group subtrees ensuring no overlap of nodes between them. We refer to this step as **VG-SubTree-**

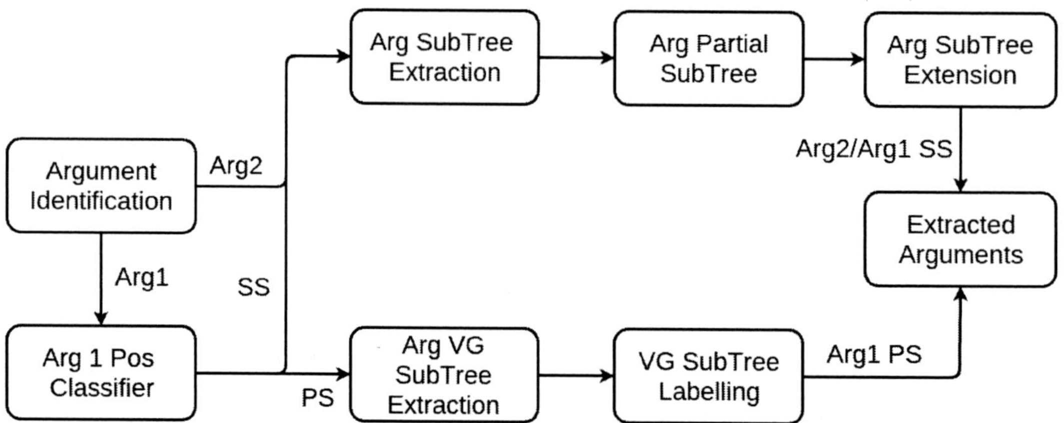

Figure 3: Argument Identication Pipeline

Extaction.

We make use of a classifier to decide whether each VG SubTree candidate is part of Arg1(PS) or not. We use *Verb-Group, Verb-Group-Compact, Verb-Root-Inflection* as features. All the nodes present in the VG SubTrees labelled as Arg1(PS) are extracted to form Arg1(PS). We refer to this step as **VG-SubTree-Labelling**.

VG-SubTree-Extraction and *VG-SubTree-Labelling* complete the pipeline for Arg1 (PS) identification. The entire pipeline for argument identification is shown below in Image 3.

5 Results

Firstly, we discuss the experimental setup, baselines and performance metrics we have considered to put the performance of our pipeline in perspective. Later on, we discuss, in detail, the performance of Arg2 and Arg1 identification pipelines.

5.1 Experimental Setup

Maximum Entropy (Fan et al., 2008) for classifier based steps and Conditional Random Fields (Lafferty et al., 2001) for linear tagging based steps were our choice of algorithms. L2 regularized Stochastic Gradient Descent (SGD) was used while training the CRF model and LibLinear solver (Fan et al., 2008) with L2 penalties was used to train the Maximum Entropy model. Maximum Entropy was implemented using Nltk toolkit[1] and Sklearn[2] whereas Conditional Random Fields was implemented using a CRFsuite[3](Okazaki, 2007).We used 5-fold cross validation to arrive at the results.

5.2 Baseline and Performance metrics

As discussed in Section 2, Arg2 is the argument occurring after the connective and Arg1 is the argument occurring before the connective. Therefore Arg2 baseline is computed by labelling Arg2 as the text span between the connective and the beginning of the next sentence. Similarly Arg1(SS) baseline is computed by labelling Arg1(SS) as the text span between the connective and the end the of the previous sentence. Arg1(PS) baseline is computed by labelling the entire previous sentence as Arg1(PS).

Ghosh et al. (2011), kong et al. (2014) and Lin et al. (2014) have reported performance using exact match metric. In addition to reporting performance using exact match metric, we introduce a new metric for measuring performance- Partial match:

$$\frac{|\,ArgResult \cup ArgGold\,| - 0.5*|\,ARgResult \cap ArgGold\,|}{|\,argGold\,|}$$

Where ArgResult is the argument labelled by the system, ArgGold is the argument labelled in the corpus. Partial match scores between 0-1 and incorporates a penalty for each missed or erroneously labelled node/chunk. Partial match is thus a more lenient scoring metric than exact match, however the

---

[1] http://www.nltk.org/
[2] http://scikit-learn.org/stable/
[3] http://www.chokkan.org/software/crfsuite/

penalty ensures the leniency is limited. Partial match allows us to measure minor performance improvements that are not captured by exact match metric.

5.3 Arg2 Results

We report Arg2 identification results in Table 2

Step	Exact	Partial
Baseline	63.2	77.95
SubTree-Extraction	58.28	69.10
Partial-SubTree	91.56	92.88
SubTree-Extension	93.28	95.37

Table 2: Arg2 identification results

We report a baseline score of 63.2 and 77.95 for exact and partial matches respectively. *SubTree-Extraction* does not reach the performance of the baseline with scores of 58.28 for exact match and 69.10 for partial match. With an increase of 33.28 for exact match and 23.78 for partial match, *Partial-SubTree* step results in the largest performance gains. *SubTree-Extension* further improves performance by 1.72 and 2.49 for exact and partial respectively. For Arg2 identification, we report a final score of 93.28 for exact match and 95.37 for partial match.

5.4 Arg1 Results

Coming to arg1 identification, we report a high accuracy of 99.1 % for *Arg1 Pos Identification* step. This is similar to the performance reported by Lin et al. (2014). We find that *Conn-Pos-Sentence* is sufficient to decide between Arg1(PS) and Arg1(SS). Other features used result in minor improvements.

Step	Exact	Partial
Baseline	43.38	71.57
SubTree-Extraction	2.05	22.63
Partial-SubTree	70.05	79.56
SubTree-Extension	71.18	80.12

Table 3: Arg1(SS) identification results

We report Arg1(SS) results in Table 3. For Arg1(SS), we report a baseline score of 43.38 and 71.57 for exact and partial matches respectively. *SubTree-Extraction* performs poorly with a score of 2.05 for exact match and 22.63 for partial match. Similar to Arg2, we find that *Partial-Subtree* results in a large increase in performance of 68 for

exact match and 56.93 for partial match. *SubTree-Extension* yields minor improvements of 1.13 and 0.56 for exact and partial respectively. For Arg1(SS) we report a final score of 70.84 for exact match and 80.12 for partial match.

Step	Exact	Partial
Baseline	71.01	72.38
System	38.55	62.07

Table 4: Arg1(PS) identification results

For Arg1(PS) we report a baseline of 71.05 and 72.38 for exact and partial matches respectively. We find that our system does not exceed the baseline scores with 38.55 for exact match and 62.07 for partial match. We believe more work is needed to successfully extract Arg1(PS).

We thus report an accuracy of 93.28% for Arg2 identification, 71.09% for Arg1 identification and 66.3% for Arg1-Arg2 identification.

6 Conclusion

In this paper, we focus on argument identification for explicit discourse relations in Hindi. In particular we propose a hybrid pipeline using both subtree extraction and linear tagging approaches. This is the first such work carried out in Hindi.

References

Evgeny A Stepanov Giuseppe Riccardi Ali and Orkan Bayer. 2015. The unitn discourse parser in conll 2015 shared task: Token-level sequence labeling with argument-specific models. *CoNLL 2015*, page 25.

Rafiya Begum, Samar Husain, Arun Dhwaj, Dipti Misra Sharma, Lakshmi Bai, and Rajeev Sangal. 2008. Dependency annotation scheme for indian languages. In *IJCNLP*, pages 721–726. Citeseer.

Nikhil Dinesh, Alan Lee, Eleni Miltsakaki, Rashmi Prasad, Aravind Joshi, and Bonnie Webber. 2005. Attribution and the (non-) alignment of syntactic and discourse arguments of connectives. In *Proceedings of the Workshop on Frontiers in Corpus Annotations II: Pie in the Sky*, pages 29–36. Association for Computational Linguistics.

Rong-En Fan, Kai-Wei Chang, Cho-Jui Hsieh, Xiang-Rui Wang, and Chih-Jen Lin. 2008. Liblinear: A library for large linear classification. *The Journal of Machine Learning Research*, 9:1871–1874.

Sucheta Ghosh, Richard Johansson, and Sara Tonelli. 2011. Shallow discourse parsing with conditional random fields. In *In Proceedings of the 5th International Joint Conference on Natural Language Processing (IJCNLP 2011*. Citeseer.

Rohit Jain, Himanshu Sharma, and Dipti Misra Sharma. 2016. Using lexical and dependency features to disambiguate discourse connectives in hindi. In *LREC*.

Sudheer Kolachina, Rashmi Prasad, Dipti Misra Sharma, and Aravind K Joshi. 2012. Evaluation of discourse relation annotation in the hindi discourse relation bank. In *LREC*, pages 823–828.

Fang Kong, Hwee Tou Ng, and Guodong Zhou. 2014. A constituent-based approach to argument labeling with joint inference in discourse parsing. In *EMNLP*, pages 68–77.

John Lafferty, Andrew McCallum, and Fernando CN Pereira. 2001. Conditional random fields: Probabilistic models for segmenting and labeling sequence data.

Ziheng Lin, Hwee Tou Ng, and Min-Yen Kan. 2014. A pdtb-styled end-to-end discourse parser. *Natural Language Engineering*, 20(02):151–184.

Eleni Miltsakaki, Rashmi Prasad, Aravind K Joshi, and Bonnie L Webber. 2004. The penn discourse treebank. In *LREC*.

Naoaki Okazaki. 2007. Crfsuite: a fast implementation of conditional random fields (crfs).

Umangi Oza, Rashmi Prasad, Sudheer Kolachina, Dipti Misra Sharma, and Aravind Joshi. 2009. The hindi discourse relation bank. In *Proceedings of the third linguistic annotation workshop*, pages 158–161. Association for Computational Linguistics.

Rashmi Prasad, Nikhil Dinesh, Alan Lee, Eleni Miltsakaki, Livio Robaldo, Aravind K Joshi, and Bonnie L Webber. 2008. The penn discourse treebank 2.0. In *LREC*. Citeseer.

Jianxiang Wang and Man Lan. 2015. A refined end-to-end discourse parser. *CoNLL 2015*, page 17.

Exploring Fine-Grained Emotion Detection in Tweets

Jasy Liew Suet Yan, Howard R. Turtle
School of Information Studies, Syracuse University
Syracuse, New York, USA
jliewsue@syr.edu, turtle@syr.edu

Abstract

We examine if common machine learning techniques known to perform well in coarse-grained emotion and sentiment classification can also be applied successfully on a set of fine-grained emotion categories. We first describe the grounded theory approach used to develop a corpus of 5,553 tweets manually annotated with 28 emotion categories. From our preliminary experiments, we have identified two machine learning algorithms that perform well in this emotion classification task and demonstrated that it is feasible to train classifiers to detect 28 emotion categories without a huge drop in performance compared to coarser-grained classification schemes.

1 Introduction

In sentiment analysis, emotion provides a promising direction for fine-grained analysis of subjective content (Aman & Szpakowicz, 2008; Chaumartin, 2007). Sentiment analysis is mainly focused on detecting the subjectivity (objective or subjective) (Wiebe et al., 2004) or semantic orientation (positive or negative) (Agarwal et al., 2011; Kouloumpis et al., 2011; Pak & Paroubek, 2010; Pang et al., 2002) of a unit of text (i.e., coarse-grained classification schemes) rather than a specific emotion. Often times, knowing exactly how one reacts emotionally towards a particular entity, topic or event does matter (Mohammad et al., 2014). For example, while anger and sadness are both negative emotions, distinguishing between them can be important so businesses can filter out angry customers and respond to them effectively.

Automatic emotion detection on Twitter presents a different set of challenges because tweets exhibit a unique set of characteristics that are not shared by other types of text. Unlike traditional text, tweets consist of short messages expressed within the limit of 140 characters. Due to the length limitation, language used to express emotions in tweets differs significantly from that found in longer documents (e.g., blogs, news, and stories). Language use on Twitter is also typically informal (Eisenstein, 2013; Baldwin et al., 2013). It is common for abbreviations, acronyms, emoticons, unusual orthographic elements, slang, and misspellings to occur in these short messages. On top of that, retweets (i.e., propagating messages of other users), referring to @username when responding to another user's tweet, and using #hashtags to represent topics are prevalent in tweets. Even though users are restricted to post only 140 characters per tweet, it is not uncommon to find a tweet containing more than one emotion.

Emotion cues are not limited to only emotion words such as *happy, amused, sad, miserable, scared*, etc. People use a variety of ways to express a wide range of emotions. For instance, a person expressing happiness may use the emotion word "happy" (Example 1), the interjection "woop" (Example 2), the emoticon ":)" (Example 3) or the emoji "😁" (Example 4).

Example 1: "I can now finally say I am at a place in my life where I am <u>happy</u> with who am and the stuff I have coming for me in the future #blessed" **[Happiness]**

Example 2: "its midnight and i am eating a lion bar <u>woop</u>" **[Happiness]**

Proceedings of NAACL-HLT 2016, pages 73–80,
San Diego, California, June 12-17, 2016. ©2016 Association for Computational Linguistics

Example 3: "Enjoying a night of #Dexter with @DomoniqueP07 :)" **[Happiness]**
Example 4: "The wait is almost over LA, will be out in just a little! 😂😂😂😂" **[Happiness]**

In addition to explicit expressions of emotion, users on Twitter also express their emotions in figurative forms through the use of idiomatic expressions (Example 5), similes (Example 6), metaphors (Example 7) or other descriptors (Example 8). In these figurative expressions of emotion, each word if treated individually does not directly convey any emotion. When combined together and, depending on the context of use, they act as implicit indicators of emotion. Automatic emotion detectors that rely solely on the recognition of emotion words will likely fail to recognize the emotions conveyed in these examples.

Example 5: "@ter2459 it was!!! I am still on cloud nine! I say and watched them for over two hours. I couldn't leave! They are incredible!" **[Happiness]**
Example 6: "Getting one of these bad boys in your cereal box and feeling like your day simply couldn't get any better http://t.co/Fae9EjyN61" **[Happiness]**
Example 7: "Loving the #IKEAHomeTour décor #ideas! Between the showroom and the catalog I am in heaven" **[Happiness]**
Example 8: "I did an adult thing by buying stylish bed sheets and not fucking it up when setting them up. *cracks beer open*" **[Happiness]**

The occurrence of an emotion word in a tweet does not always indicate the tweeter's emotion. The emotion word "happy" in Example 9 is not used to describe how the tweeter feels about the tune but is instead used to characterize the affective quality or affective property of the tune (Russell, 2003; Zhang, 2013). The tweeter attributes a happy quality to the tune but is in fact expressing anger towards the "happy" tune. Similarly, #Happiness in Example 10 is part of a book's title so the emotion word hashtag functions as a topic more than an expression or description of an individual's emotion. The common practice of using emotion word hashtags to retrieve self-annotated examples as ground truth to build emotion classifiers, a method known as "distant supervision" (Hasan et al., 2014; Mohammad, 2012; Mohammad & Ki-

ritchenko, 2014; Wang et al., 2012), is susceptible to this weakness.

Example 9: "@Anjijade I was at this party on the weekend, that happy tune was played endlessly, really not my stuff, it was like the cure's torture ha" **[Anger]**
Example 10: "Hear Carrie Goodwiler's audition for the audio version of my book #Happiness & Honey on #SoundCloud" **[No Emotion]**

These challenges associated with detecting fine-grained emotion expressions in tweets remain a virgin territory that has not been thoroughly explored. To start addressing some off these challenges, we present a manually-annotated tweet corpus that captures a diversity of emotion expressions at a fine-grained level. We describe the grounded theory approach used to develop a corpus of 5,553 tweets manually annotated with 28 emotion categories. The corpus captures a variety of explicit and implicit emotion expressions for these 28 emotion categories, including the examples described above.

Using this carefully curated gold standard corpus, we report our preliminary efforts to train and evaluate machine learning models for emotion classification. We examine if common machine learning techniques known to perform well in coarse-grained emotion and sentiment classification can also be applied successfully on this set of fine-grained emotion categories. The contributions of this paper are two-fold:

a) Identifying machine learning algorithms that generally perform well at classifying the 28 emotion categories in the corpus and comparing them to baselines
b) Comparing the machine learning performance of fine-grained to coarse-grained emotion classification

2 Empirical Study

2.1 Corpus

The corpus contains 5,553 tweets and is developed using small-scale content analysis. To ensure that the tweets included in the corpus are representative of the population on Twitter, we employed four sampling strategies: randomly sampling tweets retrieved using common stopwords (RANDOM: 1450 tweets), sampling using topical hashtags

(TOPIC: 1310 tweets), sampling using @usernames of US Senators (SEN-USER: 1493 tweets) and sampling using @usernames of average users randomly selected from Twitter (AVG-USER: 1300 tweets). Tweets were sampled from the Twitter API and two publicly available datasets: 1) the SemEval 2014 tweet data set (Nakov et al., 2013; Rosenthal et al., 2014), and 2) the 2012 US presidential elections data set (Mohammad et al., 2014). The proportion of tweets from each of the four samples is roughly balanced.

The corpus was annotated by graduate students who were interested in undertaking the task as part of a class project (e.g., Natural Language Processing course) or to gain research experience in content analysis (e.g., independent study). A total of 18 annotators worked on the annotation task over a period of ten months. Annotators were first instructed to annotate the valence of a tweet. Emotion valence can be positive, negative or neutral. Positive emotions are evoked by events causing one to express pleasure (e.g., happy, relaxed, fascination, love) while negative emotions are evoked by events causing one to express displeasure (e.g., anger, fear, sad). Emotions that were neither positive nor negative were considered to be neutral (e.g. surprise). Valence was useful to help annotators distinguish between tweets that contained emotion and those that did not.

To uncover a set of emotion categories from the tweets, we used an adapted grounded theory approach developed by Glaser & Strauss (1967) for the purpose of building theory that emerges from the data. Using this approach, annotators were not given a predefined set of labels for emotion category. Instead, the emotion categories were formed inductively based on the emotion tags or labels suggested by annotators. Annotators were required to identify emotion tag when valence for a tweet was labeled as either "Positive", "Negative" or "Neutral". For emotion tag, annotators were instructed to assign an emotion label that best described the overall emotion expressed in a tweet. In cases where a tweet contained multiple emotions, annotators were asked to first identify the primary emotion expressed in the tweet, and then also include the other emotions observed.

The annotation task was conducted in an iterative fashion. In the first iteration, also referred to as the training round, all annotators annotated the same sample of 300 tweets from the SEN-USER sample. Annotators were expected to achieve at least 70% pairwise agreement for valence with the primary researcher in order to move forward. The annotators achieved a mean pairwise agreement of 82% with the researcher. Upon passing the training round, annotators were assigned to annotate at least 1,000 tweets from one of the four samples (RANDOM, TOPIC, AVG-USER or SEN-USER) in subsequent iterations. Every week, annotators worked independently on annotating a subset of 150 − 200 tweets but met with the researcher in groups to discuss disagreements, and 100% agreement for valence and emotion tag was achieved after discussion. In these weekly meetings, the researcher also facilitated the discussions among annotators working on the same sample to merge, remove, and refine suggested emotion tags.

Annotators suggested a total 246 distinct emotion tags. To group the emotion tags into categories, annotators were asked to perform a card sorting exercise in different teams to group emotion tags that are variants of the same root word or semantically similar into the same category. Annotators were divided into 5 teams, and each team received a pack of 1' x 5' cards containing only the emotion tags used by the all members in their respective teams. This task organized the emotion tags into 48 emotion categories.

To refine the emotion categories, we collected pleasure and arousal ratings for each emotion category name from Amazon Mechanical Turk (AMT). Based on 76 usable responses, the emotion category names were mapped on a two-dimensional plot. Emotion categories that were closely clustered together on the plot and semantically related to one another were further merged resulting in a final set of 28 emotion categories. Finally, all emotion category labels in the corpus were systematically replaced by the appropriate 28 emotion category labels. Overall, annotators achieved Krippendorff's α = 0.61 for valence and α = 0.50 for the set of 28 emotion categories. Each tweet was assigned gold labels for valence and emotion category.

2.2 Emotion Distributions

This section describes the distribution of gold labels for three emotion class structures: 1) emotion/non-emotion, 2) valence, and 3) 28 emotion categories. As shown in Table 1, the overall distribution between tweets containing emotion and those that do not is roughly balanced. Slightly over half of the tweets (53%) contain emotion.

Class	n	%
Emotion	2916	53
Non-Emotion	2637	47
Total	**5553**	**100**

Table 1: Distribution of tweets with emotion and non-emotion

Class	n	%
Positive	1840	33
Negative	744	13
Neutral	155	3
Multiple Valence	177	3

Table 2: Distribution of tweets for emotion valence

Class	n	%
Admiration	132	2.38
Amusement	216	3.89
Anger	409	7.37
Boredom	10	0.18
Confidence	15	0.27
Curiosity	27	0.49
Desperation	7	0.13
Doubt	44	0.79
Excitement	228	4.11
Exhaustion	7	0.13
Fascination	47	0.85
Fear	65	1.17
Gratitude	176	3.17
Happiness	697	12.55
Hate	52	0.94
Hope	132	2.38
Indifference	24	0.43
Inspiration	16	0.29
Jealousy	5	0.09
Longing	27	0.49
Love	172	3.10
Pride	70	1.26
Regret	40	0.72
Relaxed	25	0.45
Sadness	137	2.47
Shame	22	0.40
Surprise	83	1.49
Sympathy	31	0.56

Table 3: Distribution of tweets for 28 emotion categories

The class distribution becomes more unbalanced with the finer-grained emotion classes, valence (Table 2) and 28 emotion categories (Table 3). For valence, 33% of the tweets containing emotion are positive, 13% are negative and only 3% are neutral. Emotion classes become even sparser with the 28 emotion categories. The most frequent category is *happiness* (13%) while the least frequent category is *jealousy* (0.09%).

2.3 Machine Learning Experiments

We ran a series of experiments to identify a set of machine learning algorithms that generally perform well for this task. Four machine learning algorithms were found to perform well in this problem space: support vector machines (SVM) (Alm et al., 2005; Aman & Szpakowicz, 2007; Brooks et al., 2013; Cherry et al., 2012), Bayesian networks (Sohn et al., 2012; Strapparava & Mihalcea, 2008), decision trees (Hasan et al., 2014), and k-nearest neighbor (KNN) (Hasan et al., 2014; Holzman & Pottenger, 2003). The features were held constant across different classifiers in the candidate set. As a starting point, a unigram (i.e., bag-of-words) model, which has been shown to work reasonably well for text classification in sentiment analysis (Pang et al., 2002; Salvetti et al., 2006), was chosen. Although limited, the unigram bag-of-words features captures not only emotion words but all words in a tweet, thus increasing the likelihood of the classifiers to handle the figurative expressions of emotion.

We tokenized the text in the corpus and extracted all unique terms as features. We created a custom tokenizer to better handle elements that are common in tweets. In particular, the tokenizer recognizes emoticons, emojis, URLs and HTML encoding. The tokenizer also handles common abbreviations and contractions. Text was encoded in UTF-8 in order to preserve the emojis. We then evaluated the effect of case normalization (i.e, lowercasing), stemming, and a minimum word frequency threshold ($f = 1, 3, 5$ and 10) as a means to reduce the number of features. Classifiers were evaluated using 10-fold cross validation.

To make experiments more manageable, we frame the problem as a *multi-class* classification task. Each tweet was assigned to only one emotion label. For tweets with multiple labels, only the primary label (i.e., first label) was assigned to the tweet, and the other labels were ignored. We carried out two sets of experiments. First, we created one single classifier (*multi-class-single: one versus one*) to distinguish between 29 classes (i.e., 28 emotion categories and *no emotion*). Second, we ran experiments using Weka's *MultiClassClassifier*, a meta-classifier that mapped a multi-class dataset into multiple two-class classifiers (*multi-class-binary: one versus all*), one for each emotion and one for *no emotion*, thus resulting in a setup with 29 binary classifiers in total. Unfortunately, the *multi-class-binary* setup was not designed to handle instances with multiple labels but it offered a straightforward implementation of multiple binary classifications for preliminary analysis. About 92% of the corpus contained instances with only a single label so overall classification performance is expected to be close to that of a *multi-label* classifier.

3 Evaluation and Results

3.1 Machine Learning Algorithms

We found that the use of stemming, case normalization and applying a word frequency threshold of 3 produced consistently good results.

Classifier	*MCS*	*MCB*
BayesNet	0.533	**0.574**
SVM-SMO	**0.571**	0.529
J48	0.567	0.520
KNN ($k = 1$)	0.391	0.391

Table 4: Micro-averaged F1 for *multi-class-single (MCS)* and *multi-class-binary (MCB)*

Based on the micro-averaged F1 shown in Table 4, the two machine learning algorithms that yielded the best performance were Sequential Minimal Optimization (SMO), an algorithm for training SVM (Platt, 1998) and Bayesian Networks (BayesNet) (Bouckaert, 1967). The performance ranking differs slightly between the four machine learning algorithms across the two experimental setups with SVM being the top performing classifier in *multi-class-single* while BayesNet in *multi-class-binary*. A more in-depth analysis of the best performing classifier for each emotion category also shows that BayesNet and SVM yield the best performance for over half of the emotion categories.

3.2 Comparison with Baselines

Three baselines are first established as the basis of comparison for all other classifiers.

- Majority-class baseline: The majority-class baseline simply assigns the majority class to each tweet.
- Random baseline: The random baseline classifier predicts a label randomly with no learning involved.
- OneR: OneR is a simple classifier that uses a single feature with minimum error for classification. The classifier generates a set of rules based on this single feature.

Classifier	A	P	R	F1
multi-class-single				
Majority-class	47.4	0.23	0.47	0.31
Random	0.03	0.03	0.03	0.03
OneR	49.8	0.26	0.50	0.34
BayesNet	60.1	0.54	0.60	0.51
SVM-SMO	58.9	0.57	0.59	0.57
multi-class-binary				
Majority-class	47.4	0.23	0.47	0.31
Random	0.03	0.03	0.50	0.06
OneR	51.7	0.56	0.52	0.46
BayesNet	63.0	0.60	0.63	0.57
SVM-SMO	48.9	0.61	0.49	0.53

Table 5: Comparison between best performing models and baselines (A: Accuracy, P: Precision, R: Recall)

We compare the SVM and BayesNet classifiers to the three baselines as shown in Table 5. In terms of accuracy, SVM and BayesNet outperform the majority-class and random baselines in both *multi-class-single* and *multi-class-binary*. BayesNet correctly predicts roughly 60% of the instances while SVM correctly predicts roughly 50%. In terms of F1, SVM and BayesNet exceed the performance of all the three baselines.

3.3 Levels of Granularity

Table 6 shows the performance of classifiers for fine-grained versus coarser-grained class structures across three levels of granularity: 1) emotion presence/absence (2 classes), 2) emotion valence (5 classes) and, 3) emotion category (28 classes). SVM and BayesNet perform significantly better than the majority-class baseline across all three levels of granularity using a flat classification approach. The majority class for valence and emotion category is *none*.

Level	SVM-SMO				BayesNet				Majority-class			
	A	P	R	F1	A	P	R	F1	A	P	R	F1
Emotion Presence: Emotion, None												
multi-class-single	72.7	0.73	0.73	0.73	72.2	0.73	0.72	0.72	52.6	0.28	0.53	0.36
Emotion Valence: Positive, Negative, Neutral, Multiple Valence, None												
multi-class-single	65.5	0.63	0.64	0.63	67.0	0.65	0.67	0.65	47.4	0.23	0.47	0.31
Emotion Category (28-Emo-Cat, None)												
multi-class-single	58.9	0.57	0.59	0.57	60.1	0.54	0.60	0.51	47.4	0.23	0.47	0.31
multi-class-binary	48.9	0.61	0.49	0.53	63.0	0.60	0.63	0.57	47.4	0.23	0.47	0.31

Table 6: Accuracy (A), precision (P), recall (R) and F1 across classification schemes with different levels of granularity

Comparing across the three levels of granularity, better performance is observed when there are fewer classes. For example, a classifier trained to distinguish between 2 classes (*emotion* and *none*) yields higher performance than a classifier trained to distinguish between 29 classes (28 emotion categories and *none*). The drop in classifier performance from coarser to finer levels of granularity is gradual. Note that the performance of a classifier trained to classify 29 classes is not a great deal worse than a classifier dealing with fewer classes (2 or 5). A closer analysis of the F1 per emotion category shows that the classifiers are able to correctly predict some categories better than the others. For instance, SVM and BayesNet achieve F1 greater than 0.7 for *gratitude*. The performance measures in Table 6 are micro averages across all classes. The performance results reported here are intended to show a realistic assessment of machine learning performance in classifying the 28 emotion categories that emerged from the open coding task. We included even the poor performing categories in the computation of the micro averages.

4 Discussion and Conclusion

Automatic fine-grained emotion detection is a challenging task but we have demonstrated that it is feasible to train a classifier to perform decently well in classifying as many as 28 emotion categories. Our 28 emotion categories is an extension to the six to eight emotion categories commonly-used in the state-of-the-art (Alm et al., 2005; Aman & Szpakowicz, 2007; Mohammad, 2012). Some of the 28 emotion categories overlap with those found in existing emotion theories such as Plutchik's (1962) 24 categories on the wheel of emotion and Shaver *et al.*'s (2001) tree-structured list of emotions. Existing emotion theories in psychology are not developed specifically based on emotions ex-

pressed in text. Therefore, our emotion categories offer a more fitting framework for the study of emotion in text.

Existing classifiers achieve only moderate performance in detecting emotions in tweets even those trained with a significant amount of data collected using distant supervision (Mohammad, 2012; Roberts et al., 2012; Wang et al., 2012). Our preliminary classifiers trained with less data show results that are comparable to existing coarse-grained classifiers. Results from our preliminary machine learning experiments conclude that SVM and BayesNet classifiers produce consistently good performance for fine-grained emotion classification. Therefore, we plan to continue our machine learning experiment with more sophisticated feature selection strategies, ensemble methods and more balanced training data using both SVM and BayesNet.

There is no stark difference in classifier performance between fine-grained and coarse-grained emotion classes. Classifiers perform poorly for a handful of emotion categories with very low frequency. We will need to generate more positive examples for these classes to improve classifier performance. We plan to add another 10,000 annotated tweets in the corpus to increase the size of training and evaluation data. We will make the emotion corpus available in the future.

We acknowledge that the *multi-class* setup may not be the most suitable implementation of this classification task given that the corpus contains tweets annotated with multiple emotion categories. We chose the *multi-class* setup to simplify the classification task and make the machine learning experiments more manageable in this preliminary stage. We plan to evaluate the effectiveness of these algorithms with *multi-label* classifiers in our future work.

Acknowledgments

We thank the annotators who volunteered in performing the annotation task. We are grateful to Dr. Elizabeth D. Liddy for her insights in the study.

References

Agarwal, A., Xie, B., Vovsha, I., Rambow, O., & Passonneau, R. (2011). Sentiment analysis of Twitter data. In *Proceedings of the Workshop on Languages in Social Media* (pp. 30–38). Stroudsburg, PA, USA.

Alm, C. O., Roth, D., & Sproat, R. (2005). Emotions from text: Machine learning for text-based emotion prediction. In *Proceedings of the Conference on Human Language Technology and Empirical Methods in Natural Language Processing* (pp. 579–586). Stroudsburg, PA, USA.

Aman, S., & Szpakowicz, S. (2007). Identifying expressions of emotion in text. In *Text, Speech and Dialogue* (pp. 196–205).

Aman, S., & Szpakowicz, S. (2008). Using Roget's thesaurus for fine-grained emotion recognition. In *Proceedings of the Third International Joint Conference on Natural Language Processing* (pp. 296–302).

Baldwin, T., Cook, P., Lui, M., MacKinlay, A., & Wang, L. (2013). How Noisy Social Media Text, How Diffrnt Social Media Sources? In *Proceedings of the 6th International Joint Conference on Natural Language Processing (IJCNLP 2013)* (pp. 356–364). Nagoya, Japan.

Bouckaert, R. R. (1967). *Bayesian belief networks: From construction to inference.* Universiteit Utrecht, Faculteit Wiskunde en Informatica.

Brooks, M., Kuksenok, K., Torkildson, M. K., Perry, D., Robinson, J. J., Scott, T. J., Anicello, O., Zukowski, A., Harris, P., & Aragon, C. R. (2013). Statistical affect detection in collaborative chat. Presented at the Conference on Computer Supported Cooperative Work and Social Computing, San Antonio, TX.

Chaumartin, F. R. (2007). UPAR7: A knowledge-based system for headline sentiment tagging. In *Proceedings of the Fourth International Workshop on Semantic Evaluations (SemEval-2007)* (pp. 422–425).

Cherry, C., Mohammad, S. M., & de Bruijn, B. (2012). Binary classifiers and latent sequence models for emotion detection in suicide notes. *Biomedical Informatics Insights, 5,* 147–154.

Eisenstein, J. (2013). What to do about bad language on the internet. In *Proceedings of NAACL-HLT 2013* (pp. 359–369).

Glaser, B. G., & Strauss, A. L. (1967). *The discovery of grounded theory: Strategies for qualitative research.* Chicago: Aldine.

Hasan, M., Agu, E., & Rundensteiner, E. (2014). Using hashtags as labels for supervised learning of emotions in Twitter messages.

Hasan, M., Rundensteiner, E., & Agu, E. (2014). EMOTEX: Detecting emotions in Twitter messages. Presented at the 2014 ASE BIGDATA/SOCIALCOM/CYBERSECURITY Conference, Stanford University.

Holzman, L. E., & Pottenger, W. (2003). Classification of emotions in internet chat: An application of machine learning using speech phonemes.

Kouloumpis, E., Wilson, T., & Moore, J. (2011). Twitter sentiment analysis: The good the bad and the omg! In *Proceedings of the 5th International AAAI Conference on Weblogs and Social Media (ICWSM)* (pp. 538–541).

Mohammad, S. M. (2012). #Emotional tweets. In *Proceedings of the 1st Joint Conference on Lexical and Computational Semantics* (pp. 246–255). Montreal, QC.

Mohammad, S. M., & Kiritchenko, S. (2014). Using hashtags to capture fine emotion categories from tweets. *Computational Intelligence,* 301-326.

Mohammad, S. M., Zhu, X., & Martin, J. (2014). Semantic role labeling of emotions in tweets. In *Proceedings of the ACL 2014 Workshop on Computational Approaches to Subjectivity, Sentiment, and Social Media (WASSA)* (pp. 32–41). Baltimore, MD.

Nakov, P., Kozareva, Z., Ritter, A., Rosenthal, S., Stoyanov, V., & Wilson, T. (2013). SemEval-2013 task 2: Sentiment analysis in Twitter. In *Proceedings of the 7th International Workshop on Semantic Evaluation (SemEval 2013)* (pp. 312–320).

Pak, A., & Paroubek, P. (2010). Twitter as a corpus for sentiment analysis and opinion mining. In *Seventh International Conference on Language Resources and Evaluation (LREC)* (pp. 1320–1326).

Pang, B., Lee, L., & Vaithyanathan, S. (2002). Thumbs up?: Sentiment classification using machine learning techniques. In *Proceedings of the ACL-2002 Conference on Empirical Methods in Natural Language Processing* (pp. 79–86). Stroudsburg, PA, USA.

Platt, J. C. (1998). Fast Training of Support Vector Machines Using Sequential Minimal Optimization - Microsoft Research. In *Advances in Kernel Methods - Support Vector Learning* (pp. 41–65). MIT Press.

Plutchik, R. (1962). *The Emotions: Facts, theories, and a new model.* New York: Random House.

Roberts, K., Roach, M. A., Johnson, J., Guthrie, J., & Harabagiu, S. M. (2012). EmpaTweet: Annotating and detecting emotions on Twitter. In *8th International Conference on Language Resources and Evaluation (LREC)* (pp. 3806–3813).

Rosenthal, S., Nakov, P., Ritter, A., & Stoyanov, V. (2014). Semeval-2014 task 9: Sentiment analysis in Twitter. In *Proceedings of the 8th International Workshop on Semantic Evaluation (SemEval 2014)* (pp. 73–80). Dublin, Ireland.

Russell, J. A. (2003). Core affect and the psychological construction of emotion. *Psychological Review, 110*(1), 145–172.

Salvetti, F., Reichenbach, C., & Lewis, S. (2006). Opinion polarity identification of movie reviews. *Computing Attitude and Affect in Text: Theory and Applications* (pp. 303–316).

Shaver, P., Schwartz, J., Kirson, D., & O'Connor, C. (2001). Emotion knowledge: Further exploration of a prototype approach. In *Emotions in Social Psychology* (pp. 26–56). Psychology Press.

Sohn, S., Torii, M., Li, D., Wagholikar, K., Wu, S., & Liu, H. (2012). A hybrid approach to sentiment sentence classification in suicide notes. *Biomedical Informatics Insights, 5*(Suppl. 1), 43–50.

Strapparava, C., & Mihalcea, R. (2008). Learning to identify emotions in text. In *Proceedings of the 2008 ACM Symposium on Applied Computing* (pp. 1556–1560). New York, USA.

Wang, W., Chen, L., Thirunarayan, K., & Sheth, A. P. (2012). Harnessing Twitter "big data" for automatic emotion identification. In *2012 International Conference on Privacy, Security, Risk and Trust, and 2012 International Conference on Social Computing* (pp. 587–592).

Wiebe, J. M., Wilson, T., Bruce, R., Bell, M., & Martin, M. (2004). Learning subjective language. *Computational Linguistics, 30*(3), 277–308.

Zhang, P. (2013). The Affective Response Model: A theoretical framework of affective concepts and their relationships in the ICT context. *Management Information Systems Quarterly, 37*(1), 247–274.

Extraction of Bilingual Technical Terms
for Chinese–Japanese Patent Translation

Wei Yang and **Jinghui Yan** and **Yves Lepage**
Graduate School of IPS, Waseda University,
2-7 Hibikino, Wakamatsu Kitakyushu Fukuoka, 808-0135, Japan
`{kevinyoogi@akane,jess256@suou}.waseda.jp, yves.lepage@waseda.jp`

Abstract

The translation of patents or scientific papers is a key issue that should be helped by the use of statistical machine translation (SMT). In this paper, we propose a method to improve Chinese–Japanese patent SMT by pre-marking the training corpus with aligned bilingual multi-word terms. We automatically extract multi-word terms from monolingual corpora by combining statistical and linguistic filtering methods. We use the sampling-based alignment method to identify aligned terms and set some threshold on translation probabilities to select the most promising bilingual multi-word terms. We pre-mark a Chinese–Japanese training corpus with such selected aligned bilingual multi-word terms. We obtain the performance of over 70% precision in bilingual term extraction and a significant improvement of BLEU scores in our experiments on a Chinese–Japanese patent parallel corpus.

1 Introduction

China and Japan are producing a large amount of scientific journals and patents in their respective languages. The World Intellectual Property Organization (WIPO) Indicators[1] show that China was the first country for patent applications in 2013. Japan was the first country for patent grants in 2013. Much of current scientific development in China or Japan is not readily available to non–Chinese or non–Japanese speaking scientists. Additionally, China and Japan are more efficient at converting research and development dollars into patents than the U.S. or the European countries[2]. Making Chinese patents available in Japanese, and Japanese patents available and in Chinese is a key issue for increased economical development in Asia.

In recent years, Chinese–Japanese machine translation of patents or scientific papers has made rapid progress with the large quantities of parallel corpora provided by the organizers of the Workshop on Asian Translation (WAT)[3][4]. In the "patents subtask" of WAT 2015, in (Sonoh and Kinoshita, 2015), a Chinese to Japanese translation system is described that achieves higher BLEU scores by combination of results between Statistical Post Editing (SPE) based on their rule-based translation system and SMT system equipped with a recurrent neural language model (RNNLM).

In the research by Li et al. (2012), they improved a Chinese–to–Japanese patent translation system by using English as a pivot language for three different purposes: corpus enrichment, sentence pivot translation and phrase pivot translation. Still, the availability of patent bilingual corpora between Chinese and Japanese in certain domains is a problem.

In this paper, we propose a simpler way to improve Chinese to Japanese phrase-based machine translation quality based on a small size of available bilingual patent corpus, without exploiting extra bilingual data, or using a third language, with

---

[1]`http://en.wikipedia.org/wiki/World_`
`Intellectual_Property_Indicators`

[2]`http://www.ipwatchdog.com/2013/04/04/`
`chinas-great-leap-forward-in-patents/id=`
`38625/`
[3]`http://orchid.kuee.kyoto-u.ac.jp/WAT/`
`WAT2014/index.html`
[4]`http://orchid.kuee.kyoto-u.ac.jp/WAT/`

Proceedings of NAACL-HLT 2016, pages 81–87,
San Diego, California, June 12-17, 2016. ©2016 Association for Computational Linguistics

no complex approach. Patents or scientific papers contain large amounts of domain-specific terms in words or multi-word expressions. Monolingual or bilingual term extraction is an important task for the fields of information retrieval, text categorization, clustering, machine translation, etc. There exist work on monolingual or bilingual term extraction in different languages. In (Kang et al., 2009), multi-word terms in Chinese in the information technology (IT) domain and the medicine domain are extracted based on the integration of Web information and termhood estimation. Frantzi et al. (2000) describes a combination of linguistic and statistical information method (C-value/NC-value) for the automatic extraction of multi-word terms from English corpora. In (Mima and Ananiadou, 2001), it was showed that the C-/NC-value method is an efficient domain-independent multi-word term recognition not only in English but in Japanese as well.

Some work consider the case of bilingual term extraction. In (Fan et al., 2009), Chinese–Japanese multi-word terms are extracted by re-segmenting the Chinese and Japanese bi-corpus and combining multi-word terms as one single word based on extracted monolingual terms. The word alignments containing terms are smoothed by computing the associations between pairs of bilingual term candidates.

In this paper, we propose a method to extract Chinese–Japanese bilingual multi-word terms by extracting Chinese and Japanese monolingual multi-word terms using a linguistic and statistical technique (C-value) (Frantzi et al., 2000) and the sampling-based alignment method (Lardilleux and Lepage, 2009) for bilingual multi-word term alignment. We filter the aligned candidate terms by setting thresholds on translation probabilities. We perform experiments on the Chinese–Japanese JPO patent corpus of WAT 2015. We pre-mark the extracted bilingual terms in the Chinese–Japanese training corpus of an SMT system. We compare the translation system which uses our proposed method with a baseline system. We obtain a significant improvement in translation accuracy as evaluated by BLEU (Papineni et al., 2002).

The paper is organized as follows: in Section 2, we introduce the experimental data sets used in our experiments. Section 3 gives our proposed method

to extract Chinese–Japanese bilingual multi-word terms using the C-value and the sampling-based alignment method. In Section 4, we describe our experiments and their results based on the data introduced in Section 2, and an analysis of the experimental results. Section 5 gives the conclusion and discusses future directions.

2 Chinese and Japanese Data Used

The Chinese–Japanese parallel sentences used in this paper are randomly extracted from the Chinese–Japanese JPO Patent Corpus (JPC)[5]. This corpus consists of about 1 million parallel sentences with four sections (Chemistry, Electricity, Mechanical engineering, and Physics.). It is already divided into training, tuning and test sets (1 million sentences, 4,000 sentences and 2,000 sentences respectively). For our experiments, we randomly extract 100,000 parallel sentences from the training part, 500 parallel sentences from the tuning part, and 1,000 from the test part. Table 1 shows the basic statistics on our experimental data sets.

	Baseline	Chinese	Japanese
train	sentences	100,000	100,000
	words	2,314,922	2,975,479
	mean $\pm$ std.dev.	23.29 $\pm$ 11.69	29.93 $\pm$ 13.94
tune	sentences	500	500
	words	14,251	17,904
	mean $\pm$ std.dev.	28.61 $\pm$ 21.88	35.94 $\pm$ 25.07
test	sentences	1,000	1,000
	words	27,267	34,292
	mean $\pm$ std.dev.	27.34 $\pm$ 15.59	34.38 $\pm$ 18.78

Table 1: Statistics on our experimental data sets (after tokenizing and lowercasing). Here 'mean $\pm$ std.dev.' gives the average length of the sentences in words.

In Section 3, monolingual and bilingual multi-word terms will be extracted from the training data. In Section 4, these data (train, tune and test) will be used in the baseline SMT system.

3 Bilingual Multi-word Term Extraction

This section presents our bilingual multi-word term extraction method that uses C-value (Frantzi et al., 2000) combined with the sampling-based alignment

---

[5]`http://lotus.kuee.kyoto-u.ac.jp/WAT/patent/index.html`

method (Lardilleux and Lepage, 2009). We also describe how we use these extracted bilingual multi-word terms in SMT experiments.

3.1 Monolingual Multi-word Term Extraction Using the C-value Approach

The C-value is a commonly used domain-independent method for multi-word term extraction. This method has a linguistic part and a statistical part. The linguistic part constrains the type of terms extracted. In our experiments, we extract multi-word terms which contain a sequence of nouns or adjectives followed by a noun for both Chinese and Japanese. This linguistic pattern can be written as follows using a regular expression[6]:

$$(Adjective|Noun)^+ Noun$$

The segmenter and part-of-speech tagger that we use are the Stanford parser[7] for Chinese and Juman[8] for Japanese. Examples of outputs are shown in Table 2.

The statistical part, the measure of termhood, called the C-value, is given by the following formula:

$$C\text{--}value(a) = \begin{cases} log_2|a| \cdot f(a) \\ \qquad \text{if a is not nested,} \\ log_2|a|(f(a) - \dfrac{1}{P(T_a)} \sum_{b \in T_a} f(b)) \\ \qquad \qquad \text{otherwise} \end{cases}$$

$$(1)$$

where a is the candidate string, f(.) is its frequency of occurrence in the corpus, T_a is the set of extracted candidate terms that contain a, $P(T_a)$ is the number of these candidate terms. In our experiments, we follow the basic steps of the C-value approach to extract monolingual multi-word terms from the monolingual part of the Chinese–Japanese training corpus. Then, we mark the extracted monolingual multi-word terms in the corpus by enforcing them to be considered as one token (aligned with markers).

---

[6]Pattern for Chinese: $(JJ|NN)^+ NN$, pattern for Japanese: (形容詞 | 名詞)$^+$ 名詞. 'JJ' and '形容詞' are codes for adjectives, 'NN' and '名詞' are codes for nouns in the Chinese and the Japanese annotated corpora that we use.

[7]http://nlp.stanford.edu/software/segmenter.shtml

[8]http://nlp.ist.i.kyoto-u.ac.jp/index.php?JUMAN

3.2 Bilingual Multi-word Term Extraction Using Sampling-based Method

To extract bilingual multi-word terms, we use the open source implementation of the sampling-based approach, Anymalign (Lardilleux and Lepage, 2009), to perform phrase alignment from the above marked Chinese–Japanese training corpus. We filter out any alignment ($N \times M$-grams) that is greater than 1, to obtain only word-to-word alignments[9]. In our experiments, we identify the multi-word term to multi-word term alignments between Chinese and Japanese by using the markers. We filter the aligned multi-word candidate terms by setting some threshold P for both translation probabilities of term alignments ($0 < P \leq 1$).

3.3 Bilingual Multi-word Terms Used in SMT Experiments

We train the Chinese–Japanese translation models on the training parallel pre-marked corpus with the extracted filtered aligned bilingual multi-word terms. A language model is trained with the original Japanese corpus without pre-marking annotation. We remove the markers from obtained phrase tables before performing tuning and decoding processes. We compare such a systems with a standard baseline system.

4 Experiments and Results

We extract monolingual multi-word terms from a Chinese–Japanese training corpus of 100,000 lines as indicated in Table 1 (Section 2). Table 3 shows the number of monolingual multi-word terms extracted in Chinese and Japanese respectively using C-value and the linguistic pattern given in Section 3.1. The extracted monolingual multi-word terms were ranked by decreasing order of C-values. We mark the training corpus with the same size of Chinese and Japanese monolingual multi-word terms. They are the first 80,000 monolingual multi-word terms with higher C-value in both languages.

Follow the description given in Section 3.2. Table 4 gives the number of bilingual multi-word terms obtained for different thresholds from the marked 100,000 training corpus. We randomly extract 100 bilingual multi-word terms respectively and roughly

---

[9]This is done by the option -N 1 on the command line.

Chinese or Japanese sentences	Extracted monolingual terms
Chinese: 完全/#AD 布置/#VV 在/#P 环形/#JJ 间隙/#NN 中/#LC 。/#PU	环形　间隙
Japanese: 完全に/形容詞 この/指示詞 環状/名詞 隙間/名詞 内/接尾辞 に/助詞 配置/名詞 さ/動詞 れる/接尾辞 。/特殊	環状　隙間
English meaning:　'Completely arranged in the annular gap.'	'annular gap'

Table 2: Examples of outputs on the tags used based on the linguistic pattern.

Language	♯ of Multi-word terms
Chinese	81,618
Japanese	93,105

Table 3: The number of monolingual multi-word terms extracted from Chinese–Japanese training corpus using C-value.

check how well they correspond/match manually. The precision (good match) of the extracted bilingual multi-word terms is over 70%, while threshold becomes greater than 0.4. Table 5 shows sample of bilingual multi-word terms we extracted.

4.1 Translation Accuracy in BLEU

We pre-mark the original Chinese–Japanese training corpus with the extracted bilingual multi-word terms filtering by several thresholds (Table 4) and train several Chinese to Japanese SMT systems using the standard GIZA++/MOSES pipeline (Koehn et al., 2007). The un-pre-marked (original) Japanese corpus is used to train a language model using KenLM (Heafield, 2011). After removing markers from the phrase table, we tune and test. In all experiments, the same data sets are used, the only difference being whether the training data is pre-marked or not with bilingual multi-word terms filtered by a given threshold. Table 4 shows the evaluation of the results of Chinese to Japanese translation in BLEU scores (Papineni et al., 2002). Compared with the baseline system, we obtain significant improvements as soon as the threshold becomes greater than 0.3. A statistically significant improvement of one BLEU point (p-value is 0.001) is observed when the threshold is greater than 0.6. In that case, the training corpus is pre-marked with roughly 20,000 bilingual multi-word terms.

4.2 Analysis of the Content of Phrase Tables

We further compare a system based on a pre-marked training corpus using bilingual multi-word terms (threshold of 0.6) with a baseline system. We in-

Extract or not	Chinese	Japanese
○	控制__电路 *'control circuit'*	制御__回路
×	核酸 *'nucleic acid'*	核__酸
×	粘接剂 *'adhesive'*	接着__剤
○	信息__处理__装置 *'information-processing device'*	情報__処理__装置
○	发光__二极管__元件 *'light emitting diode element'*	発光__ダイオード__素子
○	压力__传感器 *'pressure sensor'*	圧力__センサ
×	存储器__控制器 *'memory controller'*	メモリコントローラ
×	枢轴__板 *'pivot plate'*	ピボットプレート

Table 5: Extraction of bilingual multi-word terms in both languages at the same time. ○ and × show the bilingual multi-word term alignment that are kept or excluded.

vestigate the N (Chinese) $\times$ M (Japanese)-grams distribution in the reduced phrase tables[10] used in translation. In Tables 6 and 7, the statistics (Chinese→Japanese) show that the total number of potentially useful phrase pairs used in translation with the pre-marked corpus is larger than that of the baseline system. Considering the correspondence between lengths in Chinese–Japanese patent translation, we compare the number of entries, the number of phrase pairs with different lengths (like 2 (zh) $\times$ 1 (ja), 2 (zh) $\times$ 3 (ja), 2 (zh) $\times$ 4 (ja) and 3 (zh) $\times$ 4 (ja)) and observe a significant increase for these categories.

We also investigate the number of phrase alignments which the Chinese source language part containing multi-word terms in the reduced phrase table obtained when pre-marking the training corpus. There exists 8,940 phrase alignments in this case. A sample is shown in Table 8. Compared with the reduced phrase table used in the baseline system, there exist 2,503 additional phrase alignments. They con-

---

[10]The phrase table only contains the potentially useful phrase alignments used in the translation of the test set.

Thresholds $P(t\|s)$ and $P(s\|t)$	♯ of bilingual multi-word terms	Good match	BLEU	p-value
≥ 0.0	52,785	35%	32.44±1.07	0.197
≥ 0.1	31,795	52%	32.23±1.18	0.062
≥ 0.2	27,916	58%	32.00±1.16	0.072
Baseline	**Baseline**	**Baseline**	**32.35±1.15**	**Baseline**
≥ 0.3	25,404	63%	33.08±1.12	0.004
≥ 0.4	23,515	72%	32.77±1.15	0.027
≥ 0.5	21,846	76%	33.02±1.14	0.007
≥ 0.6	**20,248**	78%	**33.32±1.15**	0.001
≥ 0.7	18,759	79%	32.85±1.19	0.006
≥ 0.8	17,311	79%	33.25±1.06	0.001
≥ 0.9	15,464	80%	33.20±1.15	0.002

Table 4: Evaluation results in BLEU for Chinese to Japanese translation based on pre-marked training corpus with bilingual multi-word terms using different thresholds, tools used are Giza++/Moses 2.1.1, KenLM.

Chinese	Japanese
n型 半 导＿体层 ||| n 型
pdu＿大小 ||| pdu サイズ
新＿数据 ||| 新しい＿データ
白＿平衡 ||| ホワイト＿バランス
x＿射线 ||| x線
x＿射线 ||| x線 か゛
所 需 的 构成＿要素 ||| に 必要な 構成＿要素
个 碳＿原子 的 ||| 個 の 炭素＿原子 の
接触＿孔 ||| コンタクト＿ホール
将 反应＿混合物 ||| 反応 混合＿物 を
在 玻璃＿基板 ||| ガラス＿基板
的 视频＿信号 ||| ビデオ＿信号
负 极活性＿物质 ||| 負＿極＿物質
控制＿部 ||| 制御＿部
旋转＿量 ||| 回転＿量
新＿数据 ||| 新しい＿データ
白＿平衡 ||| ホワイト＿バランス

Table 8: Sample of phrase alignments for which the source language part (Chinese) contains multi-word terms in the reduced phrase table. We show multi-word terms as one token in the phrase table aligned with markers.

tain multi-word terms that did not exist in the reduced phrase table of the baseline system. Table 9 shows examples of more potentially useful phrase alignments obtained with our proposed method.

5 Conclusion and Future Work

We presented an approach to improve Chinese–Japanese patent machine translation performance by pre-marking the parallel training corpus with bilingual multi-word terms. We extracted monolingual multi-word terms from each monolingual part of a corpus by using the C-value method. We used the sampling-based alignment method to align the marked parallel corpus with monolingual multi-word terms and only kept the aligned bilingual multi-word terms by setting thresholds in both directions. We did not use any other additional corpus or lexicon. The results of our experiments indicate that the bilingual multi-word terms extracted have over 70% precision (the thresholds $P \geq 0.4$). Pre-marking the parallel training corpus with these terms led to statistically significant improvements in BLEU scores (the thresholds $P \geq 0.3$).

In this work, we considered only the case where multi-word terms can be found in both languages at the same time, e.g., 半导体＿芯片 (zh) 半導体＿チップ (ja) 'semiconductor chip'. However, we found many cases where a multi-word term is recognized in one of the languages, while the other side is not recognized as a multi-word term, although they may be correct translation candidates. This mainly is due to different segmentation results in Chinese and Japanese. E.g., 压缩机 (Chinese) 圧縮＿機 (Japanese) 'compressor', and 流程图 (Chinese) フロー＿チャート (Japanese) 'flow chart'. In a future work, we thus intend to address this issue and expect further improvements in translation results. We also intend to do experiments with our proposed method using a larger size of experimental training data.

References

Xiaorong Fan, Nobuyuki Shimizu, and Hiroshi Nakagawa. 2009. Automatic extraction of bilingual terms from a Chinese-Japanese parallel corpus. In *Proceed-*

ings of the 3rd International Universal Communication Symposium, pages 41–45. ACM.

Katerina Frantzi, Sophia Ananiadou, and Hideki Mima. 2000. Automatic recognition of multi-word terms:. the C-value/NC-value method. *International Journal on Digital Libraries*, 3(2):115–130.

Kenneth Heafield. 2011. Kenlm: Faster and smaller language model queries. In *Proceedings of the Sixth Workshop on Statistical Machine Translation*, pages 187–197. Association for Computational Linguistics.

Wei Kang, Zhifang Sui, and Yao Liu. 2009. Research on automatic Chinese multi-word term extraction based on integration of Web information and term component. In *Web Intelligence and Intelligent Agent Technologies, 2009. WI-IAT'09. IEEE/WIC/ACM International Joint Conferences on*, volume 3, pages 267–270. IET.

Philipp Koehn, Hieu Hoang, Alexandra Birch, Chris Callison-Burch, Marcello Federico, Nicola Bertoldi, Brooke Cowan, Wade Shen, Christine Moran, Richard Zens, and et al. 2007. Moses: Open source toolkit for statistical machine translation. In *Proceedings of the 45th Annual Meeting of the ACL on Interactive Poster and Demonstration Sessions (ACL 2007)*, pages 177–180. Association for Computational Linguistics.

Adrien Lardilleux and Yves Lepage. 2009. Sampling-based multilingual alignment. In *Recent Advances in Natural Language Processing*, pages 214–218.

Xianhua Li, Yao Meng, and Hao Yu. 2012. Improving Chinese-to-Japanese patent translation using English as pivot language. In *26th Pacific Asia Conference on Language, Information and Computation (PACLIC 26)*, pages 117–126.

Hideki Mima and Sophia Ananiadou. 2001. An application and evaluation of the C/NC-value approach for the automatic term recognition of multi-word units in Japanese. *Terminology*, 6(2):175–194.

Kishore Papineni, Salim Roukos, Todd Ward, and Wei-Jing Zhu. 2002. BLEU: a method for automatic evaluation of machine translation. In *ACL 2002*, pages 311–318.

Satoshi Sonoh and Satoshi Kinoshita. 2015. Toshiba MT system description for the WAT2015 workshop. In *Proceedings of the 2nd Workshop on Asian Translation (WAT2015)*, pages 48–53.

Source = Chinese	Target = Japanese									
	1-gram	2-gram	3-gram	4-gram	5-gram	6-gram	7-gram	8-gram	9-gram	total
1-gram	29986	**86874**	**79132**	**49514**	27936	14843	7767	149	15	296218
2-gram	**14201**	39342	**42833**	**27865**	15746	8292	4293	103	14	152690
3-gram	**1492**	**3997**	7985	**7244**	4627	2528	1290	65	3	29231
4-gram	**186**	**434**	1106	2099	1896	1310	691	23	0	7745
5-gram	27	49	163	388	659	556	392	12	0	2246
6-gram	2	6	14	60	114	180	170	10	1	557
7-gram	0	0	4	4	22	48	72	6	1	157
8-gram	0	0	0	0	0	0	0	1	0	1
9-gram	0	0	0	0	0	0	0	0	1	1
total	45894	130702	131237	87174	51000	27757	14675	369	35	**488846**

Table 6: Distribution of the reduced phrase table of a C-value/sampling-based alignment term extraction method based on GIZA++/Moses 2.1.1. The bold face numbers showing the increased N (Chinese) × M (Japanese)-grams (less than 4-grams) in the reduced phrase table, and the total number of N (Chinese) × M (Japanese)-grams, which increased compared with the baseline system.

Source = Chinese	Target = Japanese									
	1-gram	2-gram	3-gram	4-gram	5-gram	6-gram	7-gram	8-gram	9-gram	total
1-gram	32320	84308	71713	42518	22831	11726	6035	0	0	271451
2-gram	13570	39534	41775	25628	13703	6922	3518	0	0	144650
3-gram	1384	3906	8067	7117	4276	2238	1093	0	0	28081
4-gram	163	413	1124	2124	1853	1248	614	0	0	7539
5-gram	27	50	154	386	658	562	360	0	0	2197
6-gram	6	9	13	59	116	181	164	0	0	548
7-gram	1	1	3	5	20	50	73	0	0	153
8-gram	0	0	0	0	0	0	0	0	0	0
9-gram	1	0	0	0	0	0	0	0	0	0
total	47471	128221	122849	77837	43457	22927	11857	0	0	454619

Table 7: Distribution of the reduced phrase table of baseline system based on GIZA++/Moses 2.1.1.

Baseline	English meaning
传输 信道 的 ‖ 伝送 路 の	transmission channel ‖ transmission channel
位置 信息 ‖ 位置	location information ‖ location
位置 信息 ‖ 位置 の 情報	location information ‖ location information
位置 信息 ‖ 位置 は	location information ‖ location (with a auxiliary word 'は')
Pre-marked training corpus	
传输 信道 的 ‖ 伝送 路 の	transmission channel ‖ transmission channel
传输 信道 的 ‖ 、 伝送 チャネル の	**transmission channel ‖** , transmission channel of (another way of saying 'transmission channel' in Japanese)
位置 信息 ‖ 位置	location information ‖ location
位置 信息 ‖ 位置 の 情報	location information ‖ location information
位置 信息 ‖ 位置 は	location information ‖ location (with an auxiliary word 'は')
位置 信息 ‖ 位置 の 情報 である	**location information ‖ location information (with an auxiliary 'である')**
位置 信息 ‖ その 位置 情報	**location information ‖ that location information**
位置 信息 ‖ 位置 情報 は	**location information ‖ location information (with an auxiliary word 'は')**

Table 9: Samples of phrase alignments in reduced Chinese→Japanese phrase tables. Alignments given in bold face are additional phrase alignments compared with the baseline systems.

Hateful Symbols or Hateful People?
Predictive Features for Hate Speech Detection on Twitter

Zeerak Waseem
University of Copenhagen
Copenhagen, Denmark
csp265@alumni.ku.dk

Dirk Hovy
University of Copenhagen
Copenhagen, Denmark
dirk.hovy@hum.ku.dk

Abstract

Hate speech in the form of racist and sexist remarks are a common occurrence on social media. For that reason, many social media services address the problem of identifying hate speech, but the definition of hate speech varies markedly and is largely a manual effort (BBC, 2015; Lomas, 2015).

We provide a list of criteria founded in critical race theory, and use them to annotate a publicly available corpus of more than 16k tweets. We analyze the impact of various extra-linguistic features in conjunction with character n-grams for hate-speech detection. We also present a dictionary based the most indicative words in our data.

1 Introduction

Hate speech is an unfortunately common occurrence on the Internet (Eadicicco, 2014; Kettrey and Laster, 2014) and in some cases culminates in severe threats to individuals. Social media sites therefore face the problem of identifying and censoring problematic posts (Moulson, 2016) while weighing the right to freedom of speech.

The importance of detecting and moderating hate speech is evident from the strong connection between hate speech and actual hate crimes (Watch, 2014). Early identification of users promoting hate speech could enable outreach programs that attempt to prevent an escalation from speech to action.

Sites such as Twitter and Facebook have been seeking to actively combat hate speech (Lomas, 2015). Most recently, Facebook announced that they would seek to combat racism and xenophobia aimed at refugees (Moulson, 2016). Currently,

much of this moderation requires manual review of questionable documents, which not only limits how much a human annotator can be reviewed, but also introduces subjective notions of what constitutes hate speech. A reaction to the "Black Lives Matter" movement, a campaign to highlight the devaluation of lives of African-American citizens sparked by extrajudicial killings of black men and women (Matter, 2012), at the Facebook campus shows how individual biases manifest in evaluating hate speech (Wong, 2016).

In spite of these reasons, NLP research on hate speech has been very limited, primarily due to the lack of a general definition of hate speech, an analysis of its demographic influences, and an investigation of the most effective features.

While online hate speech is a growing phenomenon (Sood et al., 2012a), its distribution is not uniform across all demographics. Neither is the awareness of what constitutes hate speech (Ma, 2015). Considering that hate speech is not evenly distributed in the United States of America (Zook, 2012) and perpetrators of hate speech should be a small minority from a limited demographic group. Including available demographic information as features should thus help identification accuracy.

Our contribution We provide a data set of 16k tweets annotated for hate speech. We also investigate which of the features we use provide the best identification performance. We analyze the features that improve detection of hate speech in our corpus, and find that despite presumed differences in the geographic and word-length distribution, they have little to no positive effect on performance, and rarely improve over character-level features. The exception to this rule is gender.

2 Data

Our data set consists of tweets collected over the course of 2 months. In total, we retrieved 136,052

Proceedings of NAACL-HLT 2016, pages 88–93,
San Diego, California, June 12-17, 2016. ©2016 Association for Computational Linguistics

tweets and annotated 16,914 tweets, 3,383 of that for sexist content sent by 613 users, 1,972 for racist content sent by 9 users, and 11,559 for neither sexist or racist and is sent by 614 users.

Since hate speech is a real, but limited phenomenon, we do not balance the data, to provide as realistic a data set as possible.

Our data set will be made available as tweet IDs and labels at Github[1].

Corpus collection We bootstrapped our corpus collection, by performing an initial manual search of common slurs and terms used pertaining to religious, sexual, gender, and ethnic minorities. In the results, we identified frequently occurring terms in tweets that contain hate speech and references to specific entities, such as the term "#MKR", the hashtag for the Australian TV show *My Kitchen Rules*, which often prompts sexist tweets directed at the female participants[2]. In addition, we identified a small number of prolific users from these searches.

Based on this sample, we used the public Twitter search API to collect the entire corpus, filtering for tweets not written in English. This particular corpus construction ensures that we obtain non-offensive tweets that contain both clearly offensive words and potentially offensive words, but remain non-offensive in their use and treatment of the words. For example, even though "muslims" is one of the most frequent words in racist tweets, it also occurs in perfectly innocuous tweets, such as "you are right there are issues but banning Muslims from entering doesn't solve anything."

We manually annotated our data set, after which we had the help of an outside annotator (a 25 year old woman studying gender studies and a non-activist feminist) to review our annotations, in order to mitigate annotator bias introduced by any parties.

Identification and annotation While it is easy to identify racist and sexist slurs, hate speech is often expressed without any such terms. Furthermore, it is not trivial for humans to identify hate speech due to differences of exposure to and knowledge of hate speech. Similarly to identifying

privileges, a critical thought process is required to identify hate speech (McIntosh, 2003; DeAngelis, 2009). In order to reliably identify hate speech, we need a clear decision list to ensure that problematic tweets are identified.

We propose the following list to identify hate speech. The criteria are partially derived by negating the privileges observed in McIntosh (2003), where they occur as ways to highlight importance, ensure an audience, and ensure safety for white people, and partially derived from applying common sense.

A tweet is offensive if it

1. uses a sexist or racial slur.
2. attacks a minority.
3. seeks to silence a minority.
4. criticizes a minority (without a well founded argument).
5. promotes, but does not directly use, hate speech or violent crime.
6. criticizes a minority and uses a straw man argument.
7. blatantly misrepresents truth or seeks to distort views on a minority with unfounded claims.
8. shows support of problematic hash tags. E.g. "#BanIslam", "#whoriental", "#whitegenocide"
9. negatively stereotypes a minority.
10. defends xenophobia or sexism.
11. contains a screen name that is offensive, as per the previous criteria, the tweet is ambiguous (at best), and the tweet is on a topic that satisfies any of the above criteria.

As McIntosh (2003) highlights the way that they are privileged by being white. Many of these observations underline apparent safety and visibility granted by skin color. As such, our list highlights ways in which minorities are undercut and silenced as these occur as methods of oppression of minorities (DeAngelis, 2009).

While most of the criteria are easily identified, others such as identifying problematic hash tags is far more unclear. We define problematic hash tags as terms which fulfill the remaining one or several of other criteria.

Annotator agreement The inter-annotator agreement is $\kappa = 0.84$. 85% of all disagreements occur in annotations of sexism, with 98% of all reviewer changes being set to neither sexist nor

---

[1] http://github.com/zeerakw/hatespeech

[2] All terms queried for: "MKR", "asian drive", "feminazi", "immigrant", "nigger", "sjw", "WomenAgainstFeminism", "blameonenotall", "islam terrorism", "notallmen", "victimcard", "victim card", "arab terror", "gamergate", "jsil", "racecard", "race card"

racist, the remaining set to racist. In most of these cases we find that the disagreement is reliant on context or the lack thereof. Where our outside annotator would tend to annotate such cases lacking apparent context as not being sexist, we preferred to annotate as sexist for many of these cases. For instance, our outside annotator did not find "There just horrible #lemontarts #MKR" to be a case of sexist language whereas we had annotated it as such. Another common case of disagreement was the difference of opinion in what constitutes sexism. Where we found tweets such as ""Everyone else, despite our commentary, has fought hard too. It's not just you, Kat. #mkr"" to be singling out a single woman, our annotator found that such a comment was not coined on the gender but in fact an (assumed) expression hard work from the competitor.

3   Demographic distribution

Twitter does not directly provide fields for demographic information beyond location, so we collect this information by proxy. We extract gender by looking up names in the users profile text, the name, or the user name provided and compare them to known male and female names (Kantrowitz, 1994) as well as other indicators of gender, such as pronouns, honorifics, and gender specific nouns.

We find that the gender distributions in our hate speech are heavily skewed towards men (see Table 1).

	All	Racism	Sexism	Neither
Men	50.08%	33.33%	50.24%	50.92%
Women	02.26%	0.00 %	02.28%	01.74%
Unidentified	47.64%	66.66%	47.47%	47.32%

Table 1: Distribution of genders in hate-speech documents.

While men are over represented in our data set for all categories, the majority of users cannot be identified with our method, which heavily impairs use of gender information as features. For instance, in our racist subset, we only identify 3 out of 9, all of them men. Furthermore, (Roberts et al., 2013) find that 75% and 87% of perpetrators of hate crimes against African Caribbeans and Asians respectively, were men. Considering that hate speech is a precursor to hate crime (Watch, 2014), we find it unsurprising that such a large part of the perpetrators of hate speech in our data set are men.

And while we manage to identify 52.56% of the users in our annotated database, we find that the vast majority are users associated with sexist tweets and tweets that do not contain hate speech. Given that both have nearly the same distribution (see Table 1), we do not expect this feature to yield a substantial increase in F1 score.

4   Lexical distribution

We normalize the data by removing stop words, with the exception of "not", special markers such as "RT" (Retweet) and screen names, and punctuation.

We construct the ten most frequently occurring words by selecting the ten words with the most frequent occurrence for each class. We find that the terms frequently occurring in each class differ significantly (see Table 2). The most frequent tokens for racism are necessary in order to discuss Islam, while discussing women's issues does not require the use of most of the terms that occur most frequently.

We also see a sampling effect of the data set, as many of the tweets flagged as sexist are generated by viewers of *My Kitchen Rules*. Similarly, and more obviously, many of the tweets flagged as racist pertain to Judaism and Islam.

Lengths   Drawing inspiration from Tulkens et al. (2015), we add average and total the lengths of the tweets and the lengths of the user descriptions. We expect lengths to discriminate between tweets that contain hate speech and those that do not (see Table 3).

5   Geographic distribution

We find that using location as a feature negatively impacts the F1-score attained. In order to identify the geographical origin of a tweet, we need to consider more than just the tags Twitter provides, given that only 2% of Twitter users disclose their location (Abbas, 2015).

We therefore identify whether any location or their proxy is given in the tweet or user meta data (name given and user name). In each of these fields we extract markers indicating geographical location or time zone. Time zone is also used as a proxy for location by (Gouws et al., 2011).

If a time zone or location is identified, we map it to longitude and latitude and add to the set of tweets originating from that time zone. If a location name, such as "Sydney" is given, it is also used as a feature for classification.

Sexism	Distribution	Racism	Distribution
not	1.83%	islam	1.44%
sexist	1.68%	muslims	1.01%
#mkr	1.57%	muslim	0.65%
women	0.83%	not	0.53%
kat	0.57%	mohammed	0.52%
girls	0.48%	religion	0.40%
like	0.42%	isis	0.38%
call	0.36%	jews	0.37%
#notsexist	0.36%	prophet	0.36%
female	0.34%	#islam	0.35%

Table 2: Distribution of ten most frequently occurring terms

	Racism	Sexism	None
Mean	60.47	52.93	47.95
Std.	17.44	21.16	23.43
Min.	11.00	2.00	2.00
Max.	115.00	118.00	129.00

Table 3: Overview of lengths in characters, subtracting spaces.

6 Evaluation

We evaluate the influence of different features on prediction in a classification task. We use a logistic regression classifier and 10-fold cross validation to test the influence of various features on prediction performance, and to quantify their expressiveness.

Model Selection In order to pick the most suitable features, we perform a grid search over all possible feature set combinations, finding that using character n-grams outperforms using word n-grams by at least 5 F1-points (60.42 vs. 69.86) using similar features. For that reason, we do not consider word n-grams.

To determine whether a difference between two feature sets is statistically significant (at $p < 0.05$), we run a bootstrap sampling test on the predictions of the two systems. The test takes 10,000 samples and compares whether the better system is the same as the better system on the entire data set. The resulting (p-) value of the bootstrap test is thus the fraction of samples where the winner differs from the entire data set, giving the p-value a very intuitive interpretation.

Results We find that using character n-grams of lengths up to 4, along with gender as an additional feature provides the best results. We further find that using location or length is detrimental to our scores. By using our n-gram features we achieve the results shown in Table 4.

We find that across our features only adding gender information improves our F1-score. All other features and feature combinations are detrimental to the performance of the system. We find that gender, the only additional feature that provides an improvement, is not statistically significant, whereas the addition of location as well as gender is significant, at $p = 0.0355$.

Features We collect unigrams, bigrams, trigrams, and fourgrams for each tweet and the user description. To assess the informativeness of the features we sum the model coefficients for each feature over the 10 folds of cross validation. This allows for a more robust estimate.

We find that the most influential features for the logistic regression (see Table 5) largely correspond with the most frequent terms in Table 2. We see, for instance different n-gram lengths of the word "Islam" and "sexist".

Intuitively, it makes sense that not only will the most frequent terms be indicative, but also that character n-grams would outperform word n-grams, due to character n-gram matrices being far less sparse than the word n-gram matrices.

One of the notable differences between the n-grams for our two categories is the occurrence of a gender-based slur, and normal words pertaining to women. On the other hand, all of the racist features are n-grams of normal terms, which are re-appropriated for building a negative discourse. One such example is: "@BYRONFBERRY Good. Time to confront the cult of hatred and murder #Islam".

	char n-grams	+gender	+gender +loc	word n-grams
F1	73.89	73.93	73.62*	64.58
Precision	72.87%	72.93%	72.58%	64.39%
Recall	77.75%	77.74%	77.43%	71.93%

Table 4: F1 achieved by using different features sets.

Feature (sexism)	Feature (racism)
'xist'	'sl'
'sexi'	'sla'
'ka'	'slam'
'sex'	'isla'
'kat'	'l'
'exis'	'a'
'xis'	'isl'
'exi'	'lam'
'xi'	'i'
'bitc'	'e'
'ist'	'mu'
'bit'	's'
'itch'	'am'
'itc'	'm'
'fem'	'la'
'ex'	'is'
'bi'	'slim'
'irl'	'musl'
'wom'	'usli'
'girl'	'lim'

Table 5: Most indicative character n-gram features for hate-speech detection

Gender (*F1* 73.89) We train our model on character bi- to fourgrams and the gender information for each use obtained as described in section 3. We find that this combination yields the highest score (see Table 4), though the score only increases slightly.

Length (*F1* 73.66) This feature set contains the total of each tweet and description and average lengths of the words occurring along with the n-grams of lengths 1 to 4.

Gender + location (*F1* 73.62) In this feature set contains the locations obtained in 5 along with our 1 to 4-grams, and the gender for each user. Adding locations occurs to be slightly detrimental to the performance of the classifier.

Gender + location + length (*F1* 73.47) For completeness we train on gender, geographic information, and length features along with 1 to 4-grams. Our score decreases by the use of all features, as we expected given the results of using location in combination with gender, and length.

7   Related Work

Most related work focused on detecting profanity, using list-based methods to identify offensive words (Sood et al., 2012b; Chen et al., 2012a). While studies suggest that these are good, robust ways to identify abusive language (Sood et al., 2012b); this approach is limited by its reliance on lists. Chen et al. (2012b) addresses this by the use of character n-grams among other features, in order to identify various forms of bullying.

Sood et al. (2012b) extend their system from static lists to incorporating edit distances to find variants of slurs. This allows for finding a better recall, but does not address the core issue of detecting offensive sentences, which do not use terms that occur in the list. Chen et al. (2012a) address this by using lexical and syntactical features along with automatically generated black lists.

Warner and Hirschberg (2012) perform a similar task of detecting hate speech using a support vector machine classifier, trained on word n-grams, brown clusters, and "the occurrence of words in a 10 word window" (Warner and Hirschberg, 2012). They find that their best model produces unigrams as most indicative features, and obtains an F1 score of 63, which is similar to the F1 score we achieve using word n-grams.

8   Conclusion

We presented a list of criteria based in critical race theory to identify racist and sexist slurs. These can be used to gather more data and address the problem of a small, but highly prolific number of hateful users. While the problem is far from solved, we find that using a character n-gram based approach provides a solid foundation. Demographic information, apart from gender, brings little improvement, but this could be due to the lack of coverage. We plan to improve location and gender classification to update future data and experiments.

References

Diana Abbas. 2015. What's in a location. `https://www.youtube.com/watch?v=GN1DO9Lt8J8`, October. Talk at Twitter Flight 2015. Seen on Jan 17th 2016.

BBC. 2015. Facebook, google and twitter agree german hate speech deal. `http://www.bbc.com/news/world-europe-35105003`. Accessed on 26/11/2016.

Ying Chen, Yilu Zhou, Sencun Zhu, and Heng Xu. 2012a. Detecting offensive language in social media to protect adolescent online safety. In *Privacy, Security, Risk and Trust (PASSAT), 2012 International Conference on and 2012 International Conference on Social Computing (SocialCom)*, pages 71–80. IEEE, September.

Yunfei Chen, Lanbo Zhang, Aaron Michelony, and Yi Zhang. 2012b. 4is of social bully filtering: Identity, inference, influence, and intervention. In *Proceedings of the 21st ACM International Conference on Information and Knowledge Management*, CIKM '12, pages 2677–2679, New York, NY, USA. ACM.

Tori DeAngelis. 2009. Unmasking 'racial micro aggressions'. *Monitor on Psychology*, 40(2):42.

Lisa Eadicicco. 2014. This female game developer was harassed so severely on twitter she had to leave her home. http://www.businessinsider.com/brianna-wu-harassed-twitter-2014-10?IR=T, Oct. Seen on Jan. 25th, 2016.

Stephan Gouws, Donald Metzler, Congxing Cai, and Eduard Hovy. 2011. Contextual bearing on linguistic variation in social media. In *Proceedings of the Workshop on Languages in Social Media*, LSM '11, pages 20–29, Stroudsburg, PA, USA. Association for Computational Linguistics.

Mark Kantrowitz. 1994. Name corpus: List of male, female, and pet names. `http://www.cs.cmu.edu/afs/cs/project/ai-repository/ai/areas/nlp/corpora/names/0.html`. Last accessed on 29th February 2016.

Heather Hensman Kettrey and Whitney Nicole Laster. 2014. Staking territory in the world white web: An exploration of the roles of overt and color-blind racism in maintaining racial boundaries on a popular web site. *Social Currents*, 1(3):257–274.

Natasha Lomas. 2015. Facebook, google, twitter commit to hate speech action in germany. `http://techcrunch.com/2015/12/16/germany-fights-hate-speech-on-social-media/`, Dec. Seen on 23rd Jan. 2016.

Alexandra Ma. 2015. Global survey finds nordic countries have the most feminists. `http://www.huffingtonpost.com/entry/global-gender-equality-study-yougov_us_564604cce4b045bf3deeb96d`, November. Seen on Jan 19th.

Black Lives Matter. 2012. Guiding principles. `http://blacklivesmatter.com/guiding-principles/`. Accessed on 26/11/2016.

Peggy McIntosh, 2003. *Understanding prejudice and discrimination.*, chapter White privilege: Unpacking the invisible knapsack, pages 191–196. McGraw-Hill.

Geir Moulson. 2016. Zuckerberg in germany: No place for hate speech on facebook. `http://abcnews.go.com/Technology/wireStory/zuckerberg-place-hate-speech-facebook-37217309`. Accessed 10/03/2016.

Colin Roberts, Martin Innes, Matthew Williams, Jasmin Tregidga, and David Gadd. 2013. Understanding who commits hate crime and why they do it.

Sara Sood, Judd Antin, and Elizabeth Churchill. 2012a. Profanity use in online communities. In *Proceedings of the SIGCHI Conference on Human Factors in Computing Systems*, pages 1481–1490. ACM.

Sara Owsley Sood, Judd Antin, and Elizabeth F. Churchill. 2012b. Using crowdsourcing to improve profanity detection. In *AAAI Spring Symposium: Wisdom of the Crowd*, volume SS-12-06 of *AAAI Technical Report*. AAAI.

Stéphan Tulkens, Lisa Hilte, Elise Lodewyckx, Ben Verhoeven, and Walter Daelemans. 2015. Detecting racism in dutch social media posts, 2015/12/18.

William Warner and Julia Hirschberg. 2012. Detecting hate speech on the world wide web. In *Proceedings of the Second Workshop on Language in Social Media*, LSM '12, pages 19–26, Stroudsburg, PA, USA. Association for Computational Linguistics.

Hate Speech Watch. 2014. Hate crimes: Consequences of hate speech. `http://www.nohatespeechmovement.org/hate-speech-watch/focus/consequences-of-hate-speech`, June. Seen on on 23rd Jan. 2016.

Julia Carrie Wong. 2016. Mark Zuckerberg tells Facebook staff to stop defacing Black Lives Matter slogans. `http://www.theguardian.com/technology/2016/feb/25/mark-zuckerberg-facebook-defacing-black-lives-matter-signs`. Accessed on 10/03/2016.

Matthew Zook. 2012. Mapping racist tweets in response to president obama's re-election. `http://www.floatingsheep.org/2012/11/mapping-racist-tweets-in-response-to.html`. Accessed on 11/03/2016.

Non-decreasing Sub-modular Function for Comprehensible Summarization

Litton J Kurisinkel   Pruthwik Mishra   Vigneshwaran Muralidaran
Vasudeva Varma   Dipti Misra Sharma
International Institute of Information Technology, Hyderabad, India
{litton.jKurisinkel, pruthwik.mishra, vigneshwaran.m}@research.iiit.ac.in
{vv, dipti}@iiit.ac.in

Abstract

Extractive summarization techniques typically aim to maximize the information coverage of the summary with respect to the original corpus and report accuracies in ROUGE scores. Automated text summarization techniques should consider the dimensions of comprehensibility, coherence and readability. In the current work, we identify the discourse structure which provides the context for the creation of a sentence. We leverage the information from the structure to frame a *monotone (non-decreasing) sub-modular* scoring function for generating comprehensible summaries. Our approach improves the overall quality of comprehensibility of the summary in terms of human evaluation and gives sufficient content coverage with comparable ROUGE score. We also formulate a metric to measure summary comprehensibility in terms of *Contextual Independence of a sentence*. The metric is shown to be representative of human judgement of text comprehensibility.

1   Introduction

Extractive summarization techniques aim at selecting a subset of sentences from a corpus which can be a representative of the original corpus in the target summary space. Extensive work has been done on extractive summarization aimed at maximizing the information coverage of the summary with respect to the original corpus and accuracies have been reported in terms of ROUGE score. But, if a sentence is heavily dependent on its previous context in the original corpus, placing it in the summary in a different context can render a wrong inference to the reader of the summary.

The main intuition behind our approach begins with a crucial question about the linguistic nature of a text. *Is text a bag of words every time?* Psycholinguistic studies suggest that local coherence plays a vital role in inference formation while reading a text (McKoon and Ratcliff, 1992). Local coherence is undoubtedly necessary for global coherence and has received considerable attention in Computational Linguistics. ((Marcu, 2000), (Foltz et al., 1998), (Althaus et al., 2004), (Karamanis et al., 2004)). Linguistically, every sentence is uttered not in isolation but within a context in a given discourse. To make a coherent reading, *sentences use various discourse connectives that bind one sentence with another. A set of such structurally related sentences forms a Locally Coherent Discourse Unit (hereafter referred to as LDU).* In the current work, we suggest that it is important to leverage this structural coherence to improve the comprehensibility of the generated summary. It should be noted that the concept of LDU is different from the elementary discourse units (EDUs) as discussed in Rhetorical Structure Theory(Mann and Thompson, 1988). RST is interested in describing the structure of a text in terms of relations that hold between parts of text. Any part of the text such as nuclear discourse clauses, satellite discourse clauses can be treated as elementary discourse units. In contrast, with LDUs, we are interested in identifying which sequence of sentences make up one extractable unit that has to be taken together for an extractive summarization task. The

94

Proceedings of NAACL-HLT 2016, pages 94–101,
San Diego, California, June 12-17, 2016. ©2016 Association for Computational Linguistics

most recent works on extractive summarization can be generalized into three steps given below:-

1. Creating an intermediate representation for the target text to capture key sentence features. The possible intermediate representations are Topic Signatures, Word-frequency count, Latent Space Approaches using Matrix Factorisations or Bayesian approaches

2. Using the intermediate representation to assign scores for individual sentence features within the text

3. Selecting a set of sentences which maximizes the total score as the summary for target text

During this process, a sentence is severed from its original context in the corpus and is eventually placed in a different context. If the level of dependence of the sentence on its context is high, then it has a higher chance to deliver an erroneous reading, when placed out of context. To understand the issue, look at the below sentences in a summary.

The baroque was a style of art that existed from the late 1500s to the middle of the 18th century. In 16th century, their ruler laced the old Gothic art with a newer baroque style.

A resultant summary which contains the above two sentences one after another, can be a topically relevant summary. Both talk about 'Baroque style', 'art','century' etc and could possibly be optimal candidates for the target summary. Nevertheless, it invokes an incomprehensible reading for a human reader because the subject of the second sentence is 'their ruler' whose anaphora is not resolved in the context. Hence it is important that we do not consider a document as mere sequence of sentences or bag of words but rather as a series of LDUs.

In spite of all attempts for developing abstractive summarization techniques to mimic the human way of summarizing a text, extractive techniques still stand out as more reliable for practical purposes. So it is inevitable to enhance the extractive summarization techniques along the dimensions of readability, coherence and comprehensibility. The problem of extractive summarization can be formulated as a function maximization problem in the space of all candidate summaries as follows.

$$S^* \in argmax_{S \subseteq V} F(S) \, subject \, to \sum_{i \in S} c_i <= b$$

$$(1)$$

where F is an objective function, S^* is the summary which maximizes F with an adopted optimization method, S is a candidate summary, c_i is the cost of selecting a sentence i into summary, b is the upper bound on the total cost and V is the set of total number of sentences in the corpus.

The current work is inspired by two of the previous works namely (Lin and Bilmes, 2011) and G-Flow (Christensen et al., 2013). Lin & Bilmes observed that if the objective function to score candidate summaries is *monotone sub-modular*, a greedy approach can ensure the approximation of the summary at the global maximum by a factor of 0.632 as follows.

$$F(\hat{S}) \geq (1-1/e)*F(S_{opt}) \approx 0.632*F(S_{opt}) \quad (2)$$

where $\hat{S}$ is the summary obtained from monotone sub-modular function F and S_{opt} is the summary at the global maximum of F.

G-Flow aimed at generating coherent summaries by constructing a sentence-level discourse graph for the entire corpus and the information from the graph is utilized to quantify the coherence of candidate summaries. In a short summary space, the sentences which structurally depend on other sentences are not encouraged. So the summaries are more comprehensible than those produced by the systems which blindly aim at achieving maximum content coverage. The need to create a discourse graph can be a big hurdle to scale the summarizer to large data sets. Also the scoring function of G-Flow is not monotone sub-modular and cannot guarantee the approximation of optimum summary as per the relation 2. *The space of current work is to establish a scheme for comprehensible summarization with a monotone sub-modular objective function.* Within the scope of this paper, when we say comprehensibility we mean **how much relevant structural context does each sentence have for better conveyability of the discourse intended by the summary.**

In the current work, we try to assign a score for each sentence based on its level of contextual independence (discussed in subsequent sections). The particular score is combined as a linear component in the candidate summary scoring function of Lin and Bilmes (Lin and Bilmes, 2011) to score sentences. While adding the third component, *monotone sub-modularity* of the scoring function is not disturbed since the contextual independence of individual sentences is constant with respect to a given corpus. We observed an improvement in system-generated summary in terms of human evaluation for comprehensibility while maintaining a reasonable level of content coverage in terms of ROUGE score.

We framed a comprehensibility index to represent the level of comprehensibility of a system generated summary using contextual independence score of individual sentences. Comprehensibility index for the generated summary is **the average contextual independence score of a sentence in the summary**. We verified, through human evaluators, whether the comprehensibility index is actually representative of the human comprehensibility.

2   Previous Work

Identification of locally coherent discourse unit (LDU) and combining the information to create a comprehensible summary is a novel problem which is not attempted by any of the previous works in the field of natural language processing to the best of our knowledge. Barzilay and Lapata(Barzilay and Lapata, 2008) attempt to measure the global coherence in terms of local coherence which is measured in terms of entity role switch while G-Flow(Christensen et al., 2013) came up with a metric to measure the coherence of the generated summary with respect to a corpus level discourse graph. Still, these two works are not directly relevant to local discourse unit identification per se.

Substantial work has been done on extractive summarization which tries to achieve a proper content coverage while reducing the redundancy. Approaches include the use of Maximum Marginal Relevance (Carbonell and Goldstein, 1998), Centroid-based Summarization (Radev et al., 2002), Summarization through Keyphrase Extraction (Qazvinian et al., 2010) and Formulation as Minimum Dominating Set problem (Shen and Li, 2010), Graph centrality to estimate the salience of a sentence (Erkan and Radev, 2004). Approaches to content analysis include generative topic models (Haghighi and Vanderwende, 2009), (Celikyilmaz and Hakkani-Tur, 2010), (Li et al., 2011b) and Discriminative models (Aker et al., 2010), ILP2 (Galanis et al., 2012) Joint Optimization of the Importance and Diversity of summary's sentences (Woodsend and Lapata, 2012), Language Model based scoring function (Takamura and Okumura, 2009) as a maximum concept coverage problem with knapsack constraint(MCKP) (Wong et al., 2008). Lin and Bilmes formulated summarization as a sub-modular function maximization problem in the possible set of candidate summaries with due respect to the summary space constraint (Lin and Bilmes, 2011).

3   Contextual Independence

Identifying whether a sentence is contextually independent or not is an important step in our approach to summarization. By Contextual Independence of a sentence, we mean that the sentence can be *globally understood even when the sentences preceding/following it are not available to the reader*. Contextual dependence, signifies only the structural dependence of a sentence in a local discourse context, not the topical dependence. Topical coherence can be captured by other parameters of optimization function used for generating summary. Take a look at the below example.

1. But it never continued after the first world war.

2. The Prime Minister of France reached Delhi yesterday.

In sentence 1, it is almost impossible to make full sense of the sentence unless the anaphor 'it' is resolved. 'But' reveals a contrast relation with the previous unmentioned sentence and therefore highly contextually dependent. Whereas a sentence like 2 can safely stand alone and convey a meaningful information even if sufficient context is not revealed. In our current work, an attempt has been made to quantify this contextual independence of a sentence in terms of surface level, generic features which are described in subsection 4.1. Based on these features we arrived at a quantified score that denotes the probability of a sentence to be contextually independent.

4 Approach

4.1 LDU identification for measuring contextual independence

Any sentence can be identified to have a contextual dependence with another sentence based on some syntactic cues that trigger the discourse coherence. For example, a pronoun in the subject or object position of a clause in a sentence can more likely be an anaphora to a previous sentence. But extraction of such granular features and clause boundaries requires syntactic parsed output of every sentence in a document which is an overhead for the summarization system. Therefore, we have modelled the contextual independence identification of every sentence in a document as a sequence labelling problem using surface level features such as such as POS labels, unigram/bigram sequences of discourse connectives learnt across 3 windows of W words each. For any given sentence, we maximally take the first $3W$ words and divide them into three windows and compute the six features mentioned in Table 1 from each window.

Each of the six features signals contextual dependence. Computing these features along three windows of W words each is intended to statistically generalize that the features are located and computed across different clauses in a sentence. For instance, if a pronoun in one clause is resolved in the subsequent clause within the same sentence, one can safely conclude that the sentence is contextually independent. Instead of explicitly identifying the clause boundary and verifying if the anaphora is resolved within the sentence, one can generalize that if the first window does not begin with a pronoun and total number of pronouns is greater than the total number of Named Entities in the $3W$ word group, it is more likely to be resolved within the same sentence as an anaphora or cataphora. As another illustration, take for example determiners such as *the* modifying a noun as a part of prepositional phrase such as *the people from London*; the determiner 'the' in this phrase does not create any contextual depen-

dence. This knowledge can be learnt by tracking whether the definite determiner in one window is followed by the presence of preposition in the beginning of another window. Thus the count of each of the features mentioned in Table 1 and the W word window boundaries are both crucial to classify a sentence as contextually dependent/independent. W is varied experimentally and empirically fixed as 5.

Every locally coherent discourse unit is made up of one contextually independent sentence followed by a sequence of contextually dependent sentences and hence CRF(Lafferty et al., 2001) sequence labelling algorithm is used for learning the LDUs and in turn the sequence of LDUs in an input document. The features used for contextual independence estimation are shown in Table 1.

Feature	Description
DConnect	List of commonly occurring discourse connectives
PRPcount	Count of number of pronouns
NEcount	Count of number of named entities
CC	Coordinating conjunctions
WhCount	Question words in an interrogative sentence
NounPhrase	Presence of noun phrases starting with *the*

Table 1: Feature Selection

The model predicts the probability of contextual independence of a sentence which is later used in the scoring function. The contextual dependencies include anaphors/referents, discourse connectives and determiners. The common POS tags or sequence of POS tags that signal such discourse functions are identified to be PRP, CC, DT, WP, RB, IN, TO. The reason for the choice of the features listed out in Table 1 is explained below:

DConnect and CC - Typically, a structural connection between one sentence to the next is triggered by conjunctions such as *also, nevertheless, however, but*, discourse connectives such as *for instance, in addition, according to*. These connectives usually occur at the beginning of a sentence and the features attempt to capture that in the first window.

PRPcount and NECount - Number of Pronouns and the named Entities in a 15 word group. Their relative counts together with the fact of whether they occur in initial positions of first window helps in classification

WhCount - Question words in an interrogative sentence is a marker of contextual dependency

Using the above features we are able to model the

identification of contextual independence without resorting to the overhead associated with full syntactic parsing.

4.2 Leveraging Contextual Independence Measure for Summarization

The contextual independence score of a sentence can be useful in two ways. One is to add the score as a bias term in the candidate summary scoring function and another is to exploit the same score for calculating the comprehensibility index.

4.2.1 Adding a bias term in candidate summary scoring function

Lin and Bilmes suggested a scoring function which contains weighted linear components to capture content coverage and topical diversity of the summary (Lin and Bilmes, 2011). The scoring function is given below.

$$F(S) = L_1(S) + \lambda_1 * R_1(S) \qquad (3)$$

F is a monotone sub-modular function which guarantees the approximation of optimum summary by a factor of 0.632 using a greedy approach. The contextual independence of a sentence is added as a bias to the scoring function to enable the selection of contextually independent candidate sentences in the generated summary. The new scoring function is given below :

$$F(S) = L_1(S) + \lambda_1 * R_1(S) + \lambda_2 * CI(S) \qquad (4)$$

Here $L_1(S)$, $R_1(S)$ and $CI(S)$ are given by equations 5, 6 and 7 respectively,

$$L_1(S) = \sum_{i \in V} min\{\sum_{j \in S} w_{i,j}, \alpha \sum_{k \in V} w_{i,k}\} \qquad (5)$$

where $L_1(S)$ is the coverage function, $w_{i,j}$ is the TF-IDF cosine similarity between sentences i and j, V is the set of all sentences in the corpus, S is the set of sentences in a candidate summary, α is a learned parameter.

$$R_1(S) = \sum_{k=1}^{K} \sqrt{\sum_{j \in S \cap P_k} \frac{1}{N} \sum_{i \in V} w_{i,j}} \qquad (6)$$

where $R_1(S)$ is the diversity function, N is the total no. of documents in the corpus, $P_1, P_2, ...P_k$ are

sentence clusters formed out of applying k-means clustering on the set of sentences in the corpus with TF-IDF cosine similarity as the similarity metric.

$$CI(S) = \sum_{s \in S} CI(s) \qquad (7)$$

where $CI(s)$ probability of a sentence s being contextually independent which is obtained from the CRF model in the section 4.1.

As per the model created in section 4.1, the contextual independence of a sentence is a constant and adding it as linear component *will not disturb the monotone sub-modularity of sentence scoring function* used by Lin and Bilmes (Lin and Bilmes, 2011)[1].

4.2.2 Framing a metric for measuring the comprehensibility of generated summary

A summary S having high CI(S) in equation 7 contains more number of Contextually Independent sentences. Therefore CI(S) represents the potential of a summary to render sufficient context for the sentences , such that the reader can grasp the same contextual interpretation from the summary sentence as is conveyed in the actual corpus, without ever reading the full corpus. *The scope of the context is captured by means of Local Discourse Unit to which the sentence belongs in the original corpus.* Instead of adding CI(S) in equation 3 directly in the scoring function, it can be utilised to frame a comprehensibility index to quantify how much a summary generated by any summarization system is comprehensible to the reader.

$$Compreh(S) = \frac{CI(S)}{N} \qquad (8)$$

where Compreh(S) is the comprehensibility index, CI(S) is the contextual independence in equation 7, N is the number of sentences in the summary S.

5 Experiments and Results

We have to separately evaluate the accuracy of LDU identification, improvement of comprehensibility of system-generated summary when Contextual Independence is used as a bias term in summarization

---

[1] λ_1 and α take same values in Lin & Bilmes. With different trials λ_2 is empirically optimized to achieve better comprehensibility and ROUGE score and optimum value is 6

process and how much reliable the comprehensibility index is, as a metric to estimate the comprehensibility of the summary.

5.1 LDU Identification

Size	P	R	F-score	Acc%
2900	0.875	0.886	0.880	91.05

Table 2: Classification

For LDU identification model creation, we have taken a corpus containing narrative documents comprising of 2900 sentences. Two Computational Linguistics students were involved in annotation of the sentences in the corpus as either contextually dependent or independent. We obtained a Kappa score[2] of 0.703 (substantial agreement) between them. We extracted the features mentioned in Table 1 and created a training model using CRF++[3] by using 4-fold cross validation. The average precision (P), recall (R), F-score and Accuracy (Acc) were measured for different training sets and the results are shown in Table 2. The positive classification represents the contextual independence of a sentence.

5.2 CI(S) as a bias term in the scoring function

System	R	F
Nobata & Sekine	30.44	34.36
G-Flow	37.33	37.43
Best system in DUC-04	38.28	37.94
Takamura & Okumura	38.50	-
Lin & Bilmes	39.35	38.90
Our System	37.52	37.05

Table 3: ROUGE

Our System	Lin and Bilmes	Ambiguous
70%	10%	20%

Table 4: Preference of summary based on comprehensibility

By adding the CI(S) as a bias term in the scoring function in equation 3 to form 4, the system is constrained to choose the sentences which exhibit better contextual independence. Thus the equation 3 loses its flexibility in achieving maximum content

---

[2]https://en.wikipedia.org/wiki/Fleiss' kappa
[3]https://taku910.github.io/crfpp/

coverage by the addition of CI(S) as a bias term. We have taken DUC-2004 Task2[4] dataset as our test dataset. The results for content coverage in terms of ROUGE-1 scores are given in Table 3.

The proportional decline in content coverage in terms of ROUGE score is tolerable as shown in the table 3. We have reordered the sentences in summaries generated by our system and summaries generated by Lin and Bilmes (Lin and Bilmes, 2011) implementation using the reordering system proposed by Li et al(Li et al., 2011a). Four students of Computational Linguistics participated in our evaluation experiment where we conveyed them *what we mean by comprehensibility of a summary* as defined in section 1. For each corpus in the dataset, they were made to read the documents in the corpus and asked choose the more comprehensible of the two summaries generated by our system and Lin & Bilmes provided in a random order. Our summary[5] was chosen overwhelmingly more number of times as shown in table 4.

5.3 Evaluation of Comprehensibility Index

To evaluate the comprehensibility index, we have taken into consideration, the summaries generated by Lin& Bilmes (Li et al., 2011a) and G-Flow systems(Christensen et al., 2013) for each of the corpus in DUC-2004 dataset. The four linguists participated in another evaluation experiment where we conveyed them about comprehensibility judgement like in previous experiment. For each corpus in the dataset, they were made to choose the more comprehensible of the two summaries generated by G-Flow and Lin & Bilmes provided in a random order. For the evaluation of the comprehensibility index given by equation 8, we define the accuracy of Comprehensibility Index as the percentage of times the Compreh(S) value was greater for summaries which are chosen by humans unambiguously. The details are provided in table 5. While considering both the experiments involving human evaluators, the agreement between the evaluators was 0.79 in terms of Cohen's kappa measure(Viera et al., 2005). Considering the subjective nature of annotation, we believe

---

[4]http://www-nlpir.nist.gov/projects/duc/data/2004_data.html
[5]the code and annotated data are shared on https://bitbucket.org/littonj97/comprehensum/

% of times G-Flow was chosen	67%
% of times Lin & Bilmes was chosen	13%
Ambiguous	20%
Accuracy of Compreh(S)	79%
Average Compreh(S) for G-Flow	0.73
Average Compreh(S) for Lin& Bilmes	0.54

Table 5: Comprehensibility Index Evaluation Details

this is a reasonably good measure of how informative the human judgements were.

6 Future Work and Conclusion

LDU is identified currently by checking the contextual dependency of the current sentence with only the previous sentence. By using Recurrent Neural Networks this contextual dependency can be learnt beyond the preceding one sentence boundary. Comprehensibility index estimation can be improved by incorporating more information regarding topical context along with local discourse context.

References

Ahmet Aker, Trevor Cohn, and Robert Gaizauskas. 2010. Multi-document summarization using a* search and discriminative training. In *Proceedings of the 2010 conference on empirical methods in natural language processing*, pages 482–491. Association for Computational Linguistics.

Ernst Althaus, Nikiforos Karamanis, and Alexander Koller. 2004. Computing locally coherent discourses. In *Proceedings of the 42nd Annual Meeting on Association for Computational Linguistics*, page 399. Association for Computational Linguistics.

Regina Barzilay and Mirella Lapata. 2008. Modeling local coherence: An entity-based approach. *Computational Linguistics*, 34(1):1–34.

Jaime Carbonell and Jade Goldstein. 1998. The use of mmr, diversity-based reranking for reordering documents and producing summaries. In *Proceedings of the 21st annual international ACM SIGIR conference on Research and development in information retrieval*, pages 335–336. ACM.

Asli Celikyilmaz and Dilek Hakkani-Tur. 2010. A hybrid hierarchical model for multi-document summarization. In *Proceedings of the 48th Annual Meeting of the Association for Computational Linguistics*, pages 815–824. Association for Computational Linguistics.

Janara Christensen, Stephen Soderland Mausam, Stephen Soderland, and Oren Etzioni. 2013. Towards coherent multi-document summarization. In *HLT-NAACL*, pages 1163–1173. Citeseer.

Günes Erkan and Dragomir R Radev. 2004. Lexrank: Graph-based lexical centrality as salience in text summarization. *Journal of Artificial Intelligence Research*, pages 457–479.

Peter W Foltz, Walter Kintsch, and Thomas K Landauer. 1998. The measurement of textual coherence with latent semantic analysis. *Discourse processes*, 25(2-3):285–307.

Dimitrios Galanis, Gerasimos Lampouras, and Ion Androutsopoulos. 2012. Extractive multi-document summarization with integer linear programming and support vector regression. In *COLING*, pages 911–926. Citeseer.

Aria Haghighi and Lucy Vanderwende. 2009. Exploring content models for multi-document summarization. In *Proceedings of Human Language Technologies: The 2009 Annual Conference of the North American Chapter of the Association for Computational Linguistics*, pages 362–370. Association for Computational Linguistics.

Nikiforos Karamanis, Massimo Poesio, Chris Mellish, and Jon Oberlander. 2004. Evaluating centering-based metrics of coherence for text structuring using a reliably annotated corpus. In *Proceedings of the 42nd Annual Meeting on Association for Computational Linguistics*, page 391. Association for Computational Linguistics.

John Lafferty, Andrew McCallum, and Fernando CN Pereira. 2001. Conditional random fields: Probabilistic models for segmenting and labeling sequence data.

Peifeng Li, Guangxi Deng, and Qiaoming Zhu. 2011a. Using context inference to improve sentence ordering for multi-document summarization. In *IJCNLP*, pages 1055–1061.

Peng Li, Yinglin Wang, Wei Gao, and Jing Jiang. 2011b. Generating aspect-oriented multi-document summarization with event-aspect model. In *Proceedings of the Conference on Empirical Methods in Natural Language Processing*, pages 1137–1146. Association for Computational Linguistics.

Hui Lin and Jeff Bilmes. 2011. A class of submodular functions for document summarization. In *Proceedings of the 49th Annual Meeting of the Association for Computational Linguistics: Human Language Technologies-Volume 1*, pages 510–520. Association for Computational Linguistics.

William C Mann and Sandra A Thompson. 1988. Rhetorical structure theory: Toward a functional theory of text organization. *Text-Interdisciplinary Journal for the Study of Discourse*, 8(3):243–281.

Daniel Marcu. 2000. *The theory and practice of discourse parsing and summarization*. MIT press.

Gail McKoon and Roger Ratcliff. 1992. Inference during reading. *Psychological review*, 99(3):440.

Vahed Qazvinian, Dragomir R Radev, and Arzucan Özgür. 2010. Citation summarization through keyphrase extraction. In *Proceedings of the 23rd International Conference on Computational Linguistics*, pages 895–903. Association for Computational Linguistics.

Dragomir Radev, Adam Winkel, and Michael Topper. 2002. Multi document centroid-based text summarization. In *ACL 2002*.

Chao Shen and Tao Li. 2010. Multi-document summarization via the minimum dominating set. In *Proceedings of the 23rd International Conference on Computational Linguistics*, pages 984–992. Association for Computational Linguistics.

Hiroya Takamura and Manabu Okumura. 2009. Text summarization model based on maximum coverage problem and its variant. In *Proceedings of the 12th Conference of the European Chapter of the Association for Computational Linguistics*, pages 781–789. Association for Computational Linguistics.

Anthony J Viera, Joanne M Garrett, et al. 2005. Understanding interobserver agreement: the kappa statistic. *Fam Med*, 37(5):360–363.

Kam-Fai Wong, Mingli Wu, and Wenjie Li. 2008. Extractive summarization using supervised and semi-supervised learning. In *Proceedings of the 22nd International Conference on Computational Linguistics-Volume 1*, pages 985–992. Association for Computational Linguistics.

Kristian Woodsend and Mirella Lapata. 2012. Multiple aspect summarization using integer linear programming. In *Proceedings of the 2012 Joint Conference on Empirical Methods in Natural Language Processing and Computational Natural Language Learning*, pages 233–243. Association for Computational Linguistics.

Phylogenetic simulations over constraint-based grammar formalisms

Andrew Lamont and **Jonathan North Washington**
Indiana University
{alamont,jonwashi}@indiana.edu

Abstract

Computational phylogenetics has been shown to be effective over grammatical characteristics. Recent work suggests that constraint-based formalisms are compatible with such an approach (Eden, 2013). In this paper, we report on simulations to determine how useful constraint-based formalisms are in phylogenetic research and under what conditions.

1 Introduction

Popular computational methods for phylogenetic research (estimating the evolutionary histories of languages) primarily involve comparisons over cognate sets (Nichols and Warnow, 2008). Recent works (Dunn et al., 2005; Longobardi and Guardiano, 2009) indicate that comparing sets of grammatical parameters can be effective as well. However, generating a large number of meaningful parameters remains a formal obstacle. In this paper we argue that constraint-based grammar formalisms may be exploited for parameter generation, and explore to what extent such research is feasible.

Because the use of constraint-based grammars in phylogenetics is relatively novel, we do not know *a posteriori* how many constraints and how many languages must be considered for a computational approach to be successful. If a minimum threshold is established that is methodologically prohibitive (e.g. if such systems were only accurate given a set of 1,000 languages), we can abandon this approach as infeasible. By initially experimenting with simulated data, we establish a footing for future empirical studies.

In this paper, we report on simulations which consistently outperform two baseline models. Significantly, these results obtained with a modest number of constraints $c \geq 4$ and languages $l \geq 4$.

1.1 Grammatical parameters in phylogenetics

Longobardi and Guardiano (2009) argue that grammatical features, such as whether a language expresses a pre- or postpositional genitive, if chosen carefully, present certain advantages over lexically-based comparisons in phylogenetic work. Grammatical parameters comprise a universal set of discrete options applicable to any set of languages, especially within frameworks such as Principle and Parameters (Chomsky, 1981). Using grammatical features for phylogenetic work can be a way to avoid any difficulties associated with the collection and identification of cognate sets.

However, unlike cognate sets, there is no *a priori* assumption that correspondences between parameter settings are meaningful genetically. Instead, meaningful correspondence derives from the low probability that two languages match in a number of parameter settings by chance. Successful work therefore depends on the construction of a large set of grammatical parameters; larger sets are predicted to produce more accurate results.

1.2 Constraint-based grammar formalisms

In constraint-based theories of grammar like Optimality Theory (OT) (Prince and Smolensky, 2004), input-output relations are determined by the interaction of conflicting violable constraints.

To take a common example from phonology, a

Proceedings of NAACL-HLT 2016, pages 102–108,
San Diego, California, June 12-17, 2016. ©2016 Association for Computational Linguistics

language may require that all syllables are open, deleting consonants that would otherwise surface in coda position. In an OT analysis of such a language, the constraint NOCODA, which prohibits codas, dominates the constraint MAX, which prohibits deletion (written NOCODA $\gg$ MAX). This encodes that satisfying NOCODA is more important than satisfying MAX, though there may be additional interacting constraints complicating the analysis.

In an OT framework, the set of constraints, CON, is assumed to be universal—its members typically being grounded in typological and psycholinguistic data. Differences between grammars are encoded as different language-specific rankings of the constraint set.

OT is most often used in phonology, but has been applied widely in various linguistic sub-disciplines, including syntax, sociolinguistics, and semantics (McCarthy, 2008). Constraint-based frameworks can therefore encode diverse grammatical phenomena with minimal representation, a constraint ranking being simply a directed acyclic graph over CON.

With the exception of Eden (2013), constraint-based phylogenetic research has not yet, to our knowledge, been attempted. It remains an open question whether such a representation is useful in phylogenetics and if so, under what conditions.

1.3 Parameterizing CON

Following Longobardi and Guardiano's (2009) parametric approach, we adapt constraint rankings into binary pseudo-parameters, decomposing language-specific rankings into vectors of pairwise dominance relations (Antilla and Cho, 1998):

$$R(C_1, C_2) = \begin{cases} 1 & \text{if } C_1 \gg C_2 \\ 0 & \text{otherwise} \end{cases}$$

That is, for every pair of constraints C_1, C_2, R returns a binary value corresponding to whether C_1 dominates C_2 directly or transitively.[1] An example of a constraint ranking and its corresponding R values is shown is shown in Figure 1.

---

[1] When $R(C_1, C_2)$ returns 0, it ambiguously encodes either a non-relation between C_1 and C_2 or the dominance relation $C_2 \gg C1$. However, because R is not a symmetric relation, this ambiguity is resolved when one considers $R(C_2, C_1)$. Additionally, two constraints C_1, C_2 are unranked relative to one another if $R(C_1, C_2) = R(C_2, C_1) = 0$—i.e., there is no dominance relation, direct or transitive, between C_1 and C_2.

$$C_1 \gg C_2 \gg C_3$$

	C_1	C_2	C_3
C_1	0	1	1
C_2	0	0	1
C_3	0	0	0

$R(C_1, C_1) = 0$
$R(C_1, C_2) = 1$
$R(C_1, C_3) = 1$
$R(C_2, C_1) = 0$
$R(C_2, C_2) = 0$
$R(C_2, C_3) = 1$
$R(C_3, C_1) = 0$
$R(C_3, C_2) = 0$
$R(C_3, C_3) = 0$

Figure 1: A constraint ranking, its representation as a matrix, and as a set of binary pseudo-parameters.

We consider these to be *pseudo*-parameters because certain constraint pairs may only interact under very specific circumstances or not at all. The ranking of NOCODA and MAX, for example, is meaningful under a large number of circumstances: $R(\text{NOCODA}, \text{MAX})$ corresponds to whether a grammar deletes consonants that would otherwise surface in coda position. The ranking of NOCODA and MAX-VOICE (which prohibits deleting a voice feature), on the other hand, is less meaningful because these constraints are not expected to conflict directly (deleting a voice feature does not create an open syllable, and therefore cannot avoid a violation of NOCODA). Nevertheless, $R(\text{NOCODA}, \text{MAX-VOICE})$ may be determined via transitivity. R values therefore range from representations of a language's grammatical characteristics to higher-level artifacts of the theory as applied to its grammar. Weighting R values accordingly may be a fruitful topic for future research.

Pseudo-parameters pose certain advantages. For a set of n constraints, the size of the corresponding set of pseudo-parameters is on the order of n^2. This dramatically increases the number of comparisons one is able to make between languages with a modest number of empirically motivated constraints, as compared to a parameter set *tout court*. Because constructing a set of constraints or parameters is taxing, an approach that maximizes the impact of each additional constraint is advantageous. With pseudo-parameters, constraint $n + 1$ contributes n points of comparison, whereas parameter $n + 1$ contributes only 1 point of comparison.

A theory-internal advantage of this approach is that it faithfully represents even complex constraint rankings. Some models of OT allow for constraints to be unranked. The pseudo-parameter representation handles unranked constraints without issue, thus allowing wide theoretical coverage.

2   Related Work

Computational phylogenetic systems have taken a diverse set of inputs. Subgroup classification using cognate comparisons has been used by Ringe et al. (2002) for Indo-European (IE) and Bowern and Atkinson (2012) for Pama-Nyungan, among others. Both syntactic and phonological grammatical-level information have also been used effectively for computational phylogenetics.

Longobardi and Guardiano (2009) used sixty-three binary syntactic parameters for a phylogeny of twenty-two IE languages and six non-IE languages. Their generated trees largely agreed with the historical relations determined by traditional comparative linguistic methods. In a second experiment using fifteen languages for which lexical data were available, they found large overlap between trees generated using syntactic parameters and lexical data.

Eden (2013) replicated this study using thirteen typologically grounded parameters related to phonological stress over nineteen of the languages used by Longobardi and Guardiano (2009) as well as an additional five, demonstrating that the grammatical parameters need not be limited to the domain of syntax. A second experiment using phonotactic constraints over six languages yielded more variable results than the first experiment. The constraints used were generated by a phonotactic constraint learner (Hayes and Wilson, 2008), which differs from classic OT in several key regards: in this model, constraints are language-specific; constraints are weighted probabilistically, not ranked; and constraints only reference surface forms, not input-output relations. To utilize a single constraint set, the one hundred thirteen highest-weighted constraints that were persistently generated by the phonotactic learner across the six languages were chosen and reweighted in each language. Each language therefore had a grammar consisting of the same set of constraints. The rankings of these constraints were compared using Spearman's correlation coefficient.

Eden's (2013) study broke ground in using constraint-based grammars; however, there were certain limitations. The phonotactic learner requires a representative input corpus of at least 3,000-6,000 words, impeding the incorporation of under-resourced languages. Further, the generated constraint set is problematically language-specific. Only one constraint generated for English, for example, was active in the other five languages.

Our approach diverges from Eden's (2013) theory-internally and in scope. We assume an *a priori* universal constraint set, and our pseudo-parameter approach allows for constraints to be unranked relative to one another. We could in principle measure inter-language distance with rank correlations over topologically sorted constraint rankings, but unranked constraints are predicted to lead to highly variable results. Because our experiments in this study are over simulated languages, we are not limited by available linguistic descriptions.

3   Method

To investigate whether constraint-based formalisms are useful in phylogenetic work and under what assumptions, we conducted a large number of simulations following the procedure described by Nichols and Warnow (2008):

1. Produce a model tree T;
2. T evolves from the root, producing a set of leaves S;
3. S is used as input to the phylogeny estimation procedure, producing T';
4. T' is compared to T to calculate error.

Simulations varied with respect to the number of constraints, the size of S, and the rate of evolution.[2]

3.1   Model Tree

In these simulations, CON is defined as a set of c constraints $C_1, C_2, \ldots, C_c$. The model tree T (gold standard) is initialized with a root-node language consisting of a randomly generated full ranking of CON such that every constraint is ranked relative to every other constraint: $C_{(1)} \gg C_{(2)} \gg \ldots \gg C_{(c)}$. For c constraints, there are $c!$ possible full rankings. From this root-node, T evolves into a larger tree.

3.2   Tree Evolution

In our simulations, language change is modeled by constraint reranking (Cho, 1998), although this oversimplifies the complex processes observed in actual

---

[2]Our code and full numerical results are available at `https://github.com/lmaoaml/recon`.

data.[3] T evolves accordingly. At each evolutionary step, a leaf language either randomly changes or splits into two daughter languages inheriting the same constraint ranking according to the branching probability b.[4] The lower b is, the more changes on average a language will undergo before branching. A change entails either the addition or removal of a domination relation between two random constraints. Evolution continues until T contains a predetermined minimum number of leaves.

3.3 Phylogeny Estimation

The constraint rankings of the languages in the set of leaves S are decomposed into pseudo-parameter vectors. Inter-language distance is calculated by taking the Euclidean distance between vectors. We use Euclidean distance because it has been reported to perform well among fifteen vector similarity measures of typological distance (Rama and Prasanth, 2012), and our initial experiments found no major differences between measures. The inter-language distances serve as input to the phylogeny estimation procedure.

Because tree evolution in our model proceeds according to a lexical clock (i.e., changes accumulate over time)—or more precisely a grammatical clock—we use the Unweighted Pair Group Method with Arithmetic mean (UPGMA), a hierarchical clustering method that utilizes the average distance between clusters, as a phylogeny estimation procedure (Nichols and Warnow, 2008). For speed, we use the implementation in fastcluster (Müllner, 2013) with average linkage. The result of phylogeny estimation is a binary tree T', which is compared to T to measure accuracy.

3.4 Evaluation

Because we have access to T, the gold standard tree, we diverge from the partially qualitative evaluations of Longobardi and Guardiano (2009) and Eden (2013) and adopt a purely quantative evaluation metric based on precision and recall (van Rijsbergen, 1979). As in standard precision and recall, we measure the proportion of correct items relative

to T' and T respectively. We define correct items to be matching subtrees rooted by internal nodes as shown in Figure 2. Two subtrees are counted as matching if they dominate the same set of leaves.

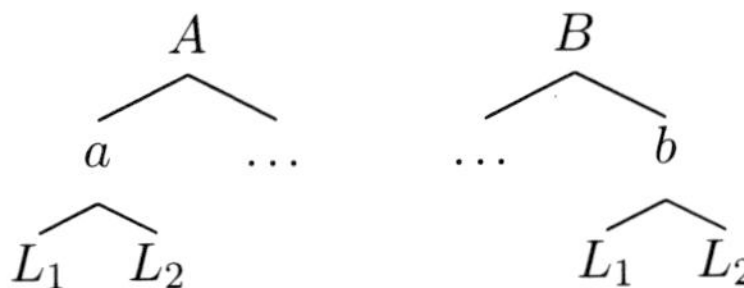

Figure 2: Subtree a in A matches subtree b in B.

T' is then compared against two null hypothesis baseline trees, BF and BR.

BF is a flat tree composed of a single internal node dominating the entire set of languages S as in Figure 3. BF encodes the empirical null hypothesis that S contains no subgroups.

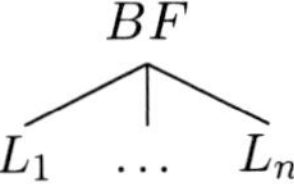

Figure 3: A random baseline tree BF with n leaves

BR is a randomly constructed binary tree encoding the null hypothesis that the phylogeny estimation procedure does not outperform chance groupings.

Precision and recall are calculated between T and the three test trees. We consider an experiment successful when T' is more accurate than BF and BR.

4 Results

Simulations were run across a wide range of settings. The number of constraints ranged exponentially from 2 to 64. The number of languages likewise ranged exponentially from 2 to 128. For each setting pair, we report precision and recall for BF, BR, and T' averaged over 1,000 independent iterations. Simulations were run with branching probability b set to 0.1, 0.01, and 0.001, as shown in Figure 4. Low branching probabilities yield more differences even between closely related languages (in the authors' opinion, this more accurately reflects actual language data).

Overall, the simulations were successful, albeit modestly. T' had a higher recall than BF and a higher precision and recall than BR in all cases except simulations with 2 constraints and 4 languages. The margin between T' and BR is promising - it indicates that this method can yield positive results.

---

[3] See Holt (2015) for an overview of approaches to language change in OT.

[4] T is limited to binary branching for simplicity, but this is not a necessary assumption for the methodology.

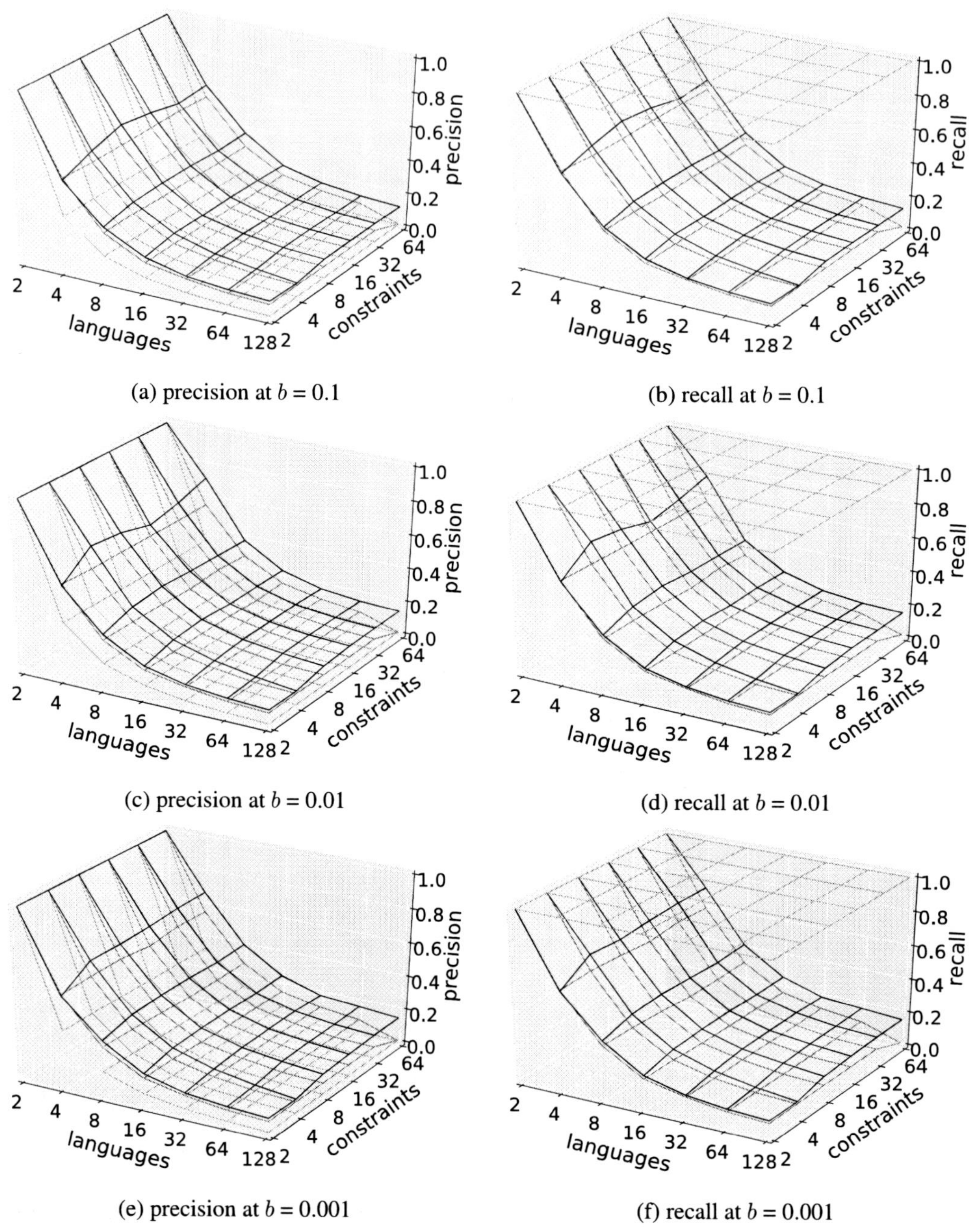

(a) precision at $b = 0.1$

(b) recall at $b = 0.1$

(c) precision at $b = 0.01$

(d) recall at $b = 0.01$

(e) precision at $b = 0.001$

(f) recall at $b = 0.001$

Figure 4: Precision and recall of BF (⸺), BR (⸺), and T' (⸺) with $b = 0.1$, $b = 0.01$, and $b = 0.001$.

5   Discussion

With 2 languages, as modeled in Figure 5, all hypotheses have perfect precision and recall. For T' and BR, because the order of the leaves does not matter, there is only one way to group 2 languages. Similarly, because there is not additional internal structure, BF has perfect recall. Trivially, BF always has perfect precision because the entire tree is the only subtree it identifies.

Figure 5: A tree A with two leaf nodes

As is expected, neither BF nor BR are affected by the number of constraints or b. However, as the number of languages increases, the probability that BR correctly identifies substructure decreases.

The accuracy of T' does interact with the numbers of constraints and languages as well as with b.

There is an overall trend that T' is more accurate with larger numbers of constraints, in accordance with the trend that phylogenetic algorithms' performances correlate with the amount of available data. This is especially clear when $b = 0.001$. Extending this method to real language data is expected to produce more accurate results with a larger number of constraints; however, this effect plateaus. Even with as few as eight constraints, our method scores around .100 higher precision and recall than BR. Ranking a set of eight constraints is within the scope of typical OT analyses.

The accuracy of T' negatively correlates with b, indicating that more grammatical distance is useful. This makes sense, as innovative traits passed down through subtrees aid in grouping.

Both precision and recall of T' decrease as the number of languages increases. We expect recall to decrease as the number of subtrees in T increases, which is the case with BF. Likewise, with more possible subtrees, the clustering algorithm makes more mistakes, leading to lower precision. These mistakes may additionally follow from the clustering method. With a large number of languages, the diversity within clusters may be especially large, leading to similar average distances between clusters, which can result in unpredictable performance

of the linkage function. However, the effect of number of languages is not more pronounced with smaller values of b. With smaller b, there are more changes to the languages and we might expect more diversity. If this is an effect of the algorithm, we expect more error high in the tree than at the leaf level. It would be worthwhile to experiment with different linkage functions at different levels in the tree.

Our method assumes that all constraint rerankings are equally likely, which is not the case in real languages; e.g., phonological evolution is frequently shaped by phonetic biases. Given that our method was successful, we anticipate that incorporating known diachronic biases will radically improve performance on natural language data.

6   Conclusion and Future Work

Our method yielded positive results for the simulations reported on in this paper. This suggests that constraint-based formalisms may be used successfully in computational phylogenetics, though this remains to be verified with natural language data. These experiments serve to establish a baseline for the use of constraint-based grammars in phylogenetic research. We believe that the results show promise for the addition of constraint-based research to the phylogenetic toolkit, though additional work is required to fully understand its usefulness.

In the future, we plan to examine the effect of different clustering algorithms, and extend this approach to actual language data. One propitious domain is the phonology of stress, because a large number of languages have already been analysed using a set of 14 core constraints (Kager, 1999). Furthermore, it presents an opportunity to compare directly a constraint-based approach with a parametric approach, such as Eden's (2013) phylogenetic results based on stress parameters.

Acknowledgements

For their helpful discussion and feedback, we thank Noor Abo Mokh, Daniel Dakota, Sandra Kübler, Lwin Moe, Larry Moss, Dragomir Radev, and audiences at the Workshop on Computational Phonology and Morphology 2015 and the CLingDing discussion group at Indiana University, as well as three anonymous reviewers.

References

Arto Antilla and Young-mee Yu Cho. 1998. Variation and change in optimality theory. *Lingua*, 104(1-2):31–56.

Claire Bowern and Quentin Atkinson. 2012. Computational phylogenetics and the internal structure of pama-nyungan. *Language*, 88(4):817–845.

Young-mee Yu Cho. 1998. Language change as reranking of constraints. In Richard M. Hogg and Linda van Bergen, editors, *Historical Linguistics 1995: Volume 2: Germanic linguistics*, pages 45–62. John Benjamins Publishing Company, Amsterdam/Philadelphia.

Noam Chomsky. 1981. *Lectures on Government and Binding*. Foris Publications, Holland.

Michael Dunn, Angela Terrill, Ger Reesink, Robert A. Foley, and Stephen C. Levinson. 2005. Structural phylogenetics and the reconstruction of ancient language history. *Science*, 309(5743):2072.

Elizabeth Eden. 2013. Measuring language distance through phonology: parameters or constraints? *UCL Working Papers in Linguistics*, 25:222–250.

Bruce Hayes and Colin Wilson. 2008. A maximum entropy model of phonotactics and phonotactic learning. *Linguistic Inquiry*, 39(3):379–440.

D. Eric Holt. 2015. Historical sound change in optimality theory: Achievements and challenges. In Patrick Honeybone and Joseph Salmons, editors, *The Oxford Handbook of Historical Phonology*, chapter 31, pages 545–562. Oxford University Press, Oxford.

René Kager. 1999. *Optimality Theory*. Cambridge University Press, Cambridge.

Giuseppe Longobardi and Christina Guardiano. 2009. Evidence for syntax as a signal of historical relatedness. *Lingua*, 119(11):1679–1706.

John J. McCarthy. 2008. *Doing Optimality Theory: Applying Theory to Data*. Blackwell Publishing, Malden, MA.

Daniel Müllner. 2013. fastcluster: Fast hierarchical, agglomerative clustering routines for R and Python. *Journal of Statistical Software*, 53(9):1–18.

Johanna Nichols and Tandy Warnow. 2008. Tutorial on computational linguistic phylogeny. *Language and Linguistics Compass*, 2(5):760–820.

Alan Prince and Paul Smolensky. 2004. *Optimality Theory: Constraint Interaction in Generative Grammar*. Blackwell Publishing.

Taraka Rama and Kolachina Prasanth. 2012. How good are typological distances for determining genealogical relationships among languages? *Proceedings of COLING 2012; Posters*, pages 975–984.

Don Ringe, Tandy Warnow, and Ann Taylor. 2002. Indoeuropean and computational cladistics. *Transactions of the Philological Society*, 100(1):59–129.

C. J. van Rijsbergen. 1979. *Information Retrieval*. Butterworth-Heinemann, Newton, MA, USA, 2nd edition.

Question Answering over Knowledge Base using Factual Memory Networks

Sarthak Jain
Department of Computer Engineering
Delhi Technological University
DL, India
successar@gmail.com

Abstract

In the task of question answering, Memory Networks have recently shown to be quite effective towards complex reasoning as well as scalability, in spite of limited range of topics covered in training data. In this paper, we introduce Factual Memory Network, which learns to answer questions by extracting and reasoning over relevant facts from a Knowledge Base. Our system generate distributed representation of questions and KB in same word vector space, extract a subset of initial candidate facts, then try to find a path to answer entity using multi-hop reasoning and refinement. Additionally, we also improve the run-time efficiency of our model using various computational heuristics.

1 Introduction

Open-domain question answering (Open QA) is a longstanding problem that has been studied for decades. Early systems took an information retrieval approach, where question answering is reduced to returning passages of text containing an answer as a substring. Recent advances in constructing large-scale knowledge bases (KBs) have enabled new systems that return an exact answer from a KB.

A key challenge in Open QA is to be robust to the high variability found in natural language and the many ways of expressing knowledge in large-scale KBs. Another challenge is to link the natural language of questions with structured semantics of KBs. In this paper, we present a novel architecture based on memory networks (Bordes et al., 2015) that can be trained end-to-end using (question, answer) pairs as training set, instead of strong supervision in the form of (question, associated facts in KB) pairs.

The major contributions of this paper are two-fold: first, we introduce factual memory networks, which are used to answer questions in natural language (e.g *"Where was Bill Gates born?"*) using facts stored in the form of (subject, predicate, object) triplets in a KB (e.g *('Bill Gates', 'place of birth', 'Seattle')*). We evaluate our system against current baselines on various benchmark datasets. Since KBs can be extremely large, making it computationally inefficient to search over all entities and paths, our second goal of this paper is to increase the efficiency of our model in terms of various performance measures and provide better coverage of relevant facts, by intelligently selecting which nodes to expand.

2 Related Work

The state-of-the-art methods for QA over a knowledge base can be classified into three classes: semantic parsing, information retrieval and embedding based.

Semantic parsing (Cai and Yates, 2013; Berant et al., 2013; Kwiatkowski et al., 2013; Berant and Liang, 2014; Fader et al., 2014) based approaches aim to learn semantic parsers which parse natural language questions into logical forms and then query knowledge base to lookup answers. Even though these approaches are difficult to train at scale because of the complexity of their inference, they tend to provide a deep interpretation of the question.

Information retrieval based systems retrieve a set of candidate answers and then conduct further analysis to rank them. Their main difference lies in select-

109

Proceedings of NAACL-HLT 2016, pages 109–115,
San Diego, California, June 12-17, 2016. ©2016 Association for Computational Linguistics

ing correct answers from the candidate set. Yao and Van Durme (2014) used rules to extract question features from dependency parse of questions, and used relations and properties in the retrieved topic graph as knowledge base features.

Embedding based approaches (Bordes et al., 2014b; Bordes et al., 2014a) learn low-dimensional vectors for words and knowledge base constitutes, and use the sum of these vectors to represent questions and candidate answers. However, simple vector addition ignores word order information and higher order n-grams. For example, the question representations of *"who killed A?"* and *"who A killed?"* are same in the vector addition model. (Bordes et al., 2015) used strong supervision signal in form of supporting facts for a question during training to improve their performance.

3   Preprocessing KB and Questions

3.1   Processing FREEBASE

Freebase : Freebase (Bollacker et al., 2008) is a huge and freely available database of factual information, organized as triplets (subject Entity, Relationship, object Entity). All Freebase entities and relationships are typed and the lexicon for types and relationships is closed. Each entity has an internal id and a set of alternative names (called aliases, e.g. JFK for John Kennedy) that can refer to that entity in text.

The overall structure of Freebase is a hypergraph, in which more than two entities can be linked together in a n-ary fact. The underlying triple storage involves dummy entities to represent such facts, effectively making actual entities involved linked through paths of length 2, instead of 1. For example, a statement like *"A starred as character B in movie C"* is represented in Freebase as (A, 'starring', dummy entity), (dummy entity, 'movie', C), (dummy entity, 'character', B), where dummy entity has same internal id in all three facts.

To obtain direct links between entities in such cases, we modify these facts by removing the dummy entities and using the second relationship as the relationship for the new condensed facts. In our example, we condense aforementioned facts into two : (A, 'character', B) and (A, 'movie', C). Also, we label these condensed facts as siblings of each other. Therefore, (A, 'character', B) is **sibling** of (A, 'movie', C) and vice versa. Moving forward, we use the term 'fact' to refer to a triplet in Freebase, containing actual entities only (no dummy entities).

After above preprocessing, we represent each entity and relationship in KB as a vector $\in \mathbb{R}^d$. Each such entity/relationship vector is computed as the average of its word vectors, where each word vector $\in \mathbb{R}^d$. In case of entities, we also include word vectors of all its aliases when calculating the average. Such a scheme has the additional advantage that we can benefit from pre-trained unsupervised word vectors (e.g. from Word2Vec), which in general capture some distributional syntactic and semantic information.

3.2   Processing Question

Let a question be given as sequence of words $(x_1, x_2, \ldots, x_{|q|})$. Each word x_i mapped to its word vector. We experimented with two different ways to compose the question embedding q out of these word-vectors:

Bag-of-words (BOW): It is sum of individual word vectors i.e. $q = \sum_{i=1}^{|q|} x_i$.

Position Encoding (PE): This heuristic take in account order of words in the question. The embedding is of form $q = \sum_{i=1}^{|q|} l_i \odot x_i$ where $\odot$ is an element-wise multiplication. For each i, l_i is a column vector $\in \mathbb{R}^d$ with the structure $l_{ij} = \min(\frac{i \times d}{j \times |q|}, \frac{j \times |q|}{i \times d})$, where d is the dimension of the embedding and j runs from 1 to d. This type of function ensures that initial part of summed vector is weighed higher for initial word vectors and vice versa. Thus, a statement like 'Who is parent of Darth Vader?' will map to a different embedding than statement like 'Who is Darth Vader parent of?'.

4   Model Description

4.1   Fact Extraction

To begin, we generate an initial list of facts (called candidate fact list) which is fed as input to our network. To generate this list, we match all possible n-grams of words of the question to aliases of Freebase entities and discard all n-grams (and their matched entities) that are a subsequence of another n-gram. All facts having one of the remaining entities as subject are added to candidate fact list.

4.2 Factual Memory Network

A L-Hop Factual Memory Network consists of L Computation Layers $C_1 \ldots C_L$ connected one after another in a linear chain, and an Output Function. The initial Computation Layer C_1 takes as input the candidate fact list (from previous step) and the initial question embedding (from Section 3.2). The Output Function takes as input the output of final Computation Layer C_L and generates a list of answers (in form of Freebase entities). Layer C_i takes as input the output of layer C_{i-1}.

4.2.1 Computation Layer

A Computation layer accesses two inputs : 1) a fact list (our 'memory') $F = \{f_1 \ldots f_{|F|}\}$, where each fact f is of form (s, R, o), s and o being the entity vectors and R the relationship vector, 2) a question embedding $q \in \mathbb{R}^d$. For each fact $f \in F$, we calculate an unnormalised score $g(f)$ and a normalized score $h(f)$.

We visualize a fact $f = (s, R, o)$ as a question-answer pair with (s, R) forming the question and o the answer. Therefore, $g(f)$ calculates similarity between the given question embedding and a hypothetical question of form $q' = (s, R)$.

$$g(f) = q^T(s + R) \tag{1}$$

For example, given a question q = *"Where was Bill Gates born?"* and a fact f = ('Bill Gates', 'place of birth', 'Seattle'), $g(f)$ will compute similarity between the question q and a hypothetical question q' of form *"Bill Gates place of birth?"*.

In case a fact f has some siblings $b_1, b_2, \ldots, b_k$ (Section 3.1), we re-calculate its $g(f)$ as follows:

$$g(f) = \text{average}(g(f), g(b_1), g(b_2), \ldots, g(b_k)) \tag{2}$$

where $g(f)$ on RHS is calculated using Eq.(1). For each sibling b_i, we calculate $g(b_i)$ using Eq.(1), but with b_i's subject replaced by its object in the formula.

Continuing with example in Section 3.1, if f = (A,'character',B) and b_1 = (A,'movie',C) is sibling of f, then this kind of processing is helpful in answering questions like *"What character does A play in movie C?"*, where fact f alone would not be enough to answer the question. Thus, above processing corresponds to a hypothetical question of form *"A character C movie ?"* for the fact f.

The normalized score $h(f)$ for a fact f is calculated using softmax function over all facts to determine their relative importance.

$$h(f) = \frac{exp(g(f))}{\sum_{f' \in F} exp(g(f'))} \tag{3}$$

Next we modify the fact list and the question embedding on basis of above calculated scores.

Step 1. Fact Pruning: We choose a threshold value ϵ and remove facts from fact list with $h(f) < \epsilon$. We found in our experiments that setting $\epsilon = \frac{\max_{f' \in F} h(f)}{2}$ gives best results. Performing pruning seems to remove non-relevant facts from subsequent computation, significantly improving our response time and allowing us to explore larger search space around the subgraphs of our question entities.

Step 2. The question embedding is modified as follows:

$$q' = q + \sum_{f \in F} h(f)(s + R) \tag{4}$$

Each such modification allows us to incorporate knowledge gathered (in form of hypothetical questions (s, R), weighted by their relevance h) at a particular layer about the question and pass it on to subsequent layer.

Step 3. Fact Addition: For each object entity o belonging to a fact f, we find all the facts (o, R', o') connected to it in KB and assign a score $h(f)q'^T(o + R')$ to each of them. If the new fact's score is $> \epsilon$, it is added to the fact list, effectively increasing path-length of our search space by 1.

The modified fact list along with the new question embedding(q') form the outputs of this layer, which are fed as input to next Computation Layer or the Output function.

4.2.2 Output Function

Output Function takes as input the output of final Computation Layer C_L (i.e. its output fact list and q') and calculate scores $h(f)$. The answer set is formed by the object entity of highest scoring fact as well as object entities of all those facts that have same s **and** R **as the highest scoring fact**.

This simple heuristic can increase utility of our model when there are multiple correct answers for a question. For example, a question like *'Who is*

Anakin Skywalker father of?' has more than one answer entities i.e. [*'Leia Organa', 'Luke Skywalker'*], and they are all linked by same s ('Anakin Skywalker') and R ('children') in Freebase. Of course, this follows the assumption that all such facts survive till this stage and atleast one of them is highest scoring fact.

4.3 Training Objectives

Let the QA training set $\mathcal{D}$ be set of question-answer pairs (q, A), where q is the question with list of correct answers A, e.g. (q = *'Who is Anakin Skywalker father of?'*, A = [*'Leia Organa', 'Luke Skywalker'*]). To train our parameters, we minimize the following loss function:

$$L_{QA} = \sum_{(q,A)} \sum_{n=1}^{L} \frac{n}{L} \|\,|F_n| \sum_{a \in A} a - |A| \sum_{f \in F_n} h(f).o\,\|^2 \tag{5}$$

Here n refers to n-th Computation Layer in our network (with F_n as its input fact list) and L is total number of Computation layers/hops in the network. This loss function defines the degree to which the object entities in fact list of a given layer are near to given answer list, weighted by $h(f)$, by taking pairwise difference between entities in answer list and objects in fact list. It was observed that minimizing this function gives higher weights to facts in which object entities are similar to answer entities as well as allow our network to generate shorter paths to reach answers from the question.

Paraphrasing Loss: Following previous work such as (Fader et al., 2013; Bordes et al., 2015), we also use the question paraphrases dataset **WikiAnswers**[1] to generalize for words and question patterns which are unseen in the training set of question-answer pairs. We minimize hinge loss so that a question and its paraphrases should map to similar representations. For the paraphrase dataset $\mathcal{P}$ of set of tuples (p, p') where p and p' are paraphrases of each other, the loss is defined as:

$$L_{PP} = \sum_{(p,p')} max\{0, 0.1 - p^T p' + p^T p''\} \tag{6}$$

where p'' is random example in $\mathcal{P}$ that is not a paraphrase of p and 0.1 is the margin hyper-parameter.

Backpropagation is used to calculate gradients while Adagrad was used to perform optimisation using max-norm regularisation. At each time step, a sample is drawn from either $\mathcal{P}$ with probability 0.25 or $\mathcal{D}$ with probability 0.75. If sample from $\mathcal{P}$ is chosen, gradient of L_{PP} is calculated. Otherwise, gradient of L_{QA} is calculated. The only parameters optimised in our model are the word vectors.

5 Experimental Setup

5.1 Baselines

We evaluate our model on following datasets:

WebQuestions[2]: This dataset, introduced in (Berant et al., 2013), contains 5,810 question-answer pairs where answer can be a list of entities, similar to (q, A) pairs described before. It was created by crawling questions through the Google Suggest API, and then obtaining answers using Amazon Mechanical Turk. WebQuestions is built on Freebase since all answers are defined as Freebase entities.

On **WebQuestions**, we evaluate against following baselines : (Berant et al., 2013; Berant and Liang, 2014; Yih et al., 2015) (semantic parsing based methods), (Fader et al., 2013) (uses a pattern matching scheme), (Bordes et al., 2014b; Bordes et al., 2014a; Bordes et al., 2015) (Embedding based approaches). Results of the baselines have been extracted from respective papers, except for (Berant et al., 2013; Berant and Liang, 2014) where we use the code provided by the author to replicate the results[2].

We compare our system in terms of F1 score as computed by the official evaluation script [2] (Berant et al., 2013), which is the average, over all test questions, of the F1-score of the sets of predicted answers.

SimpleQuestions[3]:The SimpleQuestions dataset, introduced in (Bordes et al., 2015), consists of a total of 108,442 questions written in natural language by human English-speaking annotators each paired with a corresponding Freebase fact. Our model only use the answer entity during the training, instead of whole fact. For example, {q = *'Which forest is Fires Creek in?'*, Fact = *'(fires creek, contained by, nantahala national forest)'*} could be data point in SimpleQuestions but we only use {q = *'Which forest is*

---

[1] http://knowitall.cs.washington.edu/paralex/

[2] www-nlp.stanford.edu/software/sempre/
[3] fb.ai/babi

Fires Creek in?', A = ['nantahala national forest']} for training.

On **SimpleQuestions**, we evaluate against previous result (Bordes et al., 2015) in terms of path-level accuracy, in which a prediction is correct if the subject and the relationship of highest scoring fact were correctly retrieved by the system.

5.2 Experimental Setup

The current dump of Freebase data was downloaded[4] and processed as described before. Our data contained 1.9B triplets. We used following splits of each evaluation dataset for training, validation and testing, same as (Bordes et al., 2015).
WebQuestions (WQ) : [3000, 778, 2032]
SimpleQuestions (SQ) : [75910, 10845, 21687]
We also train on automatic questions generated from the KB, which are essential to learn embeddings for the entities not appearing in either WebQuestions or SimpleQuestions. We generated one training question per fact following the same process as that used in (Bordes et al., 2014a).

The embedding dimension d was chosen 64 and max-norm cutoff was chosen as 4 using validation dataset. We pre-train our word vectors using method described by (Wang et al., 2014) to initialize our embeddings.

We experimented with variations of our model on both test sets. Specifically, we analyze the effect of question encoding (**PE vs BOW**), number of Hops and inclusion of pruning/fact-additions (**P/FA**) in our model. In subsequent section, the word 'significant' implies that the results were statistically significant ($p < 0.05$) with paired T-test

6 Results

The results of our experiments are presented in Table 1. It shows that our best model outperforms considered baselines by about 3% in case of WebQuestions and even comparable to previous results in case of SimpleQuestions. Note that the best performing system for SimpleQuestions used strong supervision (question with supporting fact) while our model used only answer entities associated with a question for training.

---

[4]https://developers.google.com/freebase/data

Setup	WQ F1	SQ Acc
Random Guess	1.9	4.9
(Berant et al., 2013)	31.3	n/a
(Bordes et al., 2014a)	39.2	n/a
(Berant and Liang, 2014)	39.9	n/a
(Yih et al., 2015)	52.5	n/a
(Bordes et al., 2015)	42.2	**63.9**
PE + 3-Hop	**55.6**	59.7
BOW + 3-Hop	48.5	54.6
PE + 2-Hop	53.8	57.3
PE + 1-Hop	47.9	55.2
without P/FA	44.3	53.8

Table 1: Results on Evaluation datasets. Acc = Accuracy

We also give the performance for the variations of our model. Position Encoding improves our performance by 7% on WQ and by 5% on SQ, validating our choice of heuristic. Also, most answers in both datasets can be found within path length of two from candidate fact list, thus a 3-Hop network shows only 2% improvement over 2-Hop network.

	WQ	SQ
Top-2	70.1	68.7
Top-3	76.4	74.5
Top-5	80.3	77.6
Top-10	88.9	85.2

Table 2: Top-K results of our best model on each test set

Top-K Performance: In Table 2, we present the top-k results on both datasets. A large majority of questions can be answered from the top two or three candidates. By providing these alternative results (in addition to the top-ranked candidate) to the user, many questions can be answered correctly.

6.1 Efficiency and Error Analysis

Efficiency: All experiments for this paper were done on an Intel Core i5 CPU @ 2.60GHz, 8GB RAM with average HDD Access time of 12.3 ms. We calculated the Average Response time / Query (ART/Q), defined as average time taken by the system from input of query till the generation of answer list, including both computational and search-and-access time for KB. ART/Q for 1, 2 and 3 Hop Networks was 200, 350 and 505 ms respectively. Also the training time (including time to search for hyper-parameters) for each of these networks was 740, 1360 and 2480 min respectively.

The major bottleneck in ART/Query for our network was the search-and-access of large amount of KB Data, therefore we implemented efficient search procedures using Prefix Trees for String Matching and pipelined different stages of the model using multi-threading (i.e. Fact Extraction, Computation and Back-Propagation were performed on individual threads) to improve our response and training time.

Effect of Pruning/Fact-Additions : From Table 1, we can see that pruning and fact-additions have significantly improved scores on all datasets. We analyzed 200 random data points from set of examples that were correctly answered only when P/FA was used (for each test set). In 97.5% of these samples, we observed that pruning allowed our model to remove spurious facts generated during initial fact extraction, making soft-max calculation in Eq. (3) more robust.

We also observed that the set of correctly answered questions using model without P/FA was proper subset of one with P/FA on each evaluation dataset, signifying that if relevant facts were scored higher in previous Computation layers, their scores are not reduced as more facts are added in subsequent layers. Removing pruning alone didn't improve our performance by more than 0.4% on any dataset while exponentially increasing the response time, signifying that pruning itself didn't remove relevant/correct fact in majority of examples.

On the computational end, we tried to determine the effect of pruning on our model response time (excluding search and access time). Including pruning improved our ART/Q by approximately 44% during test phase and by 21% during training phase for our 3 Hop network.

Manual Error Analysis : We sampled 100 examples from each test set to identify major sources of errors made by our model. Following classes of errors were determined :

Complex Questions (55%) : These types of questions involved temporal or superlative qualifier like 'first', 'after', 'largest', etc. This problem occurred in both test sets. We may be able to solve this problem using small set of rules for comparison on final answer set or better semantic representations for numerical values and qualifiers.

Question Ambiguity (20%) : This error class contains those questions that may have ambiguity in their interpretation. For example, a question like 'Where is shakira from?' generated answer as 'place_of_birth' (Baranquilla) while ground truth is 'nationality' (Colombia). This occurred mostly in WebQuestions dataset.

Ground truth Inconsistency (10%) : This type of error occurred when ground truth differed from correct entity present in Freebase KB (even though both are correct in many cases). For example, the question 'Where did eleanor roosevelt died?' have ground truth as 'New York City' whereas KB delivers the entity 'Manhattan', even though both are entities in Freebase. It occurred only in WebQuestions dataset.

Miscellaneous (15%) : This error class contains bad entity/relationship extraction (for example, mapping Anakin Skywalker to Darth Vader), bad question/answer pairs (e.g. q = "what time does american horror story air?" A = [Tom Selleck]), Typos in Question, etc.

7   Conclusion

This paper presents a Factual Memory Network model that aims to perform question-answering using facts from Knowledge bases like Freebase. The system uses a multi-hop neural network that can perform reasoning over facts generated from named entities in a given question as well as traverse the knowledge graph to include more information.

In future, we hope to extend our system so that it can work better with n-ary relations present in Freebase to deal with qualifiers, improve entity disambiguation mechanism in our model as well as include a mechanism to involve user interaction with system to improve our rates. Another goal is to add support for KBs with noisy data generated through automated relation extraction from unstructured data (for example OLLIE, etc) as well as for unstructured sources of knowledge (like Wikipedia) in our model, to extend and improve its utility.

References

Hannah Bast and Elmar Haussmann. 2015. More accurate question answering on freebase. In *Proceedings* of the 24th ACM International on Conference on Information and Knowledge Management, pages 1431–1440.

Jonathan Berant and Percy Liang. 2014. Semantic parsing via paraphrasing. In *Proceedings of the 52nd Annual Meeting of the Association for Computational Linguistics*, pages 1415–1425.

Jonathan Berant, Andrew Chou, Roy Frostig, and Percy Liang. 2013. Semantic parsing on freebase from question-answer pairs. In *Proceedings of the 2013 Conference on Empirical Methods in Natural Language Processing*, pages 1533–1544.

Kurt Bollacker, Colin Evans, Praveen Paritosh, Tim Sturge, and Jamie Taylor. 2008. Freebase: a collaboratively created graph database for structuring human knowledge. In *Proceedings of the 2008 ACM SIGMOD international conference on Management of data*, pages 1247–1250.

Antoine Bordes, Sumit Chopra, and Jason Weston. 2014a. Question answering with subgraph embeddings. In *Proceedings of the 2014 Conference on Empirical Methods in Natural Language Processing*, pages 615–620.

Antoine Bordes, Jason Weston, and Nicolas Usunier. 2014b. Open question answering with weakly supervised embedding models. In *Machine Learning and Knowledge Discovery in Databases*, pages 165–180. Springer.

Antoine Bordes, Nicolas Usunier, Sumit Chopra, and Jason Weston. 2015. Large-scale simple question answering with memory networks. *arXiv preprint arXiv:1506.02075*.

Qingqing Cai and Alexander Yates. 2013. Semantic parsing freebase: Towards open-domain semantic parsing. In *Second Joint Conference on Lexical and Computational Semantics (*SEM), Volume 1: Proceedings of the Main Conference and the Shared Task: Semantic Textual Similarity*, pages 328–338.

Li Dong, Furu Wei, Ming Zhou, and Ke Xu. 2015. Question answering over freebase with multi-column convolutional neural networks. In *Proceedings of the 53rd Annual Meeting of the Association for Computational Linguistics*, pages 260–269.

Anthony Fader, Stephen Soderland, and Oren Etzioni. 2011. Identifying relations for open information extraction. In *Proceedings of the Conference on Empirical Methods in Natural Language Processing*, pages 1535–1545.

Anthony Fader, Luke Zettlemoyer, and Oren Etzioni. 2013. Paraphrase-driven learning for open question answering. In *Proceedings of the 51st Annual Meeting of the Association for Computational Linguistics*, pages 1608–1618.

Anthony Fader, Luke Zettlemoyer, and Oren Etzioni. 2014. Open question answering over curated and extracted knowledge bases. In *Proceedings of the 20th ACM SIGKDD international conference on Knowledge discovery and data mining*, pages 1156–1165.

Tom Kwiatkowski, Eunsol Choi, Yoav Artzi, and Luke Zettlemoyer. 2013. Scaling semantic parsers with on-the-fly ontology matching. In *Proceedings of the 2013 Conference on Empirical Methods in Natural Language Processing*, pages 1545–1556.

Thomas Lin, Oren Etzioni, et al. 2012. Entity linking at web scale. In *Proceedings of the Joint Workshop on Automatic Knowledge Base Construction and Web-scale Knowledge Extraction*, pages 84–88.

Siva Reddy, Mirella Lapata, and Mark Steedman. 2014. Large-scale semantic parsing without question-answer pairs. *Transactions of the Association for Computational Linguistics*, 2:377–392.

Richard Socher, Danqi Chen, Christopher D Manning, and Andrew Ng. 2013. Reasoning with neural tensor networks for knowledge base completion. In *Advances in Neural Information Processing Systems*, pages 926–934.

Sainbayar Sukhbaatar, Jason Weston, Rob Fergus, et al. 2015. End-to-end memory networks. In *Advances in Neural Information Processing Systems*, pages 2431–2439.

Zhen Wang, Jianwen Zhang, Jianlin Feng, and Zheng Chen. 2014. Knowledge graph and text jointly embedding. In *Proceedings of the Conference on Empirical Methods in Natural Language Processing*.

Jason Weston, Sumit Chopra, and Antoine Bordes. 2014. Memory networks. *arXiv preprint arXiv:1410.3916*.

Min-Chul Yang, Nan Duan, Ming Zhou, and Hae-Chang Rim. 2014. Joint relational embeddings for knowledge-based question answering. In *Proceedings of the 2014 Conference on Empirical Methods in Natural Language Processing*, pages 645–650.

Wen-tau Yih, Ming-Wei Chang, Xiaodong He, and Jianfeng Gao. 2015. Semantic parsing via staged query graph generation: Question answering with knowledge base. In *Association for Computational Linguistics (ACL)*.

Using Related Languages to Enhance Statistical Language Models

Anna Currey, Alina Karakanta

Department of Computational Linguistics, Saarland University, Saarbrücken, Germany

`amscurrey@gmail.com, alinak@coli.uni-saarland.de`

Abstract

The success of many language modeling methods and applications relies heavily on the amount of data available. This problem is further exacerbated in statistical machine translation, where parallel data in the source and target languages is required. However, large amounts of data are only available for a small number of languages; as a result, many language modeling techniques are inadequate for the vast majority of languages. In this paper, we attempt to lessen the problem of a lack of training data for low-resource languages by adding data from related high-resource languages in three experiments. First, we interpolate language models trained on the target language and on the related language. In our second experiment, we select the sentences most similar to the target language and add them to our training corpus. Finally, we integrate data from the related language into a translation model for a statistical machine translation application. Although we do not see many significant improvements over baselines trained on a small amount of data in the target language, we discuss some further experiments that could be attempted in order to augment language models and translation models with data from related languages.

1 Introduction

Statistical language modeling methods are an essential part of many language processing applications, including automatic speech recognition (Stolcke, 2002), machine translation (Kirchhoff and Yang, 2005), and information retrieval (Liu and Croft, 2005). However, their success is heavily dependent on the availability of suitably large text resources for training (Chen and Goodman, 1996). Such data can be hard to obtain, especially for low-resource languages. This problem is especially acute when language modeling is used in statistical machine translation, where a lack of parallel resources for a language pair can be a significant detriment to quality.

Our goal is to exploit a high-resource language to improve modeling of a related low-resource language, which is applicable to cases where the target language is closely related to a language with a large amount of text data available. For example, languages that are not represented in the European Parliament, such as Catalan, can be aided by related languages that are, such as Spanish. The data available from the related high-resource language can be adapted in order to add to the translation model or the language model of the target language. This paper is an initial attempt at using minimally transformed data from a related language to enhance language models and increase parallel data for SMT.

2 Background and Previous Work

2.1 Domain Adaptation

This problem can be seen as a special case of domain adaptation, with the in-domain data being the data in the target language and the out-of-domain data being the data in the related language (Nakov and Ng, 2012). Domain adaptation is often used to leverage resources for a specific domain, such as biomedical text, from more general domains like newswire data (Dahlmeier and Ng, 2010). This idea can be applied to SMT, where data from the related lan-

116

Proceedings of NAACL-HLT 2016, pages 116–123,
San Diego, California, June 12-17, 2016. ©2016 Association for Computational Linguistics

guage can be adapted to look like data from the low-resource language. It has been shown that training on a large amount of adapted text significantly improves results compared to training on a small in-domain corpus or training on unadapted data (Wang et al., 2012). In this paper, we apply two particular domain adaptation approaches. First, we interpolate language models from in-domain and out-of-domain data, following Koehn and Schroeder (2007). We also attempt to select the best out-of-domain data using perplexity, similar to what was done in Gao et al. (2002).

2.2 Machine Translation

In contrast to transfer-based and word-based machine translation, for statistical machine translation, quality is heavily dependent on the amount of parallel resources. Given the difficulty of obtaining sufficient parallel resources, this can be a problem for many language pairs. For those cases, a third language can be used as a pivot. The process of using a third language as a bridge instead of directly translating is called triangulation (Singla et al., 2014). Character-level translation combined with word-level translation has also been shown to be an improvement over phrase-based approaches for closely related languages (Nakov and Tiedemann, 2012). Similarly, transliteration methods using cognate extraction (Nakov and Ng, 2012) and bilingual dictionaries (Kirschenbaum and Wintner, 2010) can be used to aid the low-resource language.

3 Experimental Framework

3.1 Choice of Languages

For the purpose of our experiments, we treat Spanish as if it were a low-resource language and test Spanish language models and English-Spanish translations. We use Italian and Portuguese as the closely-related languages. Using these languages for our experiments allows us to compare the results to the language models and machine translations that can be created using large corpora.

Spanish, Portuguese, and Italian all belong to the Romance family of Indo-European languages. Spanish has strong lexical similarity with both Portuguese (89%) and Italian (82%) (Lewis, 2015). Among major Romance languages, Spanish and Portuguese have been found to be the closest pair in automatic corpus comparisons (Ciobanu and Dinu, 2014) and in comprehension studies (Voigt and Gooskens, 2014), followed by Spanish and Italian.

3.2 Data

We used the Europarl corpus (Koehn, 2005) for training and testing. In order to use the data in our experiments, we tokenized[1] the corpus, converted all words to lowercase, and collapsed all numerical symbols into one special symbol. Finally, we transliterated the Italian and Portuguese corpora to make them more Spanish-like; this process is described in section 3.3.

The data that was used to train, test and develop is split as follows: 10% of the Spanish data (196,221 sentences) was used for testing, 10% for development, and the remaining 80% (1,569,771 sentences) for training. The Italian and Portuguese corpora were split similarly and training sizes for the models varied between 30K and 1,523,304 and 1,566,015 sentences for Italian and Portuguese, respectively.

3.3 Transliteration

In order to use Italian and Portuguese data to model Spanish, we first transliterated the Italian and Portuguese training corpora using a naive rule-based transliteration method consisting of word-level string transformations and a small bilingual dictionary. For the bilingual dictionary, the 200 most common words were extracted from the Italian and the Portuguese training corpora and manually given Spanish translations. In translating to Spanish, an effort was made to keep cognates where possible, and to use the most likely or common meanings.

Table 1 gives translations used for the ten most common Italian words in the data. Even in this small sample, there is a problematic translation. The Italian preposition *per* can be translated to *por* or *para*. In keeping with the desire to use a small amount of data, we briefly read the Italian texts to find the translation we felt was more likely (*para*), and chose that as the translation for all instances of *per* in the training set. We also verified that *para* was more likely in the Spanish training text overall than *por*.

---

[1] We used the Tok-tok tokenizer by Jon Dehdari: https://github.com/jonsafari/tok-tok

Italian	Spanish	Gloss
di	de	of
e	y	and
che	que	that
la	la	the (f. sg.)
in	en	in
il	el	the (m. sg.)
per	para	for
a	a	to
è	es	is
un	un	a (m. sg.)

Table 1: Sample Italian-Spanish translations.

The rule-based component of the transliteration consisted of handwritten word-initial, word-final, and general transformation rules. We applied approximately fifty such rules per language to the data. In order to come up with the rules, we examined the pan-Romance vocabulary list compiled by Euro-ComRom (Klein, 2002); however, such rules could be derived by an expert with knowledge of the relevant languages with relatively little effort. Character clusters that were impossible in Spanish were converted to their most common correspondence in Spanish (in the word list). We also identified certain strings that had consistent correspondences in Spanish and replaced them appropriately. These rules were applied to all words in the Italian and Portuguese training data except for those that were in the bilingual dictionary. See table 2 for examples of string transformation rules used for the Italian case.

Type	Original	Translit.	Example
initial	sp	esp	Spagna
initial	qua	cua	qualità
initial	st	est	stare
final	ssioni	siones	impressioni
final	are	ar	stare
final	tà	dad	qualità
general	gn	ñ	Spagna
general	vv	v	improvviso
general	ò	o	però

Table 2: Sample Italian-Spanish transliterations.

Italian text
La difficoltà di conciliare questi obiettivi risiede nel fatto che le logiche di questi settori sono contraddittorie.
Transliteration into Spanish
La dificoldad de conciliar estos obietivos risiede en el hecho que las logique de estos setores son contraditorie.

Table 3: Example of transliterated text using our approach.

4 Experiments

4.1 Experiment 1: Language Model Interpolation

Our first experiment attempted to use language models trained on the transliterated data to increase the coverage of a language model based on Spanish data; this was modeled after Koehn and Schroeder (2007). The language models in this experiment were trigram models with Good-Turing smoothing built using SRILM (Stolcke, 2002).

As baselines, we trained Spanish (*es*) LMs on a small amount (30K sentences) and a large amount (1.5M sentences) of data. We also trained language models based on 30K transliterated and standard Italian (*it*) and Portuguese (*pt*) sentences. All were tested on the Spanish test set. Table 4 shows the perplexity for each of the baselines. As expected, more Spanish training data led to a lower perplexity. However, the transliterated Italian and Portuguese baselines yielded better perplexity with less data. Note also the strong effect of transliteration.

Language	Train Size	PP
es	30K	93.49
es	1.5M	55.84
it	30K	1683.31
it translit.	30K	96.21
it translit.	1.5M	207.60
pt	30K	1877.23
pt translit.	30K	151.06
pt translit.	1.5M	251.53

Table 4: Baseline results for experiment 1.

In the experiment, we interpolated LMs trained on different amounts of transliterated data with the LM trained on 30K Spanish sentences. We used

SRILM's compute-best-mix tool to determine the interpolation weights of the models. This parameter was trained on the Spanish development set.

Table 5 shows the results for the interpolation of the Spanish LM with Italian and Portuguese, both separately and simultaneously. The lambda values are the weights given to each of the language models. None of the interpolated combinations improves on the perplexity of the smallest Spanish baseline. The best results for interpolated language models are achieved when combining the 30K-sentence Spanish model with the 1.5M-sentence Portuguese model, which almost reaches the perplexity level of the Spanish-only model. As a comparison, we also interpolated two separate language models, each trained on 30K Spanish sentences; the weight for these models was close to 0.5.

In the best-performing language model mix that used all three languages, Portuguese was weighted with a lambda of about 0.17, whereas Italian was only weighted with 0.016. That shows that Portuguese, in this setup, is a better model of Spanish.

An open question has to do with the performance of the Portuguese language model in the experiment compared to the baselines. In table 4, we see that the language model does significantly worse when trained on more Portuguese data. However, the interpolation of the Spanish and Portuguese language models yields a lower perplexity when trained on a large amount of Portuguese data. Since the data was identical in the baselines and experiments, further exploration is needed to understand this behavior.

4.2 Experiment 2: Corpus Selection

For our second experiment, our goal was to select the most "Spanish-like" data from our Italian and Portuguese corpora. We concatenated this data with the Spanish sentences in order to increase the amount of training data for the language model. This is similar to what was done by Gao et al. (2002).

First, we trained a language model on our small Spanish corpus. This language model was then queried on a concatenation of the transliterated Italian and Portuguese data. The sentences in this corpus were ranked according to their perplexity in the Spanish LM. We selected the best 30K and 5K sentences, which were then concatenated with the Spanish data to form a larger corpus. Finally, we used

KenLM (Heafield, 2011) to create a trigram language model with Kneser-Ney smoothing (Kneser and Ney, 1995) on that data. We also ran the same experiment on Italian and Portuguese separately.

Table 6 gives the results from these experiments. This table shows that the mixed-language models for each language performed better when they had a lower amount of non-Spanish data. This indicates that it is better to simply use a small amount of data in the low-resource language, rather than trying to augment it with the transliterated data from related languages. Using a smaller amount of the Spanish data, having a different strategy for selecting the non-Spanish data, using a different transliteration method, or using Italian and Portuguese data that was not a direct translation of the Spanish data may have all led to improvements. It is also interesting to note that the language models based on the corpus containing only Portuguese performed almost as well as those based on the corpus containing Portuguese and Italian. This indicates that the Portuguese data likely had more Spanish-like sentences than the Italian data. As mentioned in section 3.1, Portuguese is more similar to Spanish, so this makes intuitive sense. However, it is surprising given the results in table 4, which shows that the Italian-only language models performed better on Spanish data than the Portuguese-only language models.

4.3 Experiment 3: Statistical Machine Translation

Lastly, we experimented with translation models in order to see if our approach yielded similar results. For our baseline, we used a small parallel corpus of 30K English-Spanish (*en-es*) sentences from the Europarl corpus (Koehn, 2005). The data was preprocessed as described in section 3.2. Since SMT systems are often trained on large amounts of data, we expected poor coverage with this dataset. However, this size would be representative of the amount of data available for low-resource languages.

We used Moses (Koehn et al., 2007) to train our phrase-based SMT system on the above mentioned parallel corpus (*en-es*). We also trained a language model of 5M words of Spanish data from the same source, making sure that this data was strictly distinct from our parallel data. The language model was trained using KenLM (Heafield, 2011). The

Languages	Sentences	PP	Lambda es	Lambda it	Lambda pt
es + es	30K + 30K	86.59	0.502		
es + it	30K + 30K	95.19	0.9818	0.0182	
es + it	30K + 100K	96.08	0.9716	0.0284	
es + it	30K + 200K	96.49	0.9648	0.0352	
es + it	30K + 1.5M	96.91	0.9493	0.0507	
es + pt	30K + 30K	95.51	0.9340		0.0660
es + pt	30K + 100K	95.93	0.8939		0.1061
es + pt	30k + 200K	95.71	0.8709		0.1291
es + pt	30k + 1.5M	93.52	0.8170		0.1830
es + it + pt	30K + 30K + 30K	95.52	0.9298	0.0093	0.0608
es + it + pt	30K + 100K + 100K	95.94	0.8882	0.0126	0.0991
es + it + pt	30K + 200K + 200K	95.72	0.8655	0.0137	0.1207
es + it + pt	30K + 1.5M + 1.5M	93.53	0.8106	0.0161	0.1731

Table 5: Results of interpolated language models and optimal lambda values.

Languages	Sentences	PP
es	30K	84.57
es + it	30K + 5K	85.78
es + it	30K + 30K	94.10
es + pt	30K + 5K	85.11
es + pt	30K + 30K	90.31
es + it/pt	30K + 5K	85.13
es + it/pt	30K + 30K	90.24

Table 6: Results for the corpus selection experiment.

weights were set by optimizing BLEU using MERT on a separate development set of 2,000 sentences (English-Spanish). After decoding, we detokenized and evaluated the output. For the evaluation, we used a clean Spanish test set of 2,000 sentences from the same source. As an automatic evaluation measure, we used BLEU (Papineni et al., 2002) for quantitative evaluation.

For our experiments, we used Italian and Portuguese as auxiliary languages. We created two corpora of 30K sentences each from the Europarl corpus, *en-it* and *en-pt*. We first tokenized and transliterated the training corpus of the related language as described in section 3.3. Then, we concatenated the resulting corpora with our baseline corpus and trained our model. This is similar to what was done by Nakov and Ng (2012), although we attempt to translate into the low-resource language. We first experimented with each auxiliary language independently and then with both languages. In total we

conducted the following experiments:

- English-Spanish (*en-es*) + English-Italian transliterated (*en-es$_{it}$*)

- English-Spanish (*en-es*) + English-Portuguese transliterated (*en-es$_{pt}$*)

- English-Spanish (*en-es*) + English-Italian transliterated (*en-es$_{it}$*) + English-Portuguese transliterated (*en-es$_{pt}$*)

In this experiment, we expected to observe some improvements compared to the language modeling experiments, as the mistakes in the transliterated output could be filtered out by the language model containing clean Spanish data. Moreover, we examined whether it is possible to have gains from using multiple related languages simultaneously.

Languages	Sentences	BLEU	p-value
en-es (Baseline)	30K	0.3360	
en-es + en-es$_{it}$	30K + 30K	0.3357	0.22
en-es + en-es$_{pt}$	30K + 30K	0.3349	0.08
en-es + en-es$_{it}$ + en-es$_{pt}$	30K + 30K + 30K	0.3384	0.041

Table 7: BLEU scores obtained for the different training sets and their sizes.

Table 7 shows the BLEU scores for the experiments. To determine whether our results were significant we used the bootstrap resampling method

(Koehn, 2004), which is part of Moses. There were no significant improvements in BLEU score when only one auxiliary language was used. Nonetheless, we observed a significant improvement when data from both Italian and Portuguese is used. This may be an indication that more out-of domain data, when used in the translation model and sufficiently transformed, can actually improve performance.

One open question at this point is whether the improvement was caused by the contribution of more than one language or simply by the increase in training data. It is possible that a similar improvent could be achieved by increasing the data of one language to 60K. However, in order to support our conjecture, it will be necessary to conduct experiments with different sizes and combinations of data from the related languages.

5   Discussion

We observed that a closely-related language cannot be used to aid in modeling a low-resource language without being properly transformed. Although our naive rule-based transliteration method strongly improved over the non-transliterated closely-related language data, it performed worse than even a small amount of target language data. In addition, adding more data from the related language caused the models to do worse; this may be because there were more words in the data that were not translated using the 200-word dictionary, so there was more noise from the rule-based transliterations in the data. Thus, we were not successful in using data from a related language to improve language modeling for a low-resource language.

For statistical machine translation, our results show gains from augmenting the translation models of a low-resource language with transliterated related-language data. We expect that by taking advantage of more sophisticated transliteration and interpolation methods as well as larger amounts of data from the closely-related language(s), larger improvements in BLEU can be achieved.

6   Future Work

We plan on experimenting with more sophisticated ways of transforming related language data, including unsupervised and semi-supervised translitera-

tion methods. We would particularly like to experiment with neural network machine transliteration using a character-based LSTM network. This could be developed based on small parallel texts or lists of bilingual cognates of varying sizes. We could also use existing transliteration modules integrated in the SMT system (Durrani et al., 2014). In addition, we hope to explore using bilingual dictionaries without transliteration, as well as using phonological transcription as an intermediary between the two related languages. Finally, it would be beneficial to examine the contribution of each of the rules in our rule-based system separately.

A relatively simple modification to our experiments would be to use more data in creating the translation model (in experiment 3). While we found that using more of the high-resource language data in the language models yielded higher perplexity, the same did not carry over to BLEU scores, especially since we saw a slight improvement in BLEU score when using both Portuguese and Italian data. A similar option would be to select the best Italian and Portuguese data (as was done in experiment 2) for use in the translation model, instead of selecting random sentences.

In statistical machine translation, it would be interesting to explore methods of using data from related languages while preserving the reliable information from the low-resource language. One idea could be methods for interpolating phrase tables for the transliterated corpora as well as setting optimal weights for each of them, similar to the approach of Sennrich (2012). We would also like to improve the translation model coverage by filling up the phrase table for a low-resource language with data from a related language while keeping the useful data from the low-resource language (Bisazza et al., 2011) or by using the related languages as a back-off (Yang and Kirchhoff, 2006).

Finally, a weakness of our language modeling experiments was that we used almost parallel data between the related and the target languages. Hence, the related language was not likely to increase the vocabulary coverage of the models; instead, it just added misspellings of the target language words. In the future, we would like to run experiments with data from the related languages that is strictly distinct from the data of the low-resource language.

References

Arianna Bisazza, Nick Ruiz, and Marcello Federico. 2011. Fill-up versus interpolation methods for phrase-based SMT adaptation. In *IWSLT*, pages 136–143.

Stanley F Chen and Joshua Goodman. 1996. An empirical study of smoothing techniques for language modeling. In *Proceedings of the 34th Annual Meeting of the Association for Computational Linguistics*, pages 310–318. Association for Computational Linguistics.

Alina Maria Ciobanu and Liviu P Dinu. 2014. On the Romance languages mutual intelligibility. In *Proceedings of the 9th International Conference on Language Resources and Evaluation, LREC*, pages 3313–3318.

Daniel Dahlmeier and Hwee Tou Ng. 2010. Domain adaptation for semantic role labeling in the biomedical domain. *Bioinformatics*, 26(8):1098–1104.

Nadir Durrani, Hieu Hoang, Philipp Koehn, and Hassan Sajjad. 2014. Integrating an unsupervised transliteration model into statistical machine translation. *EACL 2014*, page 148.

Jianfeng Gao, Joshua Goodman, Mingjing Li, and Kai-Fu Lee. 2002. Toward a unified approach to statistical language modeling for Chinese. *ACM Transactions on Asian Language Information Processing (TALIP)*, 1(1):3–33.

Kenneth Heafield. 2011. KenLM: Faster and smaller language model queries. In *Proceedings of the Sixth Workshop on Statistical Machine Translation*, pages 187–197. Association for Computational Linguistics.

Katrin Kirchhoff and Mei Yang. 2005. Improved language modeling for statistical machine translation. In *Proceedings of the ACL Workshop on Building and Using Parallel Texts*, pages 125–128. Association for Computational Linguistics.

Amit Kirschenbaum and Shuly Wintner. 2010. A general method for creating a bilingual transliteration dictionary. In *LREC*.

Horst G Klein. 2002. Eurocom-Rezeptive Mehrsprachigkeit und Neue Medien.

Reinhard Kneser and Hermann Ney. 1995. Improved backing-off for m-gram language modeling. In *Acoustics, Speech, and Signal Processing, 1995. ICASSP-95., 1995 International Conference on*, volume 1, pages 181–184. IEEE.

Philipp Koehn and Josh Schroeder. 2007. Experiments in domain adaptation for statistical machine translation. In *Proceedings of the Second Workshop on Statistical Machine Translation*, pages 224–227. Association for Computational Linguistics.

Philipp Koehn, Hieu Hoang, Alexandra Birch, Chris Callison-Burch, Marcello Federico, Nicola Bertoldi, Brooke Cowan, Wade Shen, Christine Moran, Richard Zens, et al. 2007. Moses: Open source toolkit for statistical machine translation. In *Proceedings of the 45th annual meeting of the ACL on interactive poster and demonstration sessions*, pages 177–180. Association for Computational Linguistics.

Philipp Koehn. 2004. Statistical significance tests for machine translation evaluation. In Dekang Lin and Dekai Wu, editors, *Proceedings of EMNLP 2004*, pages 388–395, Barcelona, Spain, July. Association for Computational Linguistics.

Philipp Koehn. 2005. Europarl: A parallel corpus for statistical machine translation. In *MT Summit*, volume 5, pages 79–86. Citeseer.

M. Paul Lewis, editor. 2015. *Ethnologue: Languages of the World*. SIL International, Dallas, TX, USA, eighteenth edition.

Xiaoyong Liu and W Bruce Croft. 2005. Statistical language modeling for information retrieval. *Annual Review of Information Science and Technology*, 39(1):1–31.

Preslav Nakov and Hwee Tou Ng. 2012. Improving statistical machine translation for a resource-poor language using related resource-rich languages. *Journal of Artificial Intelligence Research*, pages 179–222.

Preslav Nakov and Jörg Tiedemann. 2012. Combining word-level and character-level models for machine translation between closely-related languages. In *Proceedings of the 50th Annual Meeting of the Association for Computational Linguistics: Short Papers-Volume 2*, pages 301–305. Association for Computational Linguistics.

Kishore Papineni, Salim Roukos, Todd Ward, and Wei-Jing Zhu. 2002. BLEU: a method for automatic evaluation of machine translation. In *Proceedings of the 40th Annual Meeting of the Association for Computational Linguistics*, pages 311–318. Association for Computational Linguistics.

Rico Sennrich. 2012. Perplexity minimization for translation model domain adaptation in statistical machine translation. In *Proceedings of the 13th Conference of the European Chapter of the Association for Computational Linguistics*, pages 539–549. Association for Computational Linguistics.

Karan Singla, Nishkarsh Shastri, Megha Jhunjhunwala, Anupam Singh, Srinivas Bangalore, and Dipti Misra Sharma. 2014. Exploring system combination approaches for Indo-Aryan MT systems. *LT4CloseLang 2014*, page 85.

Andreas Stolcke. 2002. SRILM - an extensible language modeling toolkit. In *Proceedings of the 7th International Conference on Spoken Language Processing (ICSLP 2002)*.

Stefanie Voigt and Charlotte Gooskens. 2014. Mutual intelligibility of closely related languages within the

Romance language family. *Language Contact: The State of the Art*, page 103.

Pidong Wang, Preslav Nakov, and Hwee Tou Ng. 2012. Source language adaptation for resource-poor machine translation. In *Proceedings of the 2012 Joint Conference on Empirical Methods in Natural Language Processing and Computational Natural Language Learning*, pages 286–296. Association for Computational Linguistics.

Mei Yang and Katrin Kirchhoff. 2006. Phrase-based backoff models for machine translation of highly inflected languages. In *EACL*, pages 3–7.